◇十八般廚藝系列◇
01

Creative
Chinese Home Dishes

創意家常菜

傅培梅／編著

編著者簡介

傅培梅女士係山東省福山縣人。民國四十六年起即教授中國烹飪，致力發揚中國飲食文化。又自民國五十一年開始擔任電視烹飪節目之教學，二十五年來示範過之美味菜點已超過一千八百多種。每年除國內教學外並屢次應邀赴世界各國做特別表演和講習，頗獲好評。著有中英文食譜十餘冊，行銷遍及海內外各地。

程安琪女士係傅培梅女士之長女，自幼即對烹飪有濃厚興趣，多年在耳濡目染及傅培梅女士細心的調教下，無論在烹飪藝術的理論或實際烹調技巧方面，均奠定了極高的造詣。程女士自中國文化大學畢業後，即投身此項工作，如今已近二十年，曾任教輔大食品營養系，也曾多次在電視上示範表演，深獲好評。

林慧懿小姐曾任華視「生活廣場」主持人，中視「早安中國」晨間烹調示範及電影《飲食男女》美食顧問等，並著有多本烹調食譜，更曾多次受邀至國外示範，在法國坎城、比利時影展中展現其精湛的烹飪技藝，讓中國美食精緻的呈現在國際友人的面前。

序

　　時光飛逝如梭，一轉眼，從事電視烹飪教學已達卅年餘，為求與過去四千五百多次節目內容之不重複，筆者絞盡腦汁，不停地在口味上、作法上求新求變。而在選料上則一本以往一貫作風，以容易購得、經濟實惠為原則，以便能深入每個家庭。而各類菜餚之收集，包括禽、畜、海鮮、蔬果、素、魚等等，既可供家常之需亦有多項適宜宴客參考。（本書之內容系採自傅培梅時間自81年～83年示範內容之精選）

　　中菜變化之多，可謂包羅萬象；一菜一格，百菜百味，浩瀚而無涯。只要膽大心細，多加練習，小心地避免火候、刀工、熱油之傷害，而在口味的調理上不必墨守成規，以合家人之鹹淡適口為依歸，如此則主中饋並非難事也。

　　烹調雖辛苦，但是除了做好菜來滿足家人的胃以外，還有什麼更能貼切表達我們的愛和耐心呢？

Preface

How time flies. It's been over 30 years since I started to demonstrate my cooking program in TV company. In order not to repeat my 4500 times recipes, I squeeze my brain to try to invent new dishes technically and flavor-wise. To choose the ingredients, I pick up those that are cheaper and easy to get, so that it will be more convenient for housewives.

The recipes includes poultry, meat, fish, sea food and Vegetables, both good for daily meal and Banquet treat.

The varieties of Chinese cookings are countless, you have to cook carefully with plenty of guts, avoid hurting from knife or hot oil, and to season according each family's different taste. Though cooking is hard and easy to get hurt. Except cooking, what else can exactly explain the love feelings and patience so deeply?

目錄

- 8・鳳翼雙味
  Two Ways Chicken Wings

- 10・香酥去骨雞
  五彩碎米雞
  Crispy Boneless Chicken
  Minced Chicken with Pop Rice

- 12・醋溜雞花
  蜜柑扣雞
  Sweet & Sour Chicken Flower
  Mold Chicken with Orange Sauce

- 14・金杯松子雞
  Chicken & Pine Nuts in Gold Cups

- 16・椰香葡國雞
  蠔油去骨雞
  Baked Chicken Portuguese Style
  Boneless Chicken with Oyster Sauce

- 18・臘味香芋雞排
  金針豉汁雞
  Chicken Chops & Smashed Taro
  Chicken & Dried Lily Flower with Fermented Bean Sauce

- 20・三絲鴨捲
  醬爆櫻桃
  Tri-Color Duck Rolls
  Frog's Legs with Sweet Soybean Sauce

- 22・紅米醬肉
  銀紙松子肉
  Pork with Red Rice Sauce
  Pine Nuts Pork in Silver Stick

- 24・什錦燴響鈴
  京都子排
  Deep Fried Bells with Assorted Ingredients
  Spareribs with King-Tu Sauce

- 26・爆羊肉雙味
  Quick Stir Fried Lamb Double Flavors

- 28・錦繡牛肉捲
  沙茶牛仔骨
  Beef Rolls
  Beef Spareribs with Sa-Cha Sauce

- 30・牛肉石榴包
  中式牛肉派
  Beef in Pomegranate Package
  Beef Pie Chinese Style

- 32・什蔬燴咖哩牛肉
  蔥油淋漢堡
  Curry Beef with Assorted Vegetables
  Chinese Hamburger with Green Onion

- 34・鍋爔牛里脊
  千層牛肉捲
  Pan Stewed Beef
  Thousand Layer Beef Rolls

- 36・生汁龍蝦球
  Lobster Balls with Mayonnaise Sauce

- 38・龍蝦粉絲煲
  扣三鮮湯
  Lobster in Casserole
  Abalone Supreme Soup

- 40・炸蛋黃蝦排
  四色鳳尾蝦
  Deep Fried Egg Prawns Batter
  Phenix Tail Prawn

- 42・香酥小蝦捲
  醬燒蝦
  Crispy Shrimp Rolls
  Stewed Shrimps with Brown Sauce

44 · 蝦片炒鮮奶
　　芥辣鮮蝦絲
　　Stir Fried Prawn with Milk Sauce
　　Shrimp Shreds with Mustard Sauce

46 · 百花鮮菇盒
　　雞絲燴翅
　　Stuffed Mushrooms with Shrimps
　　Stewed Shark's Fin with Chicken Shreds

48 · 魚翅石榴包
　　Sharks Fin in Pomegranate Package

50 · 鮑魚火腿扣通粉
　　鮑魚燴三白
　　Mold Abalone and Han
　　Braised Abalone
　　Slices with Bamboo
　　Skirt Mushroom

52 · 銀紙蒸鮮貝
　　碧綠玉筍帶子
　　Steamed Scallop
　　Fresh Scallop & Baby Corn

54 · 炒干貝蛋糕
　　鍋貼干貝酥
　　Stir-Fried Scallop Egg Cake
　　Fried Scallop Cake

56 · 金盤雙魷
　　白灼鮮魷
　　Double Squid in Golden Plate
　　Blanched Fresh Squid

58 · 果粒溜雙鮮
　　奶油焗鮮蚵
　　Squid, Shrimp with Fruits
　　Oyster with Cream Sauce

60 · 咖哩鮮蟹煲
    椒鹽焗花蟹
    Curry Sauce Crab in Casserole
    Salt & Pepper Crab

62 · 麻辣海參
    如意海參
    Spicy Sea Cucumber
    Stuffed Sea Cucumber with Chicken

64 · 香汁蝴蝶魚
    Butterfly Fish

66 · 魚中有餘
    西炸鮭魚球
    Fish in Fish's Pocket
    Deep-Fried Salmon Balls

68 · 黃魚酥方
    香菇肉燥蒸鮭魚
    Deep-Fried Fish Cake
    Steamed Salmon with Meat Sauce

70 · 鱸魚雙味
    Two Ways Fish

72 · 雙菇燜鮮魚
    四味芝麻魚
    Fish with Mushrooms
    Four Flavors Fish

74 · 脆皮五柳魚
    銀紙烤鮭魚
    Crispy Fish with Assorted Strings
    Baked Salmon in Silver Package

76 · 栗棗扣河鰻
    酥炸鰻魚捲
    Mold Eel & Walnut
    Crispy Eel Rolls

78 · 玻璃鮭魚片
    家常海鰻絲
    Transparent Package Fish
    Shredded Eel Home Style

80 · 蟹肉荷包豆腐
    酥皮豆腐捲
    Bean Curd Balls Stuffed with Crab
    Crispy Bean Curd Rolls

82 · 八寶豆腐盒
    豆腐咕咾肉
    Bean Curd Treasure Boxes
    Kou-Lou Bean Curd

84 · 香酥豆腐鬆
    油淋黃雀
    Crispy Minced Bean Curd
    Fried Crispy Packages

86 · 炸百花蛋
    蠔油蛤蜊蛋
    Deep Fried Stuffed Egg
    Steamed Egg with Clams

88 · 釀百花素雞
    燻三絲齋鵝
    Stuffed Shrimp in Bean Curd Cake
    Smoked Vegetarian Goose

90 · 金華扣四蔬
    King-Hwa Ham & Vegetables

104 · 魚香汁拌四季豆
　　　肉燥灼拌四季豆
　　　Green Bean with Szechuan Sauce
　　　Green Bean with Minced Pork Sauce

106 · 豌豆濃湯
　　　炒豌豆雞絲
　　　Snow Peas Cream Soup
　　　Chicken Strings with Snow Peas

108 · 奶油蔬菜盒
　　　三鮮盒子
　　　Cream Vegetable in Bread Boxes
　　　Fried Jumbo Dumplings

110 · 棗泥糯米球
　　　八寶芋泥捲
　　　Glutinous Rice Balls with Date Pasts
　　　Sweet Taro Rolls

112 · 饊子素菜捲
　　　歡樂滿堂彩
　　　Crispy Vegetarian Rolls
　　　Assorted Meat in Soft Cake

114 · 奶油水果淋餅
　　　French Crêpe

116 · 翡翠涼麵捲
　　　韓國涼麵
　　　Jade Color Cold Noodle Rolls
　　　Cold Noodles Korean Style

92 · 蒜汁肉捲蘆筍
　　　串炸時蔬
　　　Asparagus in Bacon Rolls
　　　Deep-Fried Vegetables Skewers

94 · 干貝扣四蔬
　　　魚酥翡翠瓜絲
　　　Mold Scallop with Four Kinds of Vegetables
　　　Jade Squash with Crispy Sole

96 · 西拌青花菜
　　　毛豆八寶醬
　　　Broccoli Salad with Assorted Dressing
　　　Eight Treasure Sauce

98 · 雞茸鮮筍紮
　　　Bamboo Shoot Bundles

100 · 碧綠三色菇
　　　魚香溜藕夾
　　　Tri-Color Mushrooms
　　　Lotus Root's Cake — Szechuan Style

102 · 什錦蔬菜沙拉
　　　什錦蔬菜沙拉捲
　　　Assorted Vegetable Salad
　　　Vegetable Salad Rolls

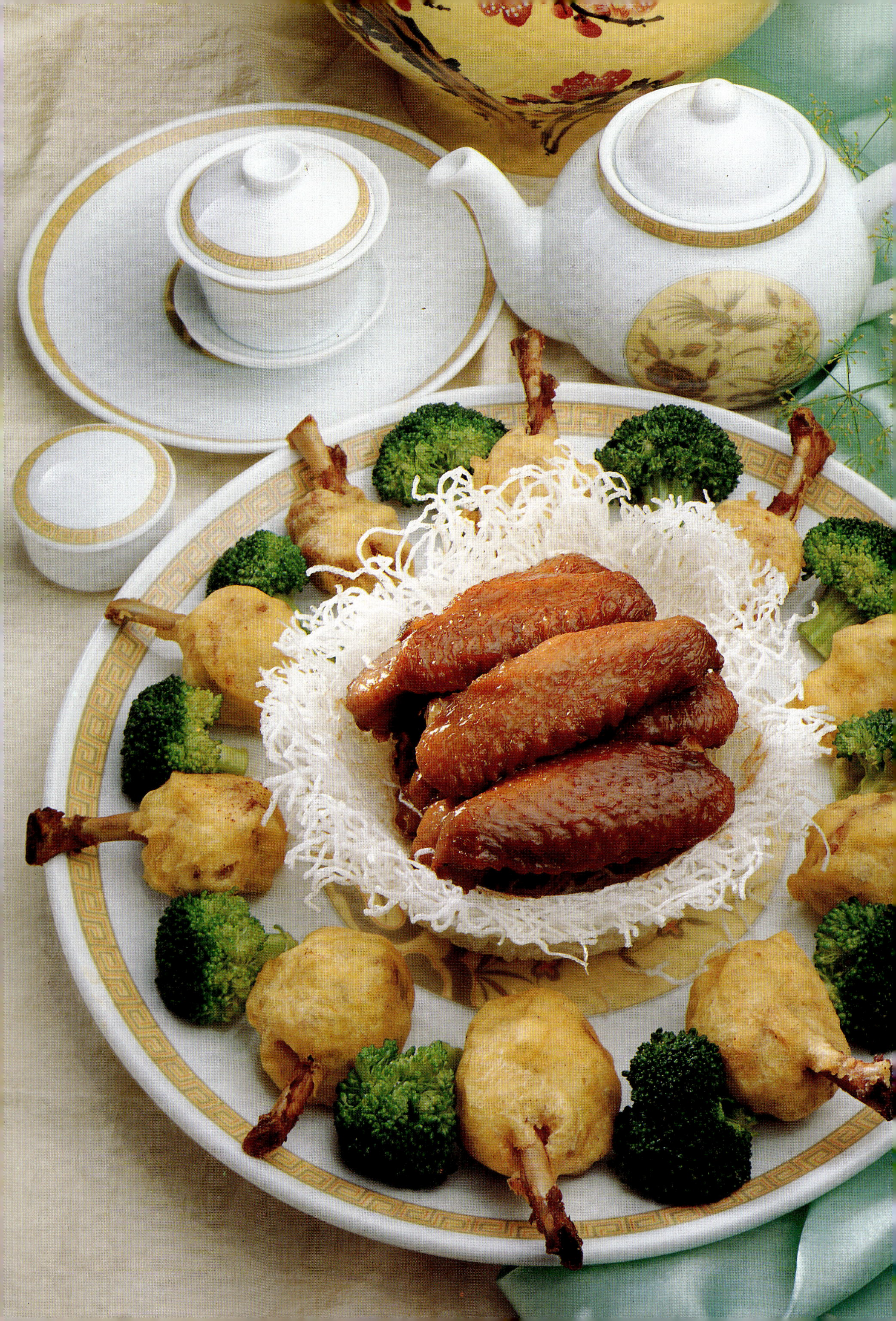

鳳翼雙味

材料
雞翅（連翅根）10支　粉絲半把（或生菜少許）

拌雞料
醬油3湯匙　酒1湯匙

紅燒料
葱2支　薑2片　八角半粒　糖1湯匙　水2杯

酥炸糊
麵粉3湯匙　太白粉2湯匙　發泡粉1茶匙　水 2/3杯

作法
1. 雞翅洗淨後，翅尖切除不用，將翅膀及翅根分割開，翅根部分將皮往下推成爲球狀，用拌雞料拌勻，放入熱油中；炸黃撈出。
2. 將炸過之翅膀、翅根加剩下之拌雞料和紅燒料一起紅燒20分鐘；將翅根球撿出。
3. 乾粉絲用熱油炸泡，瀝乾排入盤中，紅燒翅膀盛在粉絲上。
4. 翅根球裹上酥炸糊，炸黃後排在周圍便可上桌。（不用炸粉絲亦可用生菜切絲墊底）

＊乾粉絲可排在模型中炸成碗狀較美觀

Two Ways Chicken Wings

Ingredients:
10 Chicken wings, 5g Vermicelli.

Seasonings:
❶ 3T Soysauce, 1T Wine.
❷ 2 Green onion, 2 Ginger slices, 1/2 Star anise, 1T Sugar, 2C Water.
❸ 3T Flour, 2T Cornstarch, 1t Baking powder, 2/3C Water.

Methods:
1. Clean the chicken wings, cut off the ends from wings, then cut each wings into 2 parts, pull the meat to the end of the bone, like a lollipop. Marinate all with ❶, deep fry in hot oil to golden brown, drain.
2. Cook chicken with remaining ❶ and ❷ for 20 minutes.
3. Take out chicken balls (lollipop), coat with ❸ and deep fry to golden brown, arrange around the plate.
4. Deep fry vermicelli in hot oil, drain and put on center of a plate, then put the middle part of wings on vermecelli. Serve

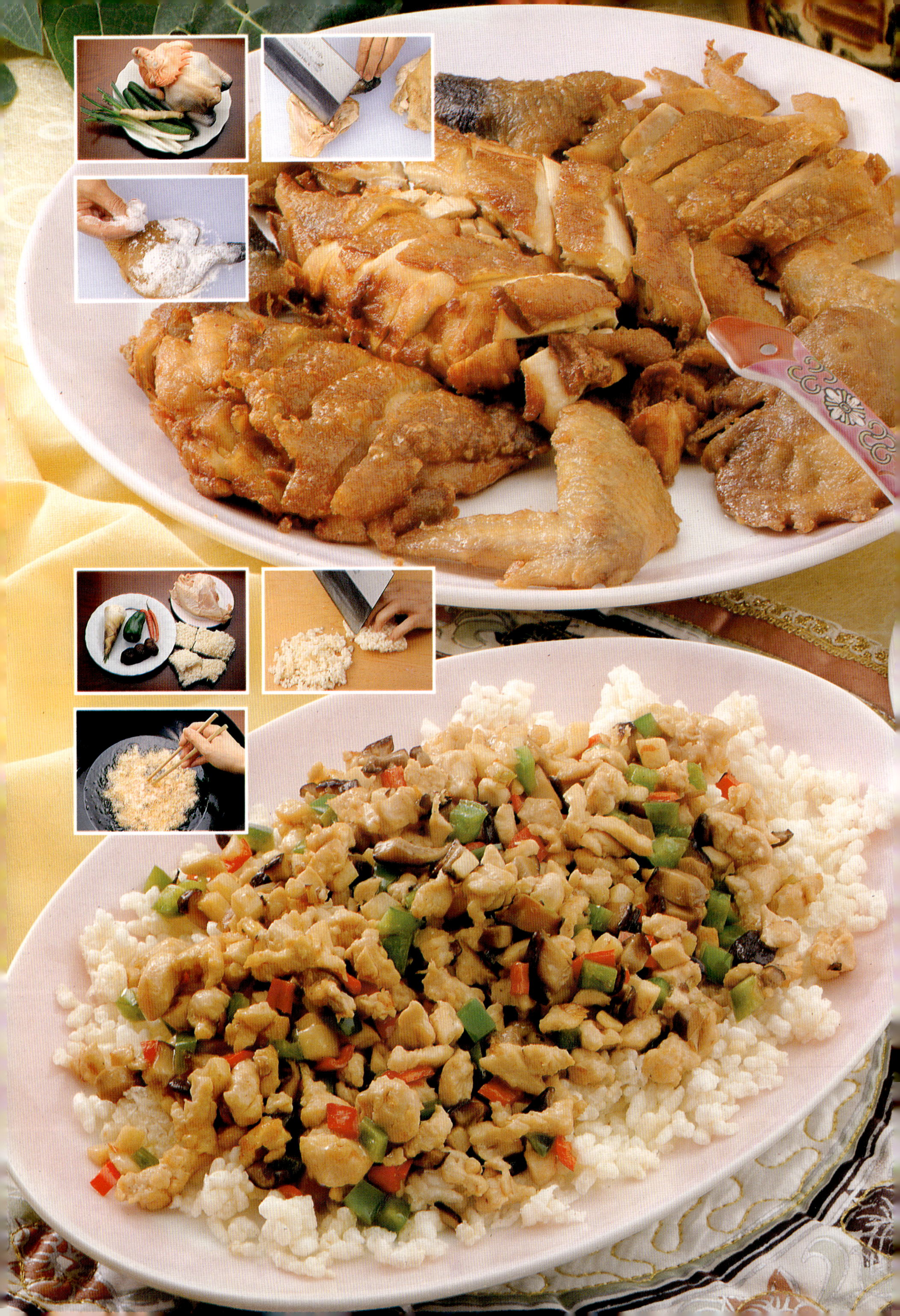

香酥去骨雞

材料
雞1隻　麵粉少許

煮雞料
花椒1湯匙　鹽1½湯匙　葱2支　薑2片
酒1湯匙　水6杯

沾雞料
煮雞湯2湯匙　葱屑1湯匙　香菜屑1湯
匙　醬油1湯匙　麻油½湯匙

作法
1. 花椒及鹽先在乾鍋中炒香後，再加葱、薑、酒及水煮滾，放入洗淨的雞，小火煮至爛，取出雞，待稍涼後拆去大骨
2. 雞表皮上塗少許醬油，並拍上一層麵粉，放入熱油中炸黃即可撈出，切塊排入盤中，附沾雞料即可上桌

* 雞也可以用醃料（煮雞料不加水）醃6～8小時，再蒸爛油炸，此法較省時，吃時附醃過的糖醋黃瓜，較不油膩

Crispy Boneless Chicken

Ingredients:
1 Chicken, 1/2C Flour

Sauce:
❶ 1T Brown pepper corn, 1-1/2T Salt, 2 Green onion, 2 Ginger slices, 1T Wine, 6C water
❷ 2T Chicken soup, 1T Green onion (chopped), 1T Parsley (chopped), 1T Soysauce, 1/2T Sesame oil

Methods:
1 Stir fry brown pepper corn and salt in a dry wok, then add green onion, ginger, wine water, bring to a boil, put chicken in and cook over low heat till tender. Take chicken out, let cool, remove bones
2 Rub soysauce on chicken's skin, coat with flour deep fry in hot oil to golden brown, cut into pieces, arrange on a plate, serve with sauce ❷

♣ You may marinate chicken with sauce ❶ for 6-8 hours, then steam to tender

五彩碎米雞

材料
雞胸肉6兩　鍋巴4片　青椒丁⅓杯　紅椒丁2湯匙　香菇丁及筍丁各½杯　葱花薑末各少許

醃雞料
淡色醬油½湯匙　太白粉½湯匙　水1湯匙

綜合調味料
醬油1湯匙　酒½湯匙　辣豆瓣醬（可免）少許　糖1茶匙　鹽、麻油各少許
太白粉1茶匙

作法
1. 雞胸肉切小丁後用醃雞料拌勻，醃10分鐘以上
2. 鍋巴用熱油炸泡，待冷後切碎放在盤中（亦可買炸好之鍋巴）
3. 炒鍋中將1杯油燒至七分熱後，放雞丁過油，待雞肉變白撈出，然後將油倒出，僅留1湯匙在鍋中
4. 用餘油先爆香葱、薑，放下香菇丁、筍丁一起炒熟，再放下雞丁和青、紅椒丁，淋下綜合調味料，大火拌炒均勻即可盛放在鍋巴上

Minced Chicken with Pop Rice

Ingredients:
225g Chicken breast, 4pcs Pop rice cake, 1/3C Green pepper, cubes, 2T Red chili, cubes, 1/2C Black mushroom, cubes, 1/2C Bamboo shoot cubes, 1T Green onion chopped, 1t Ginger chopped

Seasonings:
❶ 1T Soysauce, 1/2T Wine, 1/2T Hot bean paste 1t Sugar, 1/2t Salt, Sesame oil, 1t Cornstarch
❷ 1/2T Soysauce, 1/2T Cornstarch, 1T Water

Methods:
1. Cut chicken breast into small pieces, marinate with seasonings ❷ for 10 minutes
2. Deep fry pop rice cake in hot oil, let cool and mince, arrange on a plate
3. Heat 1C oil to deep fry chicken (about 150 C) When chicken turns white, drain. Heat 1T oil to fry green onion, ginger, mushroom, bamboo shoot, then add chicken, green & red pepper add in seasonings ❶, stir over high heat thoroughly. Pour on pop rice

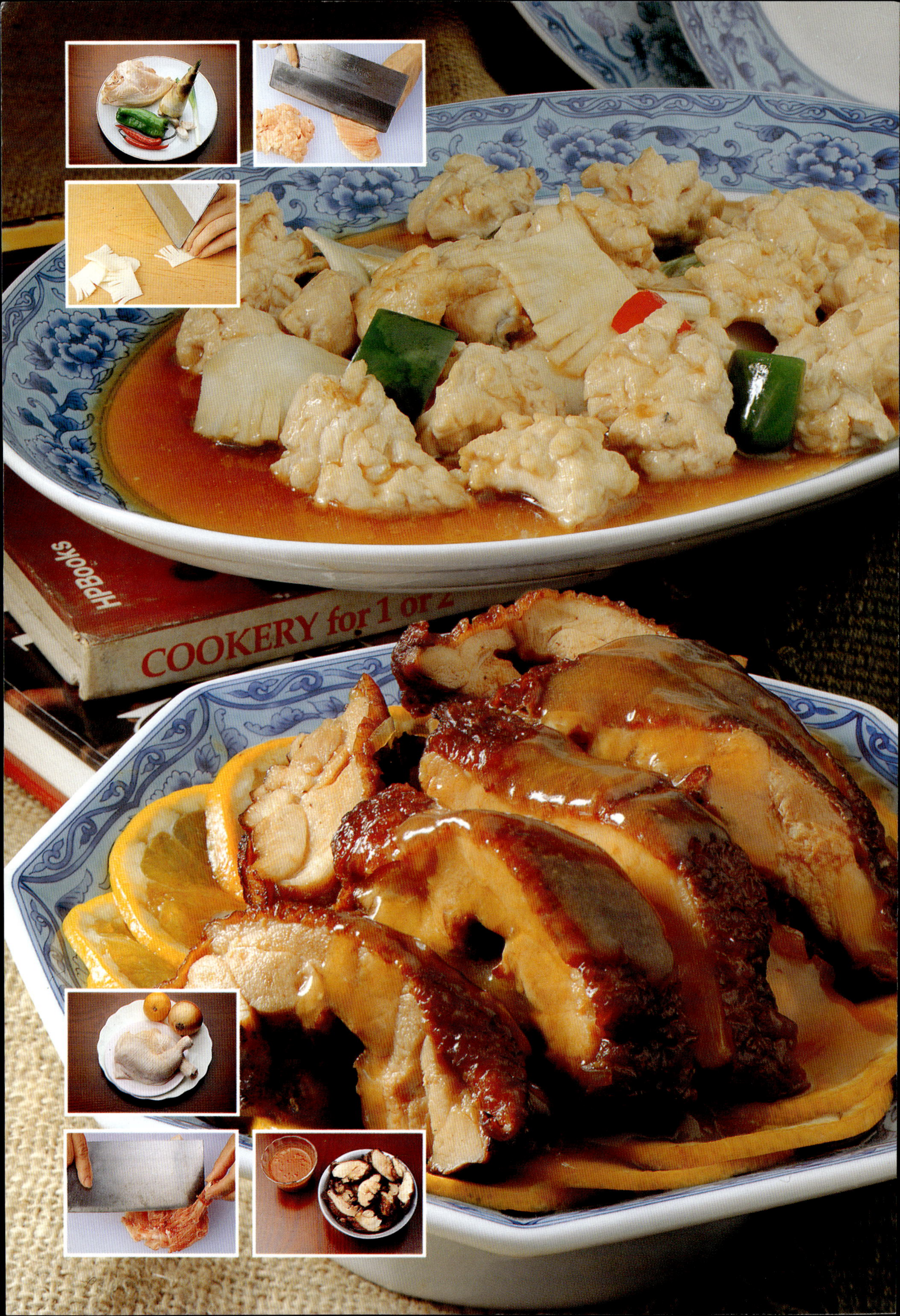
HPBooks
COOKERY for 1 or 2

醋溜雞花

材料
雞胸肉1個或雞腿2支　青椒1個　筍半支　紅辣椒2支　葱段、薑片、大蒜片各少許

醃雞料
蛋白半個　酒½湯匙　鹽½茶匙　胡椒粉少許　太白粉1湯匙　油1湯匙

綜合調味料
醬油、醋各1½湯匙　酒1湯匙　糖1茶匙　太白粉½湯匙　水2湯匙

作法
1. 雞胸(或腿)去骨，皮朝下平放在砧板上，直刀在雞肉上切細密交叉刀口，再分割成1寸大小塊狀，用醃雞料拌勻後醃20分鐘
2. 青椒、紅椒切小片，筍切成梳子片備用
3. 鍋中將2杯油燒至八分熱，放入雞肉泡熟瀝出。然後另起油鍋，用2湯匙油爆香葱、薑及蒜片，加入青、紅椒及筍片，大火炒一會兒後，加入雞肉和綜合調味料，拌炒均勻即可盛盤

Sweet & Sour Chicken Flower

Ingredients:
1 Chicken breast, 1 Green pepper, 1/2 Bamboo shoot, 2 Red chili, 1T Green onion, 1t Ginger slices, 1T Garlic slices.

Seasonings:
❶ 1/2 Egg white, 1/2T Wine, 1/2t Salt, pepper, 1T Cornstarch, 1T Oil.
❷ 1-1/2T Soysauce, 1-1/2T Vinegar, 1T Wine, 1t Sugar, 1/2T Cornstarch, 2T Water.

Methods:
1. Remove bones from chicken breast, place on a board, scare the meat part crisscrossly, then cut into 1" cubes, marinate with seasoning ❶ for 20 minutes.
2. Cut green pepper, red chili into small pieces Slice the bamboo shoot thinly and cut each piece into a comb shape.
3. Heat 2C oil to 160°C, deep fry the chicken till done, drain. Heat 2T oil to stir fry green onion, ginger and garlic, add green & red pepper, bamboo shoot, stir fry over high heat, add chicken, and seasoning ❷, mix evenly. Serve

蜜柑扣雞

材料
雞腿2支　柳丁1個　洋葱丁½杯

調味料
番茄醬½湯匙　酒½湯匙　糖2茶匙　鹽½茶匙　水½杯　濕太白粉酌量

作法
1. 將雞腿去骨後，用醬油略拌，用熱油將表面炸黃，撈出切塊鋪在湯碗中。
2. 柳丁擠汁約1湯匙量，皮切細條。
3. 用1湯匙油將洋葱丁炒軟，加入番茄醬炒紅。另淋入酒、糖、鹽和水，煮滾後淋入1.項的湯碗中，大火蒸半小時
4. 將蒸好的湯汁再泌入鍋中，加入柳丁汁及皮煮滾後，將汁中的渣質撈棄，淋下濕太白粉勾芡，澆至扣在盤中的雞腿上即可

Mold Chicken with Orange Sauce

Ingredients:
2 Chicken legs, 1 Orange, 1/2C Onion, Chopped

Seasonings:
1/2T Ketchup, 1/2T Wine, 2t Sugar, 1/2t Salt, 1/2C Water, 1T Cornstarch paste.

Methods:
1. Remove bones from chicken legs, marinate the meat with soysauce and deep fry in hot oil cut into cubes and arrange in a bowl.
2. Squeeze juice out of the orange for later use Peel the skin, use the very outer part (fine and thin as if you can see it through) to cut into fine shreds.
3. Heat 1T oil to stir fry onion, add ketchup, wine, sugar, salt and water, bring to a boil, pour over chicken. Steam for 1/2 hour with high heat.
4. Pour the steamed chicken soup in the pan, add orange juice and peel, bring to a boil drain the peel, thicken with cornstarch paste, pour on chicken Serve.

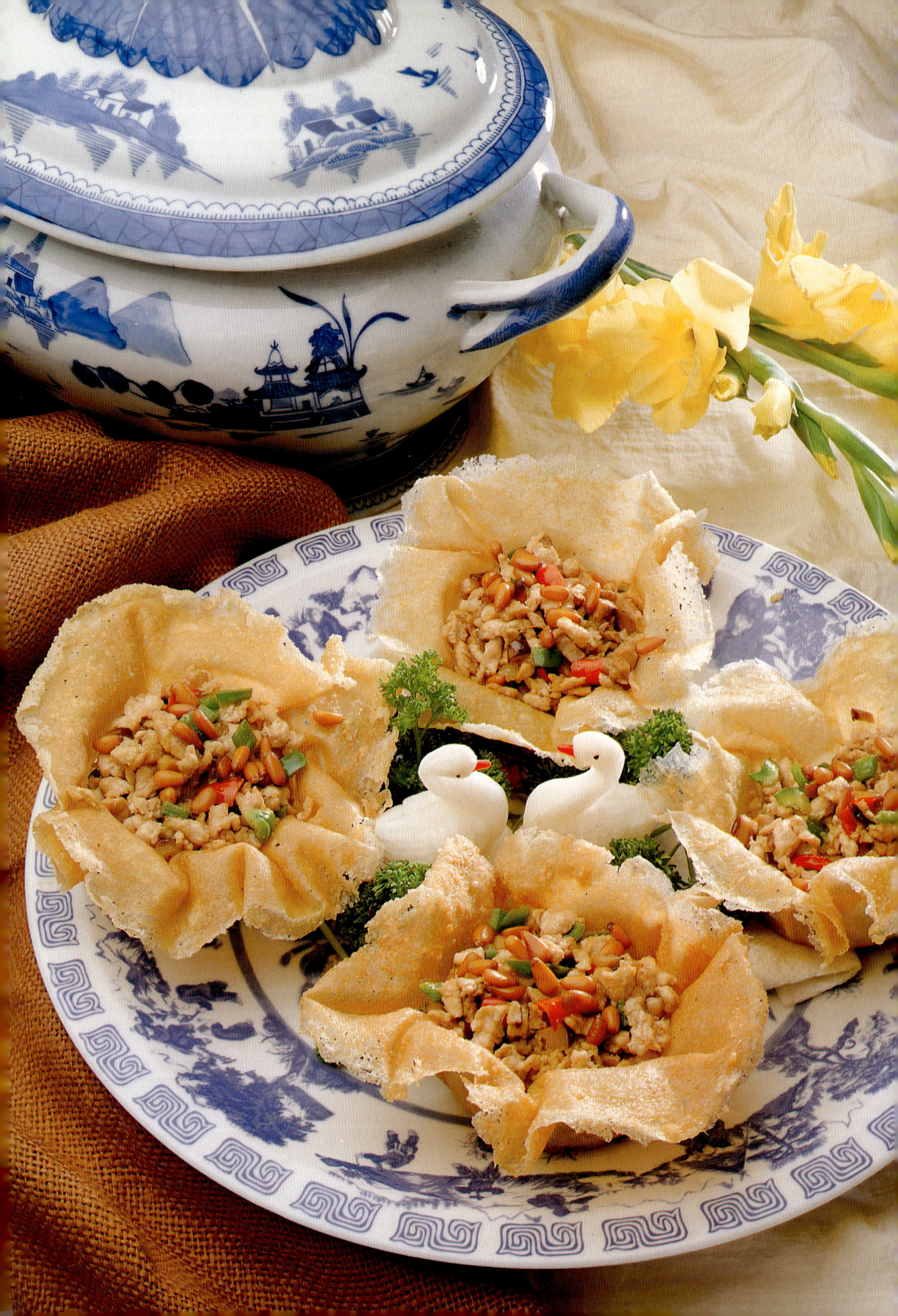

金杯松子雞

材料
青瓜(大黃瓜)1條　春捲皮4張　雞肉6兩　香菇丁、青椒丁各½杯　紅椒丁2湯匙　松子2湯匙　蔥小段、薑小片酌量

醃雞料
醬油½湯匙　太白粉1茶匙　水½湯匙

綜合調味料
淡色醬油、酒、水各½湯匙　鹽¼茶匙　糖½茶匙　胡椒粉、麻油各少許　太白粉1茶匙

作法
1. 青瓜在最粗的地方切成兩半，用鋁箔紙包裹，並將底部壓平
2. 春捲皮(修剪成直徑約20公分圓形)平放到熱油中，並用青瓜棒由中間壓下，使春捲皮捲成杯子狀，待成形後，使青瓜與春捲皮分離，續將春捲皮炸成金黃色，撈出瀝乾
3. 雞肉切小丁，用醃雞料拌醃10分鐘以上，用熱油將雞肉泡熟後瀝出
4. 另起油鍋，用1湯匙油爆香蔥段、薑片，並加入雞丁等料同炒，淋下綜合調味料拌勻便熄火，麗下炸過之松子便分別盛入金杯中裝盤上桌

＊松子先用糖水泡20分鐘，瀝乾再用小火溫油炸酥，撈出後鋪在紙上待冷即可

Chicken & Pine Nuts in Gold Cups

Ingredients:
1 Big cucumber, 4 pcs Spring roll skin, 225g Chicken breast, 1/2C Black mushroom, cubed, 1/2C Green pepper, cubed, 2T Red chili, 2T Pine nuts, 2 Green onion, sectioned , 3 pcs Ginger, sliced

Seasonings:
❶ 1/2T Soysauce, 1t Cornstarch, 1/2T Water
❷ 1/2T Soysauce, 1/2T Wine, 1/2T Water, 1/4t Salt, 1/2t Sugar, Pepper, Sesame oil, 1t Cornstarch

Methods:
1. Cut big cucumber into 2, wrap by a piece of aluminum foil, flat the bottom.
2. Heat 5C oil to very hot, place a piece of spring roll skin on surface of oil, press down immediately from center with the cucumber stick, to make the spring roll skin into a cup shape (with edges fry to a skirt) When the cup is firm, take out cucumber and drain the gold cup.
3. Dice chicken, marinate with seasoning ❶ for 10 minutes, deep fry in hot oil to done, drain.
4. Heat 1T oil, stir fry green onion, ginger, add chicken, all ingredients and seasoning ❷, mix well with fried pine nuts, pour in cups, serve.

✤ Soak pine nuts in sweet water, drain & deep fry in warm oil over low heat until crispy. Remove

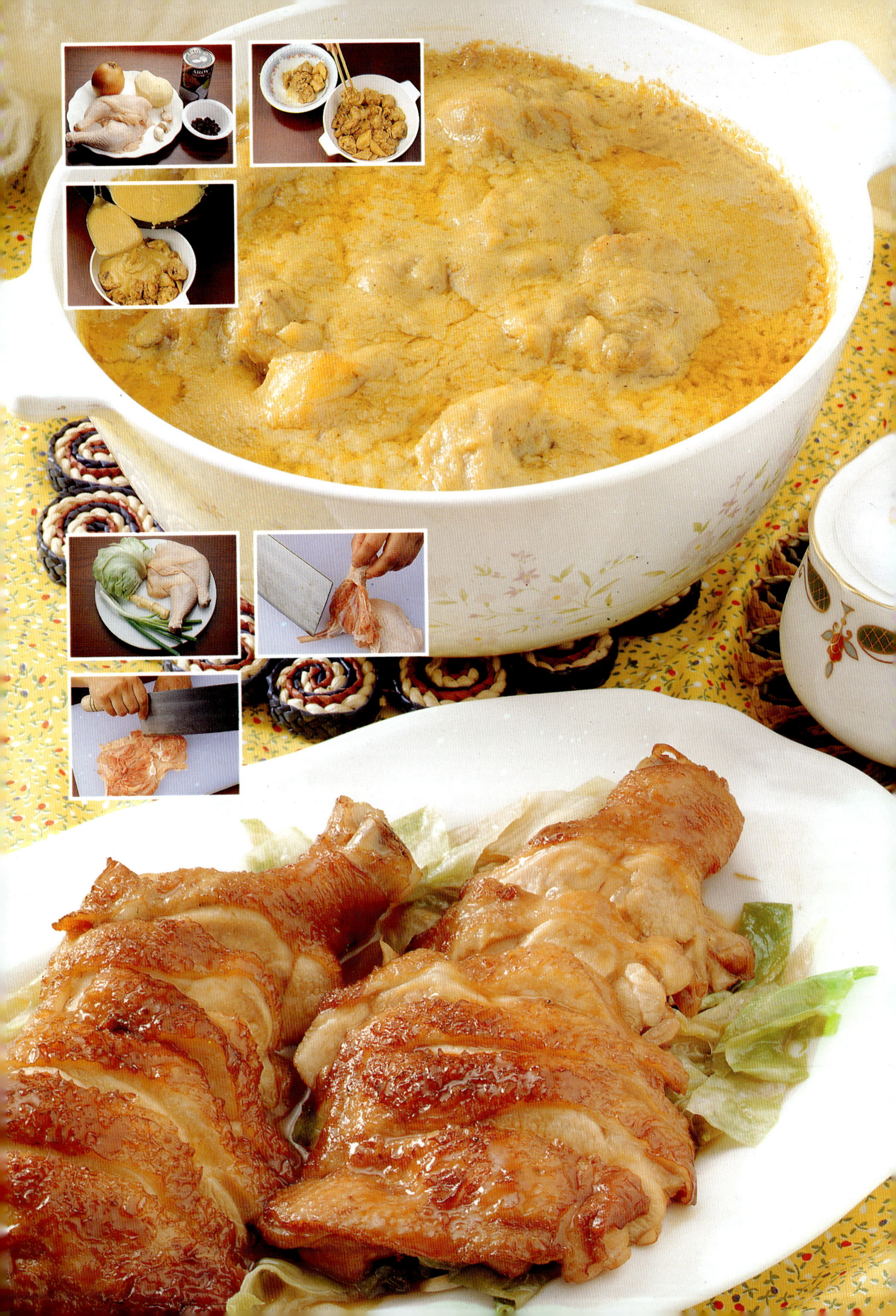

椰香葡國雞

材料
雞腿2支　大馬鈴薯1個　洋蔥丁2/3杯
大蒜屑1湯匙　葡萄乾(泡軟)約20粒

調味料
咖哩粉1½湯匙　水4杯　酒½湯匙　鹽1茶匙　糖½茶匙

麵糊料
油4湯匙　麵粉4湯匙　牛奶¼杯　椰漿¼杯

作法
1. 雞腿斬成小塊，沾上麵粉炸黃，馬鈴薯切滾刀塊也炸黃。
2. 用2湯匙油爆香大蒜屑及洋蔥丁，再加入咖哩粉炒香，注入清水等調味料，加入雞塊及馬鈴薯，小火煮30分鐘。然後撿出雞塊及馬鈴薯放入烤碗中，麗入葡萄乾。
3. 用火炒香麵粉，倒入過濾後的湯汁，慢慢攪勻並加入牛奶及椰漿，調成糊狀淋到烤碗中，放烤箱中以小火烤至微乾黃即可

Baked Chicken Portuguese Style

Ingredients:
2 Chicken legs, 1 Potato, 2/3C Onion, chopped, 1T Garlic, chopped, 20 pcs Raisin.

Seasonings:
❶ 1-1/2T Curry powder, 4C Water, 1/2T Wine, 1t Salt, 1/2t Sugar.
❷ 4T Oil, 4T Flour, 1/4C Milk, 1/4C Coconut milk.

Methods:
1. Cut chicken leg into small cubes, coat with flour and deep fry together with potato cubes to golden brown.
2. Heat 2T oil to stir fry garlic, onion and curry powder, add water and seasoning ❶, then add chicken & potato, cook over low heat for 30 minutes, strain the soup for later use, put chicken and potato in a bake ware, sprinkle raisins on top.
3. Heat 4T oil to stir fry flour then add the curry soup in, stir and mix with milk and coconut milk to a paste, pour on top of chicken, bake for 10 minutes until surface turns to golden brown. Serve.

蠔油去骨雞

材料
雞腿2支　西洋生菜半棵

醃雞料
醬油2湯匙　酒1湯匙　蔥支、薑片酌量

調味料
蠔油1湯匙　濕太白粉1茶匙

作法
1. 雞腿剔除骨頭，用刀將白筋斬斷，放入醃雞料中醃半小時。
2. 生菜切寬條，在滾水中川燙一下(水中放油½湯匙，鹽½茶匙)撈出，瀝乾水分，鋪在盤中。
3. 燒熱2杯油，雞皮面朝下，放入油中炸熟(或用5湯匙熱油將雞腿煎熟)，趁熱切小塊，排放生菜上。
4. 剩餘的醃雞料加水半杯倒入鍋中煮滾，撈棄蔥薑，勾芡後加入蠔油拌勻，淋到雞肉上。

Boneless Chicken with Oyster Sauce

Ingredients:
2 Chicken legs, 1/2 head. Lettuce.

Seasonings:
❶ 2T Soysauce, 1T Wine, Green onion, Ginger.
❷ 1T Oyster sauce, 1t Cornstarch paste.

Methods:
1. Remove bones from chicken, chop meat and cut off the tendon, marinate with ❶ for 1/2 hour.
2. Shred lettuce, blench in boiling water, (add 1/2T oil & 1/2t salt in water previously) drain, put on a plate.
3. Heat 2C oil to deep fry chicken until done, remove and cut into pieces and arrange on lettuce.
4. Add 1/2C water to cook with seasoning ❶, bring to a boil, mix with oyster sauce and thicken by cornstarch paste, pour over chicken.

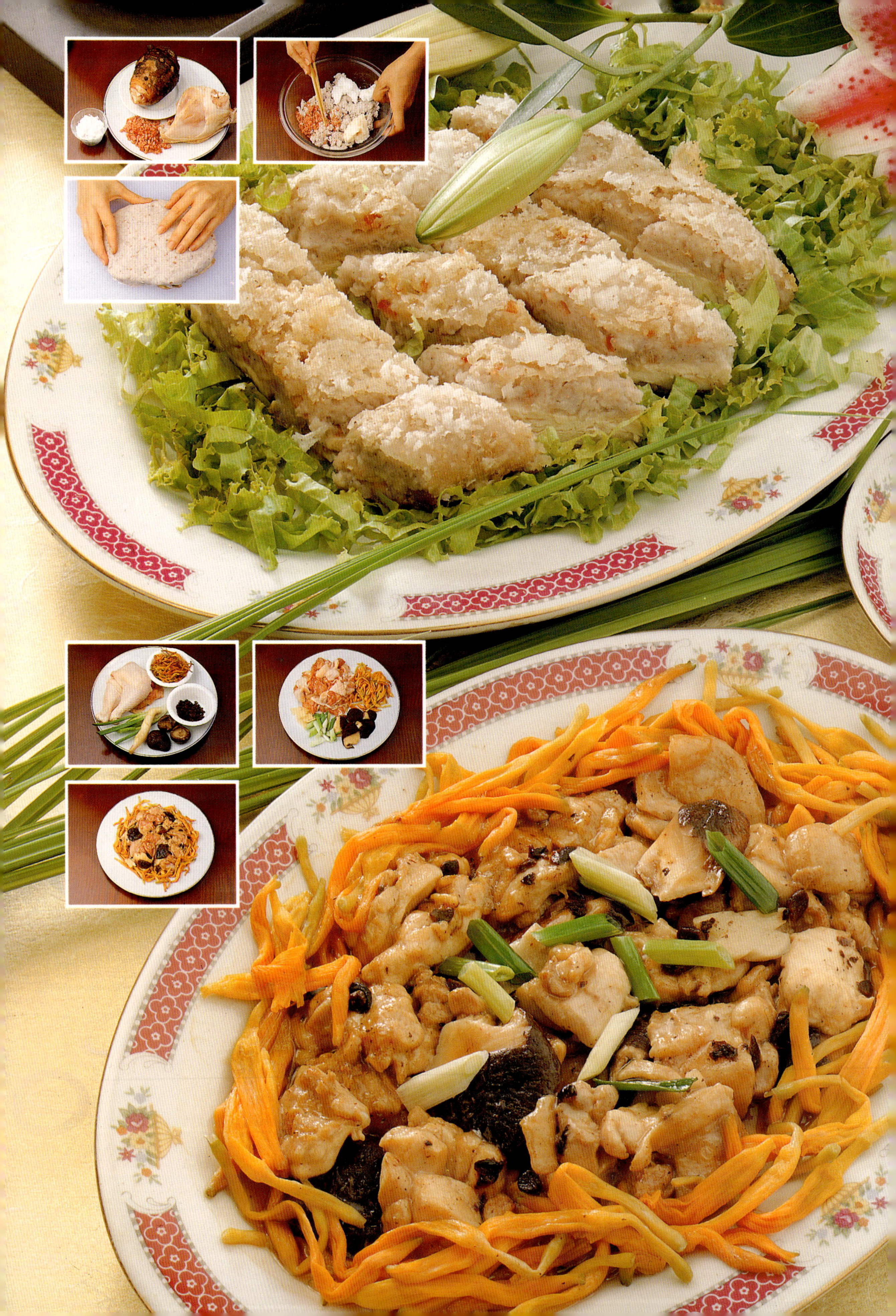

臘味香芋雞排

材料
大雞胸1個　大芋頭1斤　熟臘腸丁½杯

芋泥料
澄粉(或玉米粉)3湯匙　油2湯匙　鹽¼茶匙　胡椒粉少許

蠔油沾汁
蠔油1湯匙　蒸雞汁(或水)2湯匙　蔥花少許　麻油1茶匙

作法
1. 雞胸肉用拍碎之蔥、薑及鹽和酒抹勻醃片刻，入鍋蒸熟。
2. 芋頭切厚片一起蒸熟，趁熱壓成泥狀，拌入臘腸丁及其他芋泥料(澄粉或玉米粉先用半杯滾水燙過，略拌)。
3. 雞肉稍涼後剔除大骨，並將雞肉較厚的地方片切開，攤成厚度均勻的雞排，撒上太白粉，再將芋泥平鋪在雞肉上，再撒一層太白粉，放入熱油中炸酥。
4. 撈出雞排，瀝乾油，趁熱切塊，排入盤中，附上蠔油沾汁上桌。

Chicken Chops & Smashed Taro

Ingredients:
1 Chicken breast, 600g Taro, 1/2C Chinese sausage, diced.

Seasonings:
❶ 3T Flour starch, 2T Oil, 1/4t Salt, Pepper.
❷ 1T Oyster sauce, 2T Chicken broth, 1t Sesame oil, 1T Green onion, chopped.

Methods:
1. Marinate chicken with green onion, ginger, wine & salt for 10 minutes, steam to done.
2. Peel taro and cut into thick slices, steam to done, smash and mix with sausage and ❶, (mix flour starch with boiling water first).
3. Remove bones from chicken, shread chicken to a large piece, sprinkle cornstarch, spread taro on evenly, press and then sprinkle cornstarch on top. Deep fry in hot oil to crispy Drain.
4. Cut chicken into rectangle, arrange on a plate, serve with dipping sauce ❷.

金針豉汁雞

材料
雞腿2支　香菇4朵　金針⅓兩　嫩薑15小片　蔥段2湯匙

調味料
豆豉1湯匙　醬油、酒、蠔油各½湯匙　糖、鹽各¼茶匙　胡椒粉、麻油各少許　太白粉1茶匙

作法
1. 雞腿去骨，肉切成1寸大小塊狀。香菇泡軟切斜片，金針泡軟，擠乾水分放在蒸盤中。
2. 用油1湯匙炒香豆豉，並加入其他調味料，放下雞肉嫩薑及香菇拌勻，平鋪放在金針菜上，大火蒸15分鐘。
3. 另熱1½湯匙油，放下蔥段煎香，趁熱淋到雞肉上，略加拌合，盛入盤中。

Chicken & Dried Lily Flower with Fermented Bean Sauce

Ingredients:
2 Chicken legs, 4 Black mushroom, 12g Dried lily flower, 15pcs Young ginger slices, 2T Green onion, sectioned.

Seasonings:
1T Fermented black beans, 1/2T Soysauce, 1/2T Wine, 1/2T Oyster sauce, 1/4t Salt, 1/4t Sugar, 1t Cornstarch, Pepper, Sesame oil.

Methods:
1. Remove bones from chicken, cut meat into 1 cubes. Slice soaked black mushrooms into halves. Soak dried lily flowers, squeeze and put on a plate.
2. Heat 1T oil, stir fry fermented black beans, add all seasonings, mix with chicken, black mushroom, ginger. Pour on lily flower, steam over high heat for 15 minutes.
3. Heat 1-1/2T oil, fry green onion till good smell rises, pour on chicken. Serve.

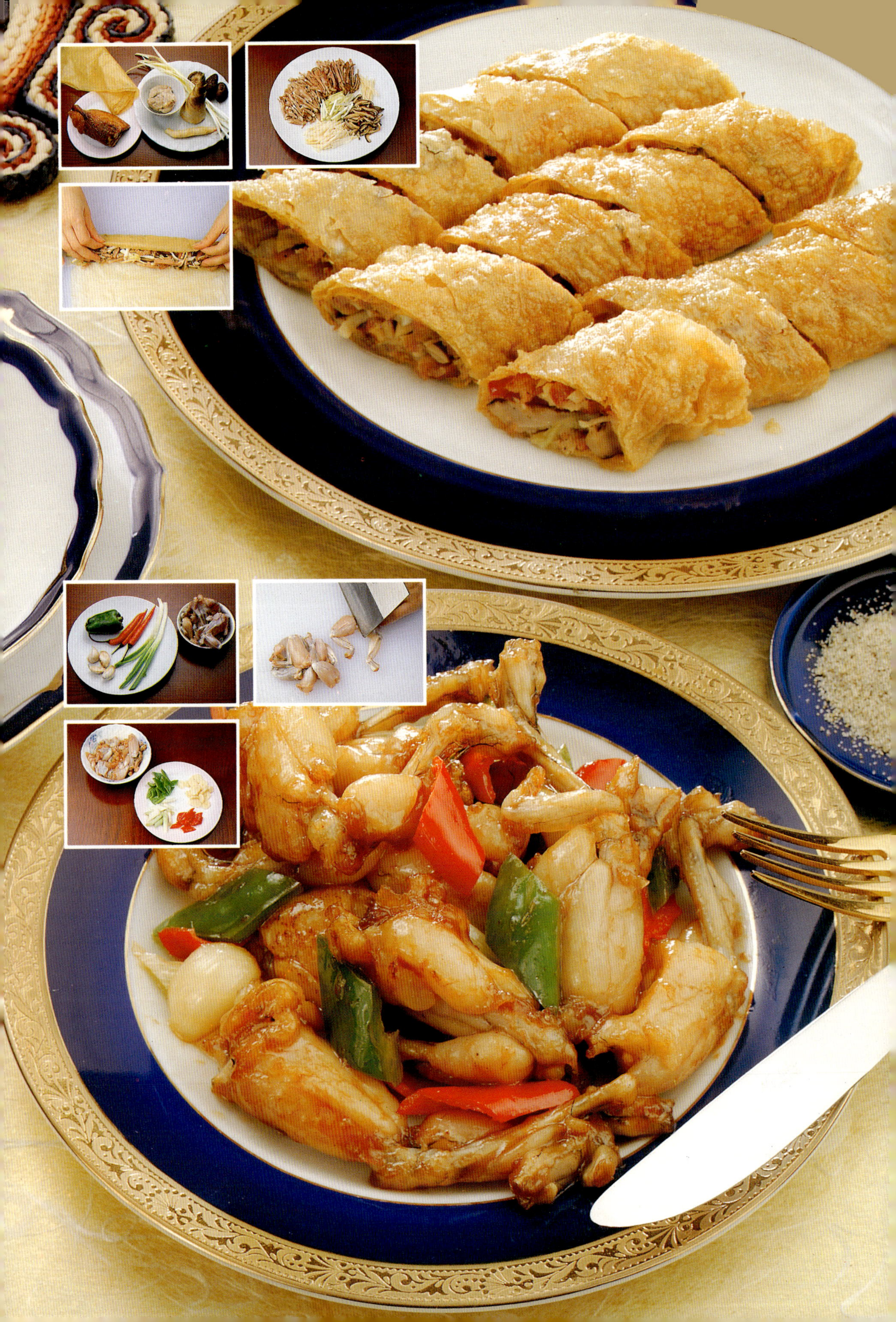

三絲鴨捲

材料
鹽水鴨（或燒鴨）¼隻　瘦豬肉3兩　筍1支　香菇3朵　韭黃5支　嫩薑少許　豆腐衣3張

拌鴨料
蛋1個　醬油½湯匙　酒1茶匙　鹽½茶匙　麻油1茶匙　糖¼茶匙　胡椒粉少許

作法
1. 鴨去骨取肉，切成2寸長之細條，豬肉煮熟也切成相同大小，嫩薑、煮熟的筍、泡軟的香菇，均切成絲狀，韭黃切成1寸長段。
2. 上項各料盛在大碗中，加入拌鴨料拌勻，分別用豆腐衣包捲成長條筒狀（3條）
3. 油2杯燒至七分熱，放下鴨肉捲，用中火慢炸至外層酥脆即可撈出，切段盛盤（可附上花椒鹽或甜酸醬以供沾食）

Tri-Color Duck Rolls

Ingredients:
1/4 Roast duck, 112.5g Lean pork, 1 Bamboo shoot, 3pcs Black mushroom, 5pcs White leek, Young ginger, shredded, 3pcs Bean curd sheet

Seasonings:
1 Egg, 1/2T Soysauce, 1t Wine, 1/2t Salt, 1t Sesame oil, 1/4t Sugar, Pepper.

Methods:
1. Remove bones from duck, cut into 2" long strips. Cut boiled pork into same size, shred the cooked bamboo shoot, shred the soaked black mushroom. Cut white leek into 1" sections.
2. Mix the above ingredients with seasonings, wrap and fold with dried bean curd sheet to a roll. Make 3 rolls.
3. Deep fry rolls in warm oil over medium heat till crispy, drain and cut into sections. Serve with sweet & sour sauce or brown pepper corn salt

醬爆櫻桃

材料
田雞1斤　青椒1支　紅辣椒2支　蔥2支　大蒜片15片

醃料
醬油½湯匙　太白粉2茶匙

綜合調味料
甜麵醬1湯匙　水、酒、醬油各½湯匙　糖1茶匙　番茄醬1茶匙　麻油少許

作法
1. 田雞僅取用雙腿，分割後用醃料醃20分鐘以上（放入冰箱中）。蔥、紅辣椒切斜段，青椒切斜塊。
2. 燒熱1杯油，將田雞腿過油炸熟瀝出。
3. 另起油鍋，用1湯匙油爆香大蒜片及蔥段，再將綜合調味料倒入炒香，放下青、紅椒及田雞腿，大火快炒，拌炒均勻便可裝盤。

* 菜名之「櫻桃」係江浙人見田雞腿炸熟後腿肉漲圓而稱之。故本菜僅用田雞腿。家庭中烹調可將有肉的部分切塊來爆炒。亦可以雞肉來做「醬爆雞丁」。

Frog's Legs with Sweet Soybean Sauce

Ingredients:
600g Frog's legs, 1 Green pepper, 2 Red chilli, 2 Green onion, 15pcs Garlic slices.

Seasonings:
❶ 1/2T Soysauce, 2t Cornstarch.
❷ 1T Sweet soybean paste, 1/2T Wine, 1/2T Water, 1/2T Soysauce, 1t Sugar, 1t Ketchup. 1/2t Sesame oil.

Methods:
1. Cut each frog's leg into 2 parts, marinate with ❶ for 20 minutes.
2. Heat 1C oil to fry frog's legs to done, drain.
3. Heat 1T oil to fry garlic and green onion, add seasonings ❷, bring to a boil, put green pepper, red chili, frog's legs, stir fry over high heat, mix evenly. Serve.

✤ Shanghai cuisine call this dish "Cherry with Sweet Soybean Sauce" because the frog's legs shrink after fried till done and look like cherries.

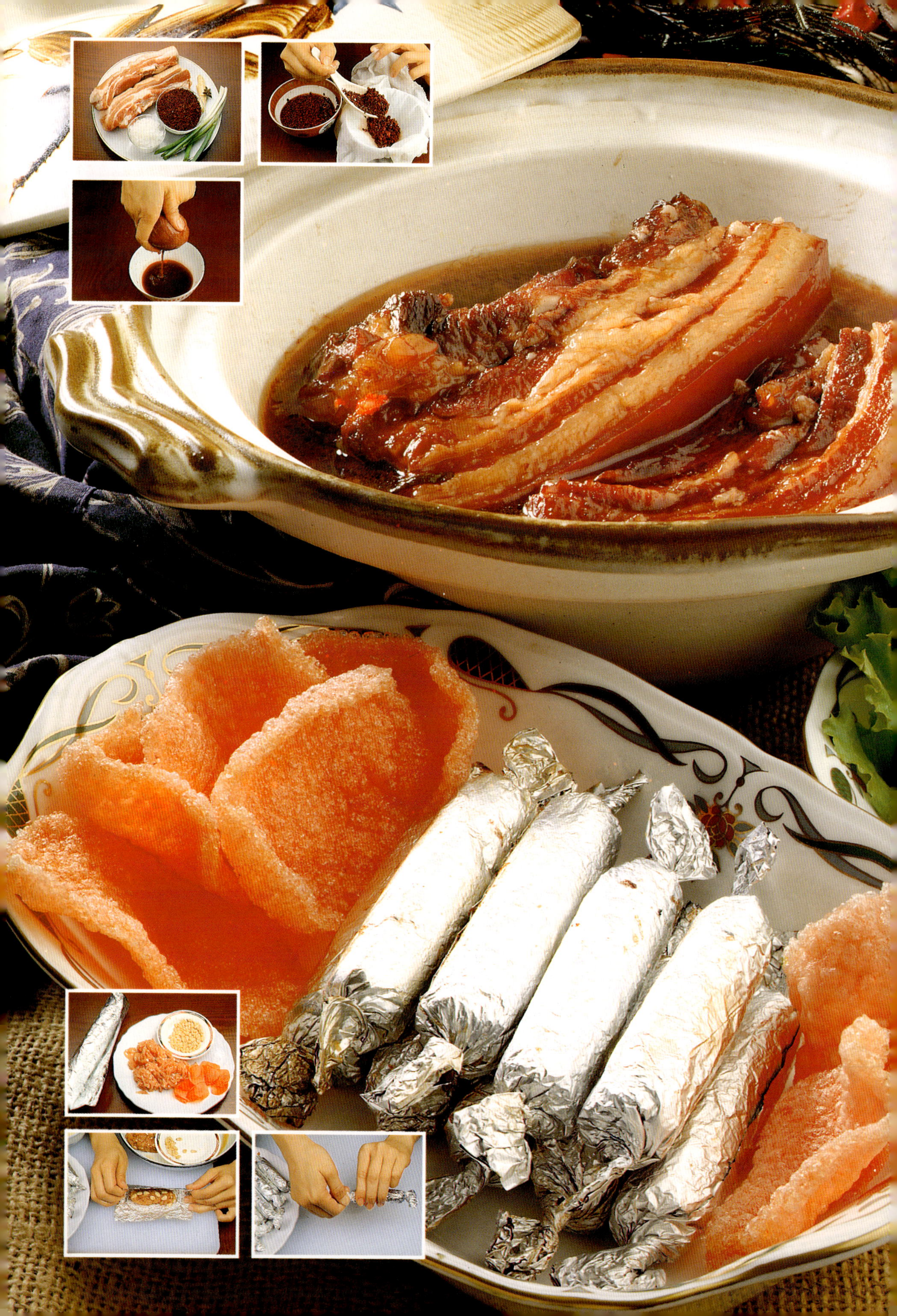

紅米醬肉

材料
五花肉1½斤　紅米½杯　葱4支　薑2片　八角1顆

調味料
淡色醬油4湯匙　酒½杯　冰糖½杯

作法
1. 五花肉整塊連皮切成3長條，用開水燙過，放入墊上葱段、薑片之砂鍋或湯鍋中，加入滾水3杯及八角，小火煮半小時以上至肉已半爛爲止。
2. 紅米用2杯水泡軟後，用紗布袋包紮，將紅米汁擠入鍋中，紗布包亦放入，再加調味料。先用大火煮滾數分鐘，繼續用小火燒煮1小時半以上至肉已十分軟爛。
3. 食前取出，切成約2公分寬度，裝盤淋上肉汁即可上桌。
* 這道菜因烹調較費時，因此一次可做多些，燒好浸泡在湯汁中，食前另行加熱

Pork with Red Rice Sauce

Ingredients:
900g Pork (bacon part), 1/2C Red rice, 4 Green onion, 2pcs Ginger, 1 Star anise.

Seasonings:
4T Soysauce, 1/2C Wine, 1/2C Rock sugar.

Methods:
1. Cut pork belly into 2" thick slices about 10" long. Make 3 pieces, blench in boiling water, drain, put into a casserole with green onion, ginger, 3C boiling water & star anise, cook over low heat for 1/2 hour.
2. Soak red rice with 2C water until soft, wrap in a cloth, tie up and squeeze the juice out, pour this juice and rice package to the casserole, add seasonings and cook over high heat for 5 minutes. Then cook over low heat for 1-1/2 hour till pork is tender.
3. When serve, cut into 2cm cubes.
♣ This dish needs long time to cook, you may cook a large portion and serve separately.

銀紙松子肉

材料
豬肉(梅花肉或夾心肉)半斤　松子2湯匙　鋁箔紙(8公分見方)8張　蝦片酌量　葱2支　薑2片

調味料
醬油1湯匙　糖½茶匙　鹽¼茶匙　胡椒粉、五香粉各少許

作法
1. 豬肉切成細條，葱、薑拍碎加水2湯匙，擠出葱薑水拌入肉中，再加調味料拌攪，加入松子。
2. 鋁箔紙刷上少許麻油，放入約1½湯匙的1.項料，包捲成小棒狀。
3. 投入熱油中炸約2分鐘即可，另以炸蝦片圍飾。

Pine Nuts Pork in Silver Stick

Ingredients:
300g Pork, 2T Pine nuts, 8pcs Aluminum foil (8cm x 8cm), Dried shrimp chip, 2 Green onion, 2pcs Ginger slices.

Seasonings:
1T Soysauce, 1/2t Sugar, 1/4t Salt, Pepper, Five-spicy powder, Meat tenderizer (optional).

Methods:
1. Cut pork into fine shreds. Pat the green onion & ginger, soak with 2T water, squeeze out the to mix with pork & seasonings, then mix with the pine nuts.
2. Brush some sesame oil on the aluminum foil, put in 1-1/2T pork mixture. Wrap & fold into a roll.
3. Deep fry in hot oil for 2 minutes. Put on a plate. Serve with deep fried shrimp chip.

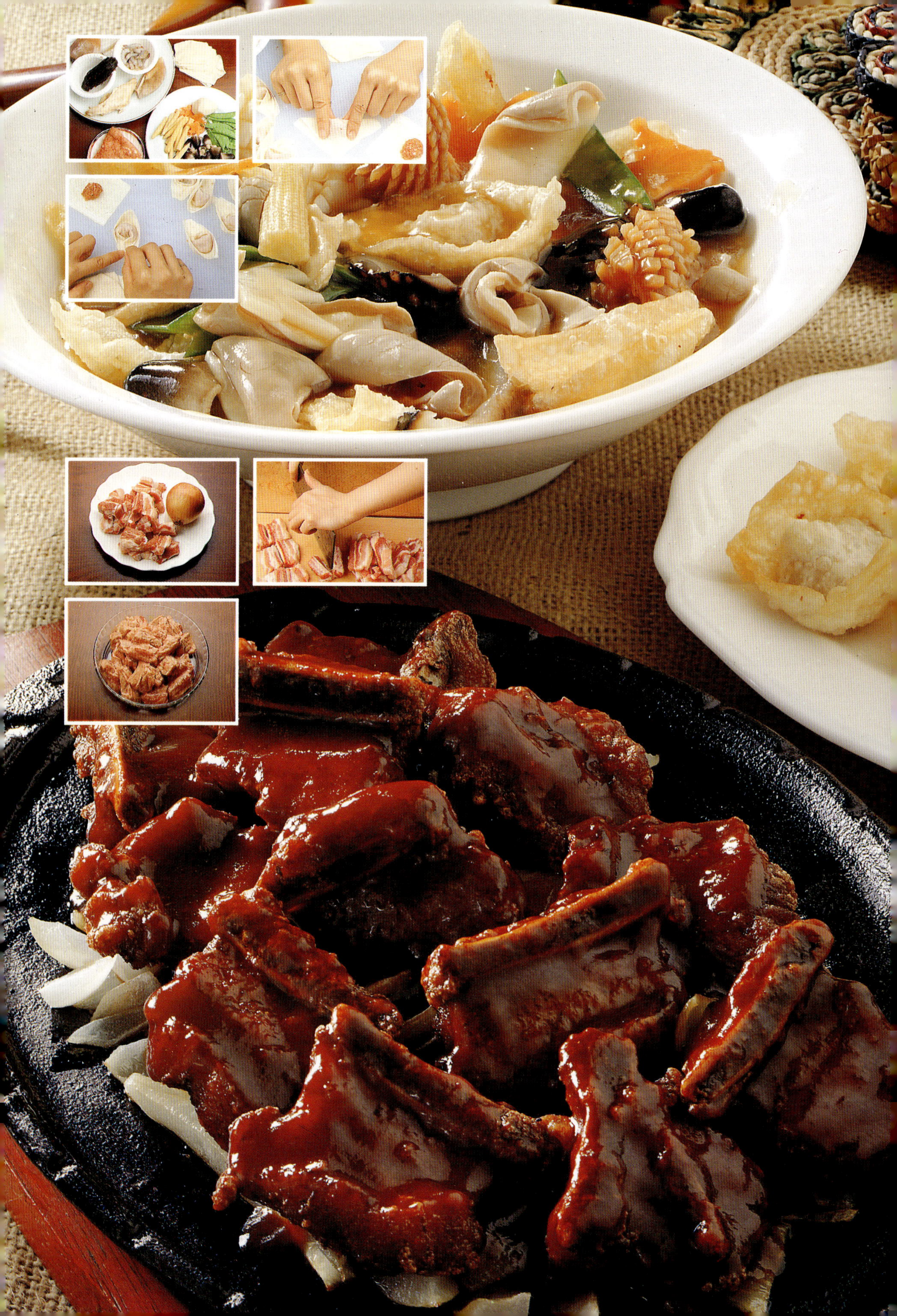

什錦燴響鈴

材料
豬肉或雞肉片、魷魚、花枝、蝦仁、豬肚、海參等各酌量　筍片、胡蘿蔔片、豌豆夾等蔬菜料隨意　蔥、薑各少許　餛飩皮12張　絞肉3兩

調味料
高湯3杯　醬油½湯匙　鹽1茶匙　胡椒粉少許　濕太白粉1湯匙

作法
1. 絞肉加少許醬油及鹽，調成絞肉餡，用餛飩皮包成小餛飩。
2. 將選用的各種材料分別切成片狀，用滾水川燙一下撈出。
3. 起油鍋爆香蔥、薑後，淋入高湯煮滾，再將各種材料依硬度先後下鍋，調味後勾芡，裝在大碗中保溫。
4. 熱油將小餛飩炸熟成金黃色，裝在大碗中，淋入3.項，使其有響聲，快速分食。

＊什錦料不拘種類，可隨意挑選調配

Deep Fried Bells with Assorted Ingredients

Ingredients:
Pork, Chicken & squid, Cuttlefish, Shrimp, Pork stomach, Sea cucumber, Bamboo shoot, Carrot, Snow peas, Black mushroom, Straw mushroom, Babycorn, Green onion, Ginger, 12pcs Won-Ton skin, 112.5g Minced pork.

Seasonings:
3T Soupstock, 1/2T Soysauce, 1t Salt, Pepper, 1T Cornstarch paste.

Methods:
1. Mix minced pork with soysauce & salt, stir till very sticky, wrap in Won-Ton skins.
2. Cut every ingredient into slices. Blench in boiling water.
3. Heat 2T oil to stir fry green onion & ginger, add in soup stock. When boiling, add all ingredients (putting in a sequence according to each ingredient's hard texture), season and thicken
4. Deep fry Won-Ton to golden brown, put in a plate. Pour over the thicken assorted ingredients while serving.

♣ You may add no matter what kind of ingredients.

京都子排

材料
豬小排12兩　洋蔥絲1杯

醃肉料
醬油2湯匙　太白粉、麵粉1½湯匙　水2湯匙　小蘇打粉¼茶匙

綜合調味料
番茄醬、辣醬油、A1牛排醬各1湯匙　清水2湯匙　糖½湯匙　麻油½茶匙

作法
1. 將豬小排切成2寸寬，骨頭粗的由中間劈開，用醃肉料醃1小時以上。
2. 用少量油炒熟洋蔥絲，加鹽調味盛盤內。
3. 炸油燒熱放入豬小排，大火炸2～3分鐘，見外皮酥脆即可撈起。
4. 另用1湯匙油炒煮綜合調味料，煮滾後將排骨下鍋拌合即可盛放洋蔥上。

Spareribs with King-Tu Sauce

Ingredients:
450g Spareribs, 1C Onion, shredded.

Seasoning:
❶ 2T Soysauce, 1-1/2T Cornstarch, 1-1/2T Flour, 2T Water, 1/4t Baking soda.
❷ 1T Ketchup, 1T A1 Sauce, 1T Worcester sauce, 2T Water, 1/2T Sugar, 1/2t Sesame oil.

Methods:
1. Cut spareribs into 2" sections, cut and split (from the bone) into 2 parts, marinate with sauce ❶ for 1 hour.
2. Stir fry onion with 2T hot oil, season with salt. Remove to a plate.
3. Deep fry spareribs over high heat for 2~3 minutes till golden brown.
4. Heat 1T oil to fry sauce ❷. When boiling, mix with fried spareribs. Put on fried onion.

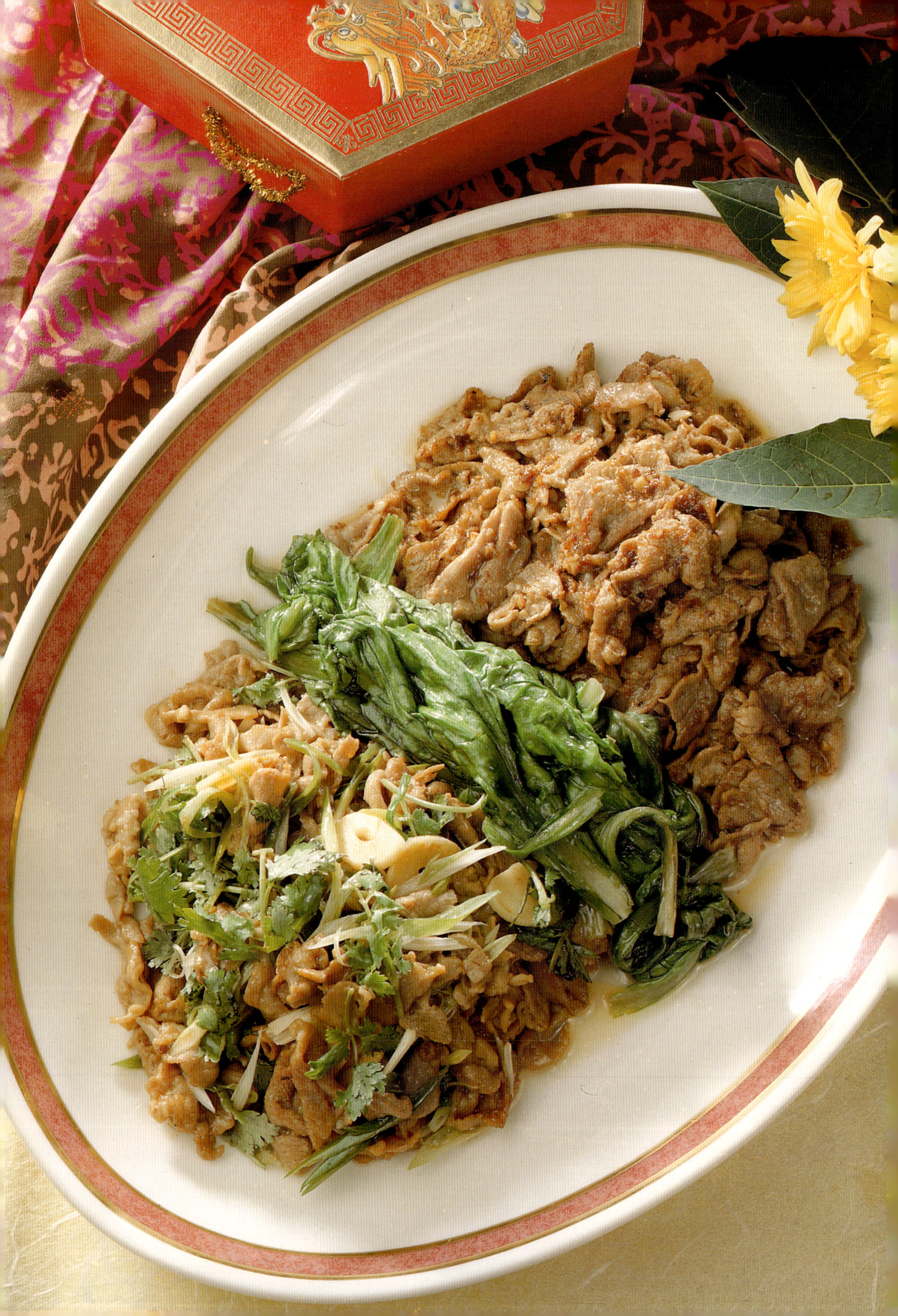

爆羊肉雙味

沙茶羊肉片材料
羊肉片6兩　大蒜屑1湯匙　青菜隨意

調味料
沙茶醬1½湯匙　醬油、酒各½湯匙　糖¼茶匙

作法
1. 小碗中先將調味料調勻備用。
2. 起油鍋炒熟青菜，瀝乾湯汁，排放在盤中間。
3. 用2湯匙油爆香大蒜屑，放下羊肉片大火爆炒至熟，淋入1.項調味料拌勻，盛在青菜的一邊。

葱爆羊肉材料
羊肉片6兩　大蒜片1湯匙　葱絲1杯　香菜半杯

醃肉料
醬油1湯匙　酒½湯匙　花椒粉少許　油½湯匙

調味料
醬油½湯匙　麻油1茶匙　醋2茶匙

作法
1. 羊肉用醃肉料醃10分鐘以上。
2. 燒熱2湯匙油爆香大蒜片，馬上放下羊肉片，大火拌炒，見肉片轉白，放下葱絲續炒，淋下調味料快速炒勻便可盛出。也可在最後加入香菜段少許一起拌合。

Quick Stir Fried Lamb Double Flavors

A. Lamb with Sa-Cha Sauce
Ingredients:
225g Lamb slices, 1T Garlic, chopped, Green vegetables.

Seasonings:
1-1/2T Sa-Cha Sauce, 1/2T Soysauce, 1/2T Wine, 1/4t Sugar.

Methods:
1. Mix seasonings in a bowl.
2. Stir fry the vegetable and put on center of a plate.
3. Heat 2T oil, stir fry garlic, add lamb and stir fry quickly over high heat until done, mix with seasonings and pour on the vegetables.

B. Lamb with Green Onion
Ingredients:
225g Lamb slices, 1T Garlic, sliced, 1C Green onion, 1/2C Chinese parsley.

Seasonings:
❶ 1T Soysauce, 1/2T Wine, 1/2T Oil, Brown pepper corn powder.
❷ 1/2T Soysauce, 1t Sesame oil, 2t Vinegar.

Methods:
1. Marinate lamb with seasoning ❶ for 10 minutes.
2. Fry garlic in 2T heated oil, add lamb and fry over high heat. When meat turns white, add green onion & seasonings ❷. Mix well and serve. You may add Chinese parsley to fry at last.

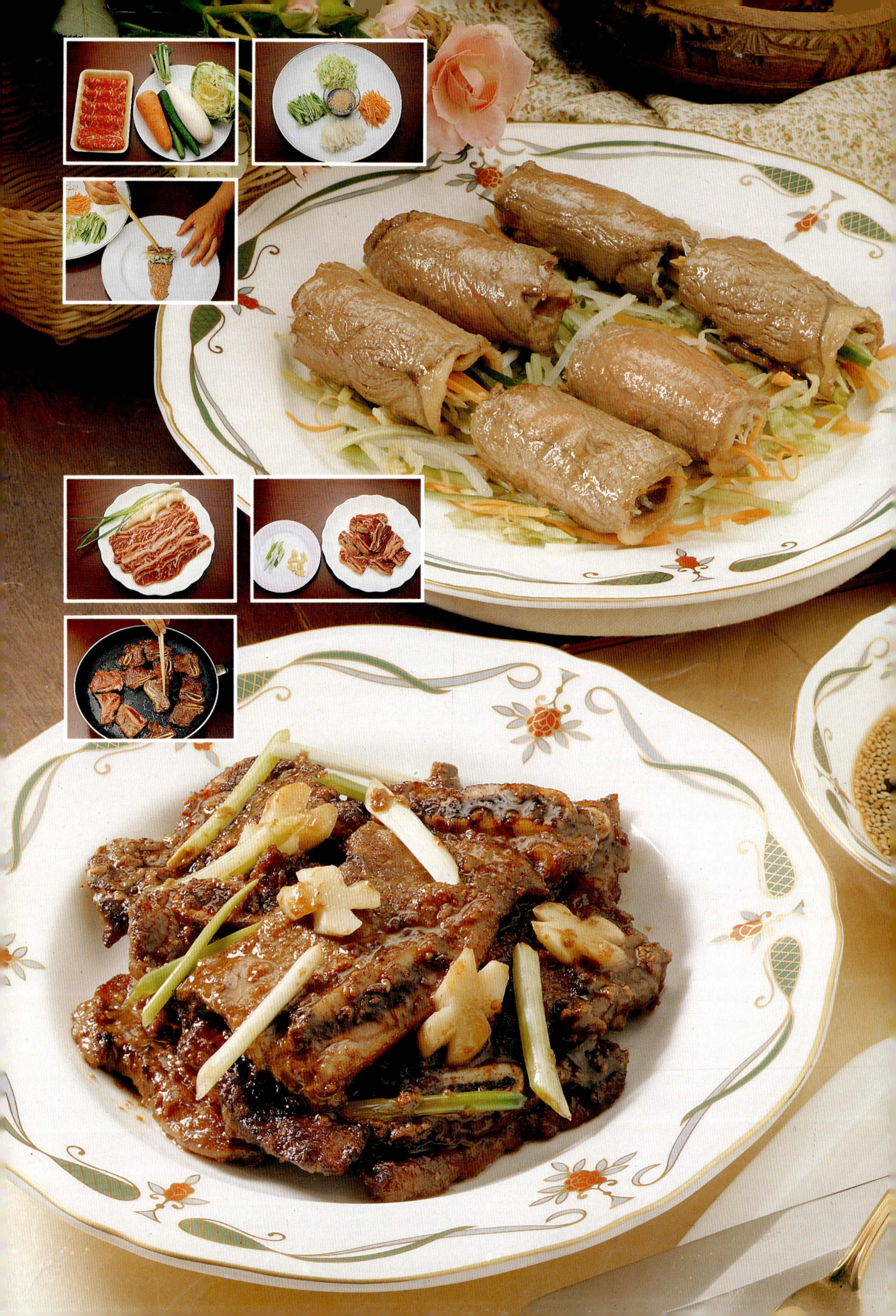

錦繡牛肉捲

材料
大薄片嫩牛肉6片　白蘿蔔絲、胡蘿蔔絲、小黃瓜絲、生菜絲、香菜絲各酌量

沾料
醬油1湯匙　麻油½湯匙　清湯3湯匙　炒過的芝麻1茶匙

作法
1. 將牛肉片攤開，撒下少許鹽、胡椒粉，逐片用少許油煎熟。
2. 蘿蔔絲、胡蘿蔔絲、小黃瓜絲、香菜絲及生菜絲先混合後，包在牛肉片中，分別捲成筒狀，放在盤中。
3. 將調好的沾料淋到牛肉捲上即可。

Beef Rolls

Ingredients:
6 pcs Beef tenderloin slices, Turnip, shredded, Carrot, shredded, Cucumber, shredded, Lettuce, shredded, Chinese parsley, shredded.

Dipping sauce:
1T Soysauce, 1/2T Sesame oil, 3T Soup stock, 1t Fried sesame seeds.

Methods:
1. Spread the beef, sprinkle some salt & pepper, fry both sides with a little oil.
2. Mix turnip, carrot, cucumber, lettuce and parsley, arrange on the beef, roll into a cylinder, put on a plate.
3. Pour the mixed dipping sauce on beef rolls and serve.

沙茶牛仔骨

材料
牛小排4片　葱段1湯匙　薑片4小片

醃料
醬油1湯匙　太白粉1茶匙　水少許

調味料
沙茶醬1湯匙　醬油½湯匙　酒½湯匙　水½湯匙

作法
1. 將牛小排按骨縫分割成小塊，全部放入大碗中，用醃料拌醃。
2. 用熱油5～6湯匙將牛小排大火煎熟瀝出（或用多量油炸熟）。
3. 用1湯匙油爆香葱段及薑片，放入牛小排再加入調味料，大火炒煮均勻，淋少許油即可盛盤。

Beef Spareribs with Sa-Cha Sauce

Ingredients:
4 Beef spareribs, 1T Green onion, sectioned, 4pcs Ginger slices.

Seasonings:
❶ 1T Soysauce, 1t Cornstarch, 2t Water.
❷ 1T Sa-Cha Sauce, 1/2T Soysauce, 1/2T Wine, 1/2T Water.

Methods:
1. Cut beef spareribs into small sections, marinate with seasonings ❶.
2. Heat 5T oil to fry both sides of spareribs over high heat, drain.
3. Heat 1T oil to stir fry green onion & ginger, add spareribs & seasonings ❷, fry over high heat, mix evenly and serve. (Decorated with green vegetables).

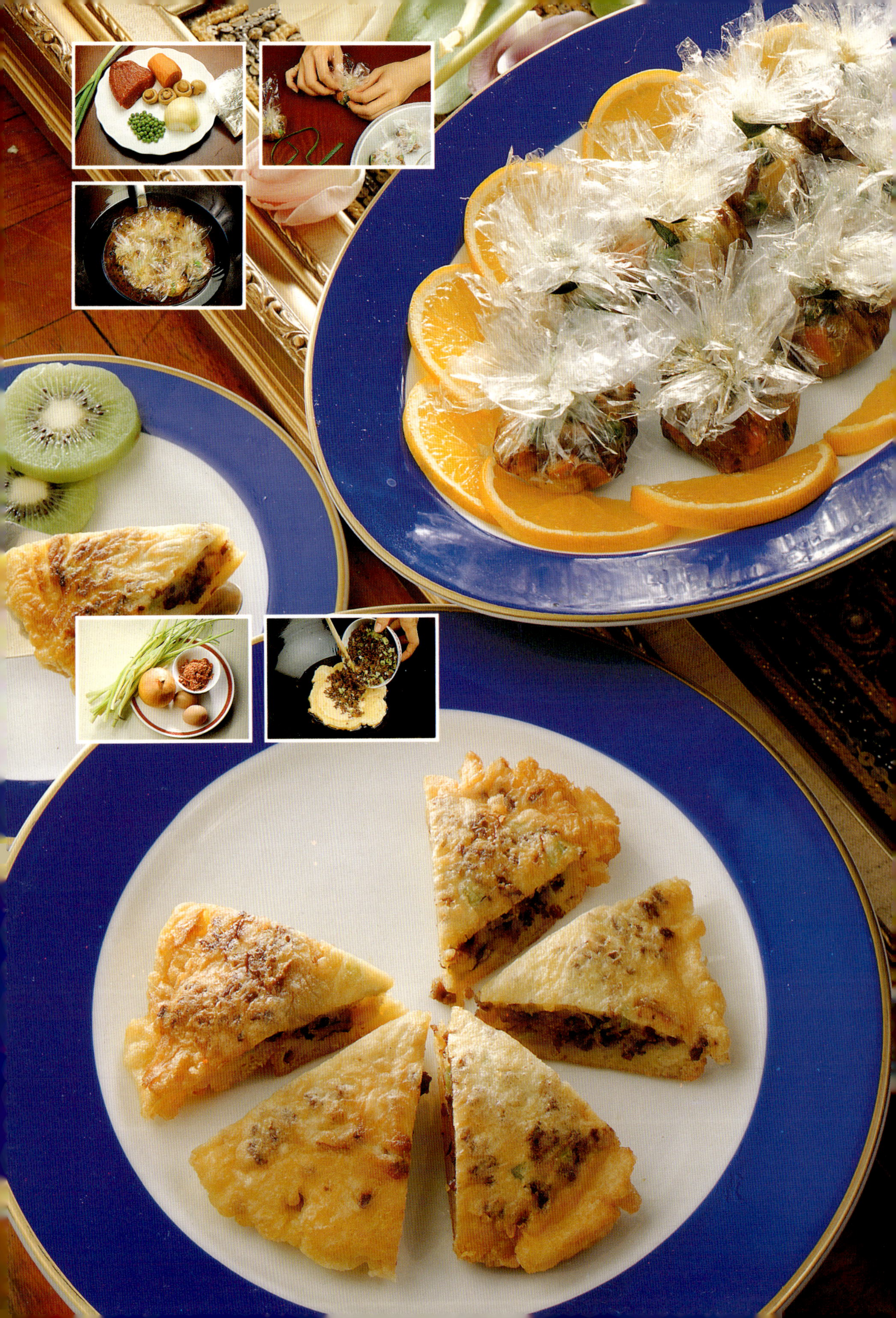

牛肉石榴包

材料

嫩牛肉6兩　洋蔥丁½杯　熟胡蘿蔔片少許　洋菇片⅓杯　豌豆2湯匙　青蒜葉或韭菜數支　玻璃紙（12公分四方）10張

醃肉料

醬油、酒各½湯匙　鹽½茶匙　糖¼茶匙　胡椒粉少許　麻油1茶匙　太白粉1茶匙

調味料

蠔油1湯匙　麻油1茶匙

作法

1. 將牛肉切片，用醃料拌勻醃10分鐘以上，用熱油泡熟。
2. 用1湯匙油爆香洋蔥丁，加入洋菇片、胡蘿蔔片等同炒，淋下蠔油，放入牛肉片下鍋，大火炒勻，撒下豌豆及麻油，拌勻即可盛出。
3. 每張玻璃紙上刷少許油，包入牛肉餡料約1½湯匙，收口後用燙過的青蒜條紮住，翻開紙角便成石榴狀，全部排在大漏勺中。
4. 用熱油或熱水浸泡牛肉包（連漏勺）至內部夠熱即可瀝出裝盤。

Beef in Pomegranate Package

Ingredients:
225g Beef tenderloin, 1/2C Onion & Carrot slices, 1/3C Mushroom , 2T Snow peas , 10pcs Cellophane paper (12cm square), leek.

Seasonings:
❶ 1/2T Soysauce, 1/2T Wine, 1/2t Salt, 1/4t Sugar, Pepper, 1t Sesame oil, Constarch.
❷ 1T Oyster sauce, 1t Sesame oil .

Methods:
1. Slice the beef, marinate with ❶ for 10 minutes. Deep fry in hot oil.
2. Heat 1T oil to stir fry onion, mushroom, carrot, add oyster oil, beef, stir evenly over high heat, finally add snow peas, sesame oil. This is the stuffing.
3. Brush some oil on each cellophane paper. Fill in 1-1/2T stuffing and wrap, fasten with boiled leek, put all packages in a strainer.
4. Soak all packages (together with the strainer) in hot oil or hot water until the stuffing gets hot, drain and serve.

中式牛肉派

材料

絞牛肉4兩　洋蔥屑⅓杯　芹菜屑¼杯

調味料

醬油、酒各½湯匙　鹽¼茶匙　胡椒粉少許

蛋麵糊

蛋3個　麵粉3湯匙　太白粉1湯匙　鹽½茶匙　發泡粉½茶匙

作法

1. 先用熱油2湯匙炒香洋蔥屑，再加入絞牛肉大火炒熟，加調味料後，撒下芹菜屑即盛出。
2. 在大碗中將蛋打鬆後，將蛋麵糊調勻。
3. 用平底鍋將3湯匙油燒熱，倒入一半的蛋麵糊料，中火煎成半熟時，放下牛肉料平均鋪平，再將另一半之蛋麵糊料淋下，蓋住牛肉餡，用小火燜煎至熟。煎時分數次淋下一些油，且中途需翻面，以使兩面均呈金黃色。取出切成尖角型，排入盤中。

Beef Pie Chinese Style

Ingredients:
150g Minced beef, 1/3C Onion, chopped, 1/4C Celery, chopped.

Seasonings:
❶ 1/2T Soysauce, 1/2T Wine, 1/4t Salt, pepper

Batter:
3 Eggs, 3T Flour, 1T Cornstarch, 1/2t Salt, 1/2t Baking powder.

Methods:
1. Heat 2T oil to fry onion, add beef and seasonings, fry over high heat, mix finally with celery.
2. Mix the batter.
3. Heat 3T oil in a pan, pour half of batter, fry to medium, add beef, pour another half of batter, fry over low heat to form a cake. (Add some oil intermediately) when the color turns golden brown, take out and cut into pieces. Serve.

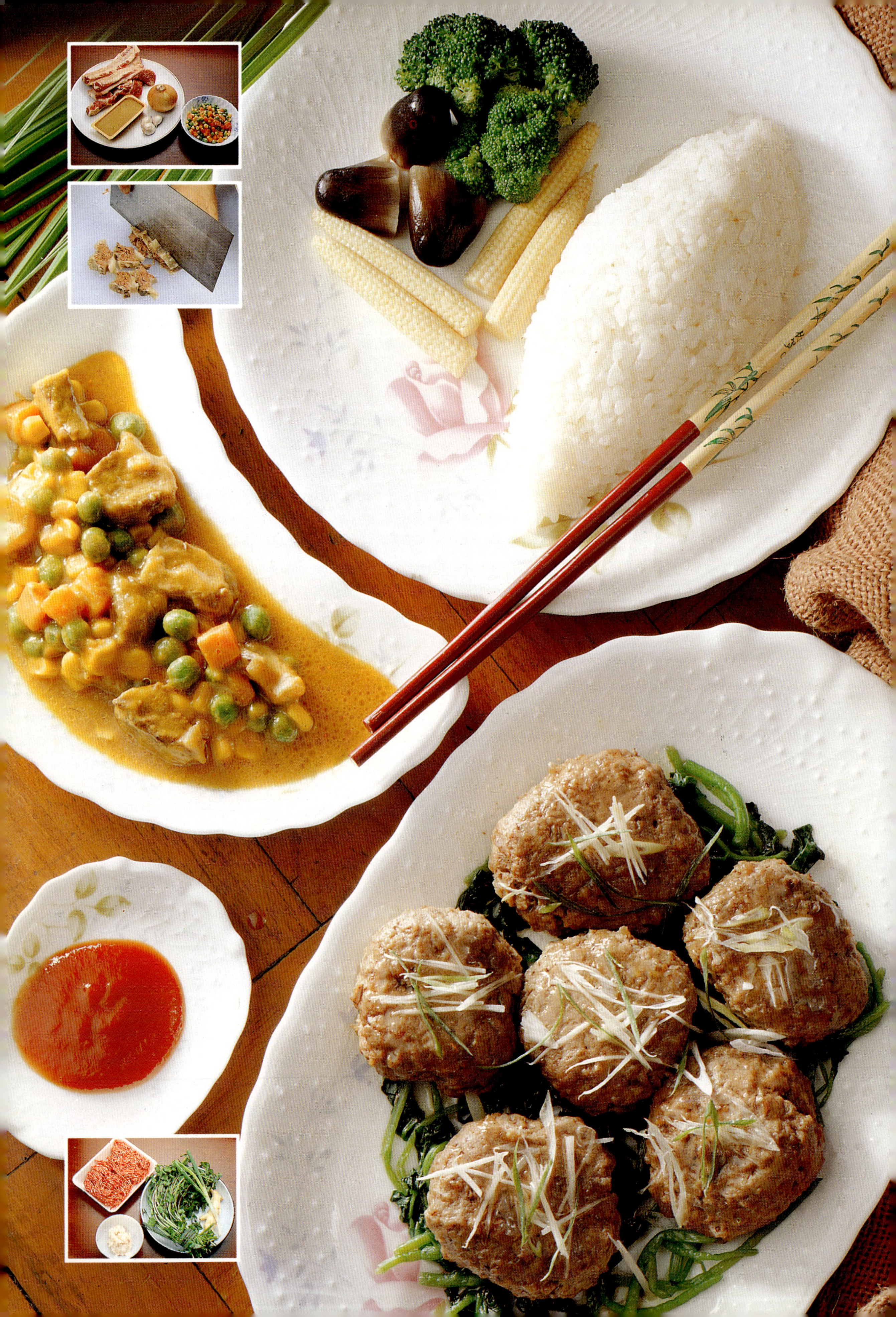

什蔬燴咖哩牛肉

材料
牛肋條或牛腱1斤　洋葱屑½杯　大蒜屑1湯匙　冷凍什錦蔬菜1½杯

煮牛肉料
水4杯　葱2支　薑2片　八角1粒　酒1湯匙

調味料
咖哩粉1½湯匙　鹽1茶匙　糖½茶匙　濕太白粉酌量

作法
1. 牛肉用開水燙煮滾後撈出。煮牛肉料先煮開後，放下牛肉煮至八分爛，取出切成1寸四方大小。
2. 用2湯匙油炒香洋葱屑、大蒜屑及咖哩粉，加入牛肉及湯汁（約1杯，不足可加水），再煮5分鐘。
3. 放下冷凍蔬菜料再煮滾，加鹽、糖調味，勾芡後即可裝盤上桌，淋在白飯、熟麵條或通心粉上均可。

* 目前市面有售已調味之咖哩塊，可挑選喜愛口味，不需再調味及勾芡。

Curry Beef with Assorted Vegetables

Ingredients:
600g Beef brisket, 1/2C Onion, chopped, 1T Garlic, chopped, 1-1/2C Frozen assorted vegetables.

Seasonings:
❶ 4C Water, 2 Green onion, 2 Ginger slices, 1 Star anise, 1T Wine.
❷ 1-1/2T Curry powder, 1t Salt, 1/2t Sugar, Cornstarch paste.

Methods:
1. Blanch beef in boiling water, drian. Boil seasoning ❶, add beef and cook for 1 hour, take out and cut into 1" cubes.
2. Heat 2T oil, stir fry onion, garlic & curry powder, add beef and soup, cook for 5 more minutes.
3. Add frozen vegetables, sugar, salt, thicken and serve with rice, or noodles.

♣ The curry cube cake can be used as a substitute for powder.

葱油淋漢堡

材料
全瘦絞牛肉半斤　絞肥豬肉2兩　西洋菜1把　葱絲、嫩薑絲各½杯

拌肉料
葱薑水⅓杯　嫩精⅓茶匙　酒½湯匙　醬油½湯匙　鹽½茶匙　胡椒粉少許　太白粉1湯匙

作法
1. 絞牛肉與肥肉混合均勻，加入葱薑水（葱2支、薑3片拍碎，泡入⅓杯水中）等拌肉料，用手抓拌摔擲多次，使肉增加彈性。
2. 西洋菜切短，在開水中燙煮一下撈出，冷開水沖涼後，鋪在深盤中。
3. 牛肉做成6個圓球，壓成扁圓形的漢堡排，放在西洋菜上，大火蒸8分鐘，再撒下葱、薑絲，淋入燒得極熱之油，透出香氣即可。

Chinese Hamburger with Green Onion

Ingredients:
300g Minced lean beef, 75g Minced pork fat, Watercress, 1/2C Green onion, shredded, 1/2C Ginger, shedded.

Seasonings:
1/3t Meat tenderizer, 1/2T Wine, 1/2T Soysauce, 1/3C Ginger & green onion juice, 1T Cornstarch, 1/4t Pepper.

Methods:
1. Mix minced beef and pork fat, add seasonings and mix well, stir to sticky.
2. Cut watercress into sections 2" long, blanch and rinse cool, put on the plate.
3. Use beef to make 6 balls, press flat a little bit, arrange on the watercress, steam for 8 minutes.
4. Sprinkle ginger & green onion shreds, splash hot oil on top, serve.

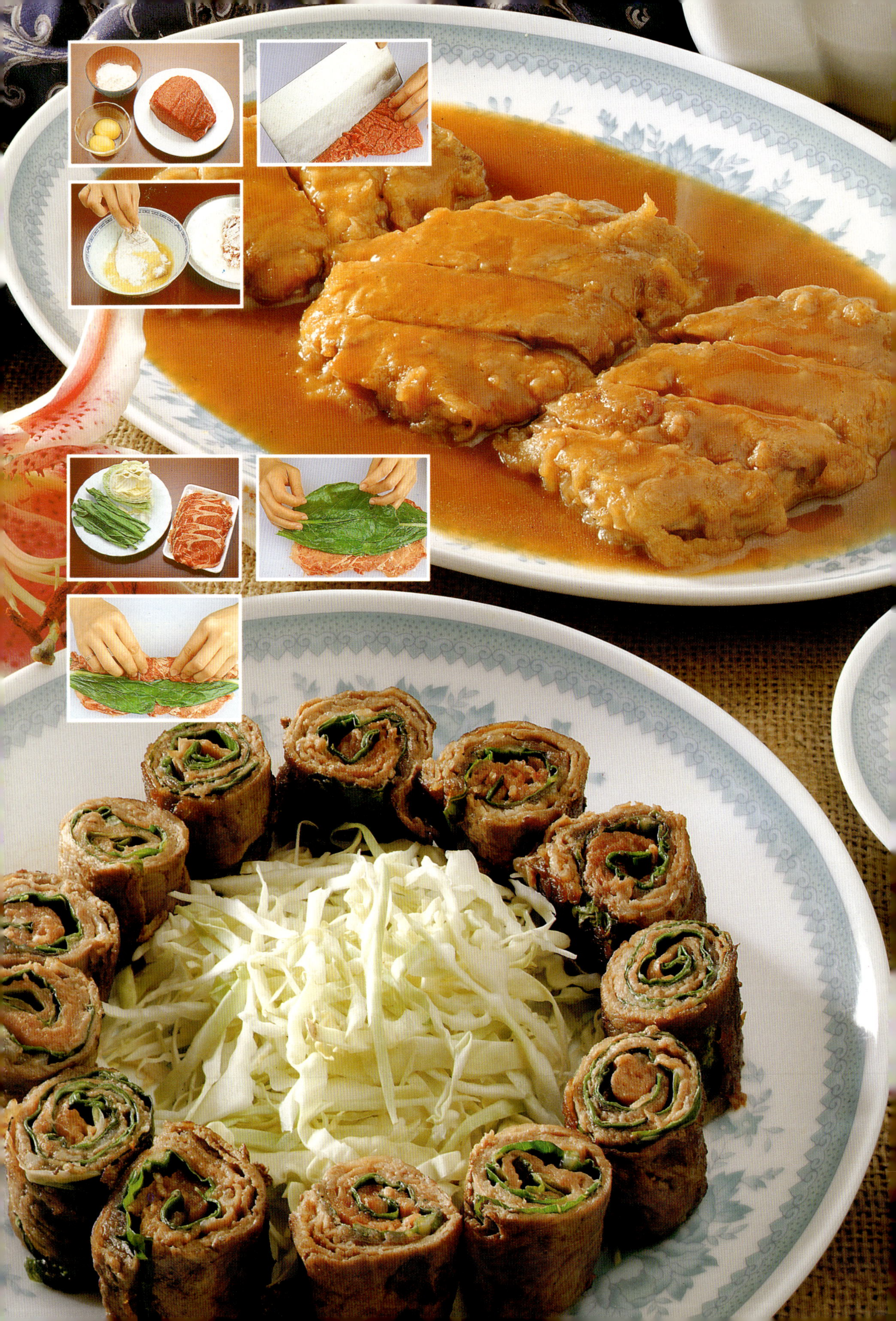

鍋燼牛里脊

材料
牛里脊肉6兩　麵粉2湯匙　蛋黃2個

醃肉料
葱、薑末各少許　太白粉1湯匙　水1湯匙

調味料
清湯(或水)2/3杯　醬油2湯匙　酒1/2湯匙　糖1茶匙　鹽1/4茶匙　胡椒粉少許

作法
1. 將牛里脊肉橫片成1/3寸厚的大片(可買切好之牛排再橫切成1/3寸厚片)，在肉面上劃切交叉刀口，用醃肉料醃10分鐘以上
2. 牛肉先沾麵粉再沾滿蛋黃，用熱油煎黃
3. 用1湯匙油炒煮調味料，煮滾後將牛肉入鍋，小火燜煮約2分鐘
4. 夾出牛肉切寬條裝盤，淋入肉汁即可

Pan Stewed Beef

Ingredients:
225g Beef tenderloin, 2T Flour, 2 Egg yolk

Seasonings:
❶ Green onion, Ginger (chopped), 1T Cornstarch, 1T Water.
❷ 2/3C Soup stock, 2T Soysauce, 1/2T Wine, 1t Sugar, 1/4t Salt, Pepper.

Methods:
1. Cut beef into 1/3" thick slices, score crisscross on surface, marinate with sauce ❶ for 10 minutes.
2. Sprinkle flour on beef, dip in egg yolk, fry in hot oil.
3. Heat 1T oil to fry seasonings ❷, when boiling add beef in and cook over low heat for 2 minutes.
4. Take out beef and cut into thick sticks, put on a plate, pour the sauce on

千層牛肉捲

材料
大薄片牛肉8片　芥蘭菜葉4枚　包心菜絲1杯

醃肉料
酒1/2湯匙　醬油1/2湯匙　胡椒粉1/4茶匙

作法
1. 將牛肉片用醃肉料拌醃一下。以4片為一單位，半重疊，鋪成大片狀，撒下少許太白粉，放上2張燙過的芥蘭菜葉，用手推捲成筒狀，做成2捲。
2. 用平底鍋燒熱油少許，放下牛肉捲煎黃(如喜歡極熟，可淋下少許水燜煮片刻)。
3. 趁熱切成半寸寬厚度，切口向上裝碟，包心菜或生菜絲作墊底，附上喜愛之醬料蘸用即可

* 沾料可選用如芥末醬加醬油、葱、薑絲加醬油、辣醬油或牛排醬均可

Thousand Layer Beef Rolls

Ingredients:
8 pcs Beef tenderloin large thin slices, 4 pcs Mustard green vegetable leaves, 1C Cabbage shredded.

Seasonings:
1/2T Wine, 1/2T Soysauce, 1/4t Pepper.

Methods:
1. Marinate beef with seasonings for 10 minutes. Arrange 4 pieces one overlap the other, sprinkle cornstarch, cover the beef with blanched mustard green leaves, roll tightly into a cylinder.
2. Heat 2T oil in a pan, fry the beef rolls to done
3. Cut into 1/2" sections, arrange on a plate, decorated by cabbage shreds. Serve with dipping sauce.
♣ Worchester sauce, A1 sauce, mustard sauce or green onion & soysauce can be the dipping sauce

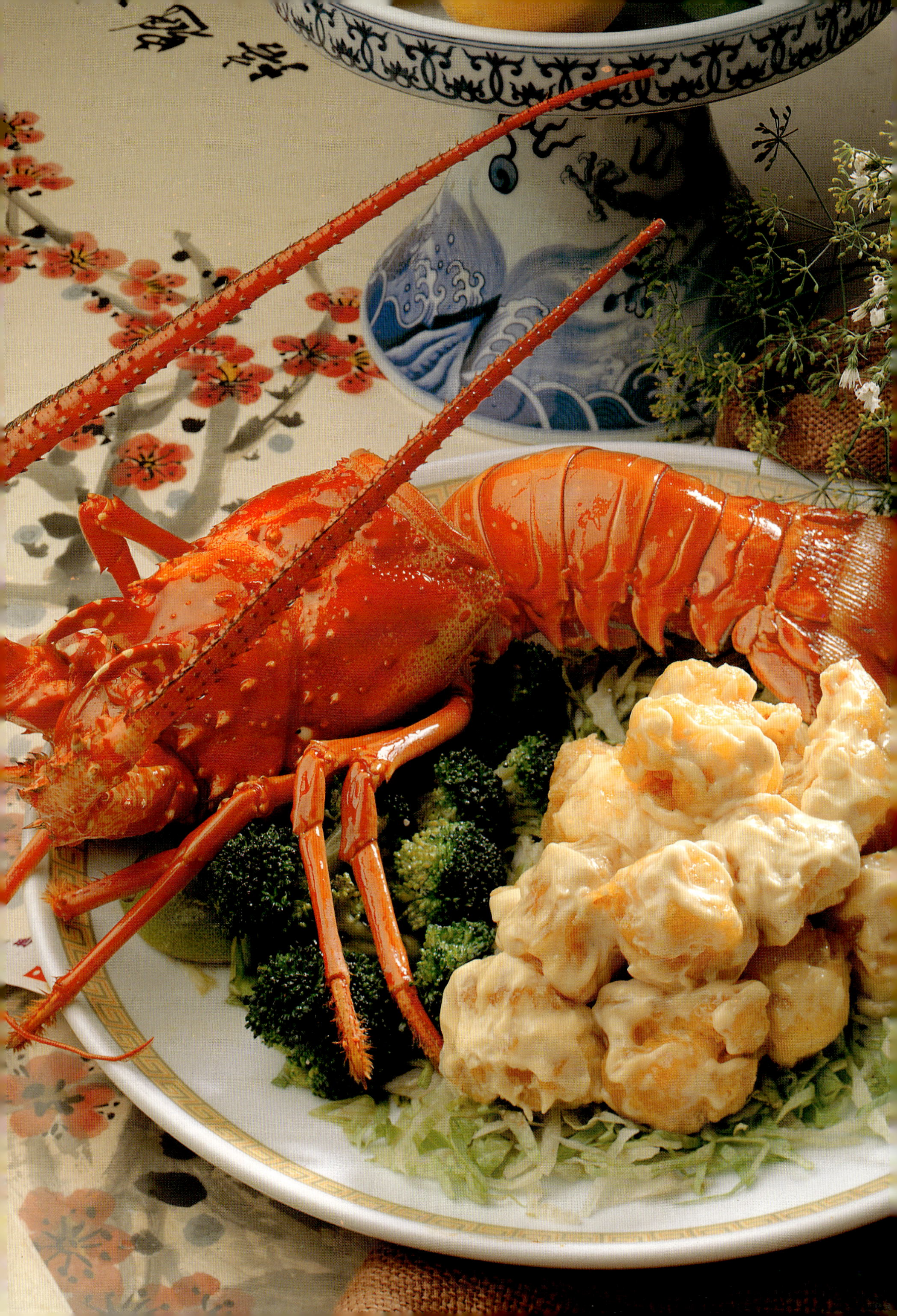

生汁龍蝦球

材料
龍蝦1隻　明蝦3隻　玉米粉½杯　青花菜1棵
生菜絲1½杯

醃蝦料
蛋白1個　鹽¼茶匙

拌蝦料
沙拉醬½杯　芥末醬1茶匙　牛奶1湯匙

作法
1. 龍蝦及明蝦剝殼取肉後，切成2公分四方大小，用醃蝦料拌醃10分鐘以上。
2. 生菜絲墊盤底，將龍蝦頭與尾蒸熟後刷上少許油，使其光亮後排於兩端。
3. 蝦肉沾滿玉米粉後投入熱油中炸酥，撈出後放入調勻拌蝦料的碗中，抖動碗使蝦肉均沾上醬料，排入盤中央，可用燙過的青花菜圍飾。

＊用明蝦是使蝦肉份量增加，也可以都用龍蝦或用明蝦來做。

Lobster Balls with Mayonnaise Sauce

Ingredients:
2 Lobsters, 5 Prawns, 1/2C Cornstarch, 1 Broccoli, 1-1/2C Lettuce leaves.

Sauce:
❶ 1 Egg white, 1/4t Salt.
❷ 1/2C Mayonnaise, 1t Mustard, 1T Milk.

Methods:
1. Shell the lobster & prawns, cut into 2" long sections, marinate with ❶ for 10 minutes.
2. Steam the head & tail of lobster and put on two sides of a plate. Arrange lettuce leaves (shredded) on center of the plate.
3. Mix sauce ❷.
4. Coat lobster & prawns with cornstarch, deep fry in hot oil to crispy, drain and mix with sauce ❷, pour over lettuce. Decorate with boiled broccoli.

♣ The prawns added can increase the quantity of lobster meat.

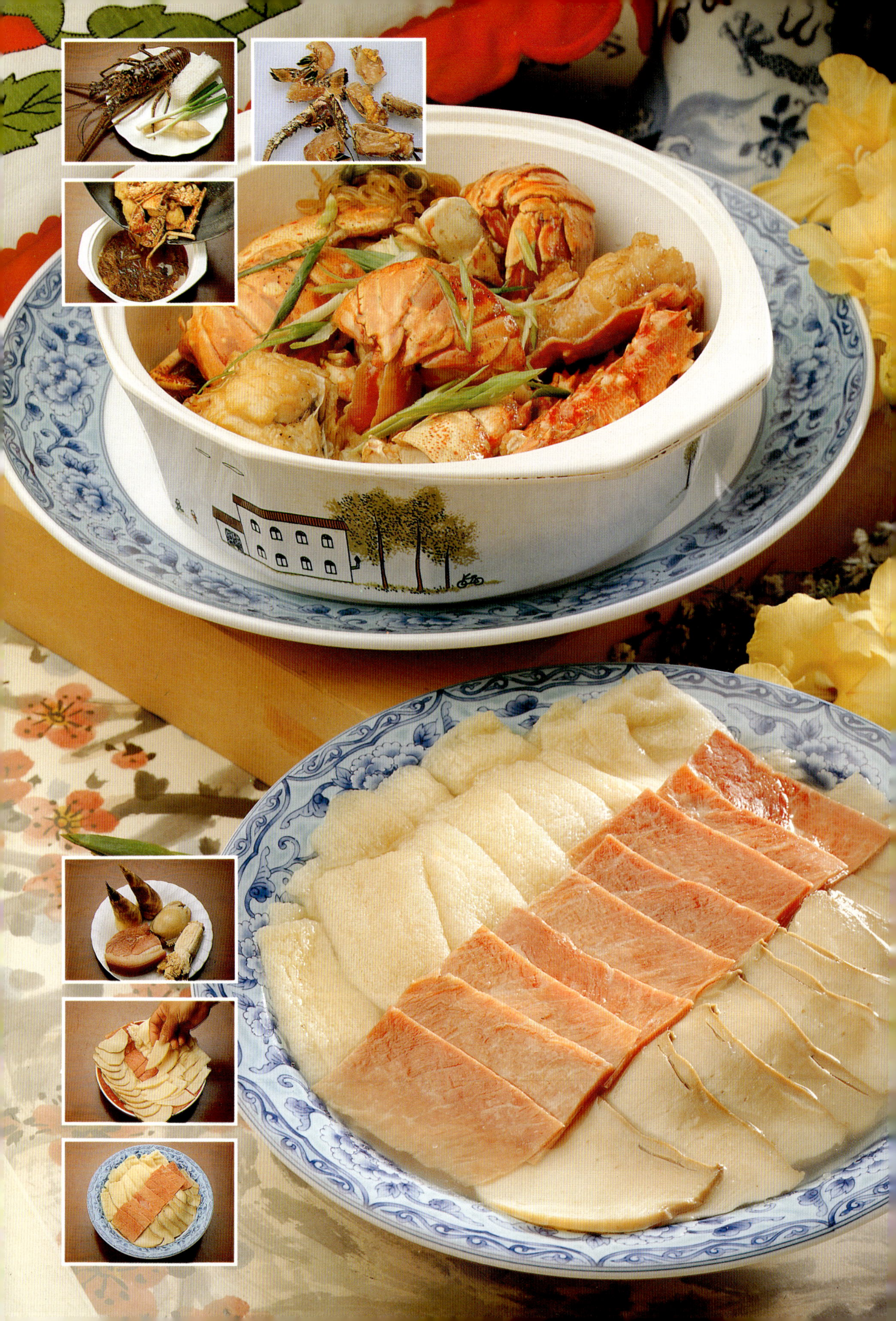

龍蝦粉絲煲

材料
活龍蝦1隻(約1斤多重)　葱3支　薑10片　粉絲2把　青蒜絲少許

調味料
酒1湯匙　醬油2湯匙　鹽¼茶匙　糖½茶匙　胡椒粉¼茶匙　水2杯

作法
1. 龍蝦處理後，分斬成10～12小塊，沾上少許麵粉，用熱油煎過，葱3支切段。
2. 另燒熱3湯匙油，爆香葱段及薑片，放下龍蝦及調味料，大火煮滾。
3. 粉絲用冷水泡軟，剪短。起油鍋爆香葱段，淋醬油1湯匙、水1杯，放入粉絲煮至半透明，倒入砂鍋中，再倒下2.項料，大火燒1分鐘，撒下青蒜絲即可

Lobster in Casserole

Ingredients:
1 Live lobster, 3 Green onion, sectioned, 10 pcs Ginger slices, 2 Mungbean threds, Parsley.

Seasonings:
1T Wine, 2T Soysauce, 1/4t Salt, 1/2t Sugar, 1/4t Pepper, 2C Water.

Methods:
1. Kill the live lobster, cut into 10 pieces. Coat with flour & fry in hot oil.
2. Heat 3T oil to stir fry ginger & green onion, add lobster, then add in seasonings, bring to a boil
3. Soak mung bean threads to soft, cut into small sections about 4" long, put into a casserole. pour the lobster & soup in, cook over medium heat until the mung bean threds turns transparent and the soup reduced. turn off heat, sprinkle the parsley. Serve

扣三鮮湯

材料
中國火腿4兩　鮑魚(罐頭裝)12片　竹笙8條　筍2支　雞湯5杯

作法
1. 中國火腿買2寸寬一條，整條洗淨蒸熟，切12片備用，鮑魚切12薄片，竹笙泡軟，切除頭尾後，用開水川燙一次，沖洗並擠乾，筍切片。
2. 蒸碗中，火腿排在中間，兩邊分別排鮑魚及竹笙，中間空處填上筍片，淋下半杯雞湯，大火蒸半小時，泌出湯汁到雞湯中，扣在大湯碗內，淋入調味過之雞湯即可上桌

Abalone Supreme Soup

Ingredients:
112.5g Chinese ham, 12pcs Abalone slices, 8pcs Dried bamboo skirt mushroom, 2 Bamboo shoot 5C Soup stock, Salt.

Methods:
1. Rinse and brush clean the Chinese ham, steam to done, cut into 12 slices. Soak bamboo skirt mushroom to soft, cut off 2 ends blanch in boiling water, rinse and squeeze Slice thinly the bamboo shoot.
2. Arrange ham slices in the middle of a large bowl. Put abalone and bamboo skirt mushroom on two sides, stuff center with bamboo shoot, add soup stock in, steam for 1/2 hour, pour soup out into the soup stock, bring to a boil add salt is soup. Reverse the whole thing on a plate. Pour the soup on top Serve

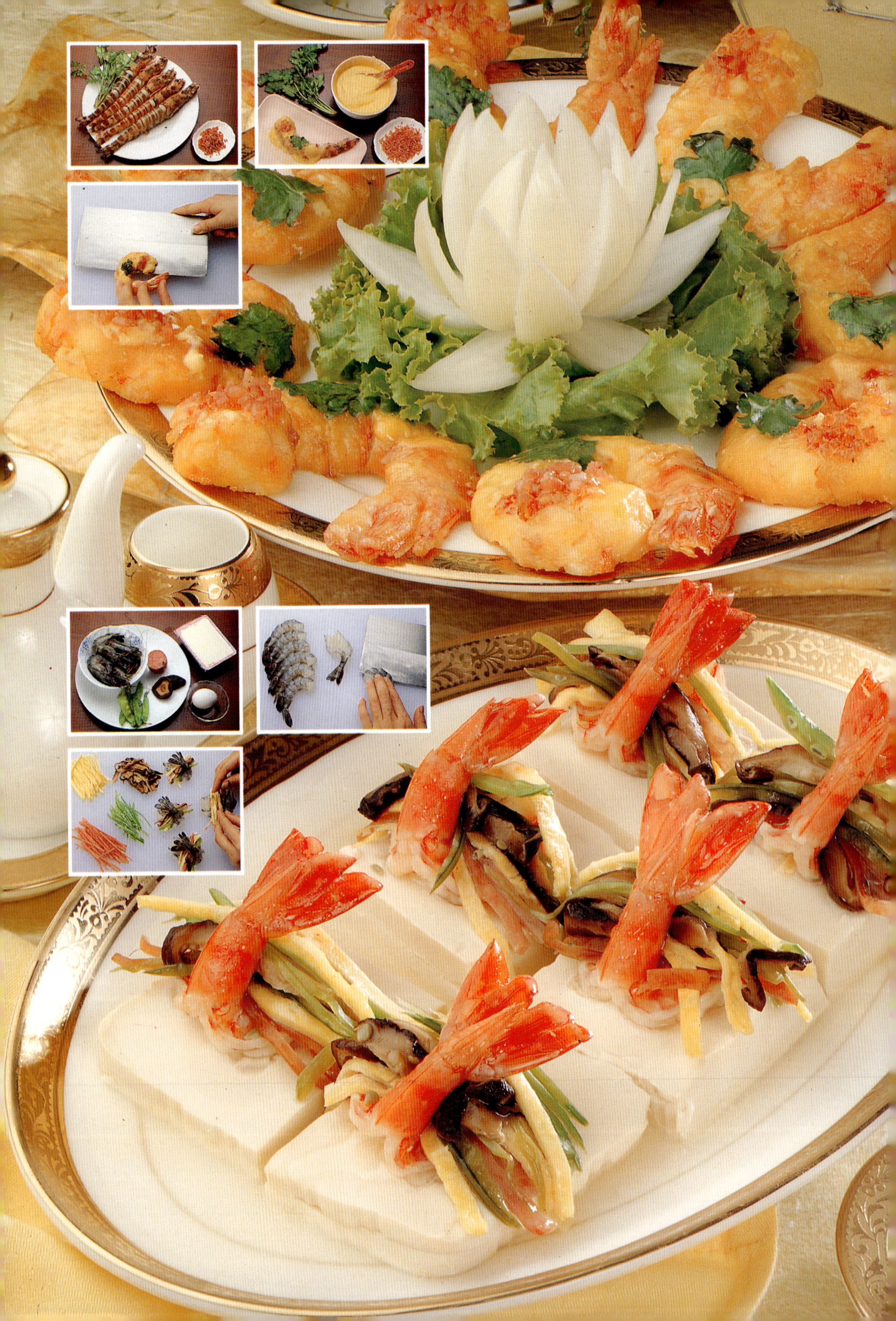

炸蛋黃蝦排

材料
草蝦或小明蝦10隻　火腿屑2湯匙　香菜葉10片

醃蝦料
酒1茶匙　鹽¼茶匙　糖、麻油各少許　太白粉1茶匙　葱1支　薑1片

蛋黃糊
蛋黃2個　鹽少許　麵粉2湯匙

作法
1. 蝦去殼僅留尾部，抽除砂筋後，用醃蝦料醃片刻，並調好蛋黃糊備用。
2. 將醃過之蝦肉，撒少許太白粉後，每隻沾上蛋黃糊並在兩面撒下火腿屑和香菜葉片。
3. 將蝦投入熱油中炸熟，瀝淨油後，由背部平刀片切成兩半排列在盤中，附上花椒鹽及番茄醬上桌。

Deep Fried Egg Prawns Batter

Ingredients:
10 pcs Prawns, 2T Ham (chopped), Chinese parsley leaves.

Sauce :
❶ 1t Wine, 1/4t Salt, 1/2t Sugar, 1/2t Sesame oil, 1t Cornstarch, 1 Green onion, 1 Ginger slice.
❷ 2 Egg yolk, 1/2t Salt, 2T Flour.

Methods:
1. Shell the prawns, (leave tail shell), marinate with ❶. Mix ❷.
2. Pat prawns with cornstarch, coat with ❷ batter, then sprinkle the ham and parsley on both sides.
3. Deep fry prawns in hot oil to golden brown, drain and slice horizontally into halves, arrange on a plate. Serve with ketchup and brown pepper corn powder.

四色鳳尾蝦

材料
小明蝦或大草蝦6隻　香菇2朶　熟火腿絲2湯匙　蛋1個　營養豆腐半盒　豌豆夾酌量　清湯半杯

醃蝦料
鹽¼茶匙　太白粉1茶匙　酒1茶匙

蒸香菇料
醬油1湯匙　糖¼茶匙　油1茶匙

作法
1. 蝦剝殼，僅留尾部，由蝦背剖開成一大片，並用刀面拍平，用醃蝦料拌醃一下。
2. 香菇泡軟連汁與蒸香菇料蒸15分鐘，取出切絲。蛋做成蛋皮切絲，豌豆夾切絲，豆腐半盒先對半切為二後，再橫片2刀，共6片，平舖盤底，上面撒上少許鹽。
3. 4種絲料各取3、4條，橫放在蝦身上，再將蝦尾彎曲一下，排在豆腐上，大火蒸4分鐘，取出後湯汁泌到鍋中，再加清湯半杯及鹽少許，煮滾勾芡，澆到蝦上即可。

＊蝦腹部之白筋不可抽斷，否則蝦尾熟後就不會彎曲了。

Phenix Tail Prawn

Ingredients:
6pcs Prawns, 2pcs Black mushroom, 2T Ham. shredded, 1 Egg, Peas, Bean curd.

Sauce:
❶ 1/4t Salt, 1t Cornstarch. 1t Wine.
❷ 1T Soysauce, 1/4t Sugar, 1t Oil.

Methods:
1. Shell the prawns, (leave the tail shell on), cut the back of prawns to let prawn spread to a large piece, pat with the cleaver side, marinate with ❶ for 10 minutes.
2. Soak the mushroom in a bowl with water to soft, add ❷ and steam for 15 minutes, drain and cut into fine shreds. Beat the egg and fry into a sheet, cut into shreds. Cut peas into shreds. Cut bean curd into 6 thick slices, arrange on a plate, sprinkle some salt.
3. Put 4 strings of mushroom, ham, peas & egg on belly part of prawn, pierce the tail to the head meat part, to make a ring style, place one prawn ring on each bean curd slice. Steam for 4 minutes. Thicken the steamed soup and add some salt, pour on prawns.

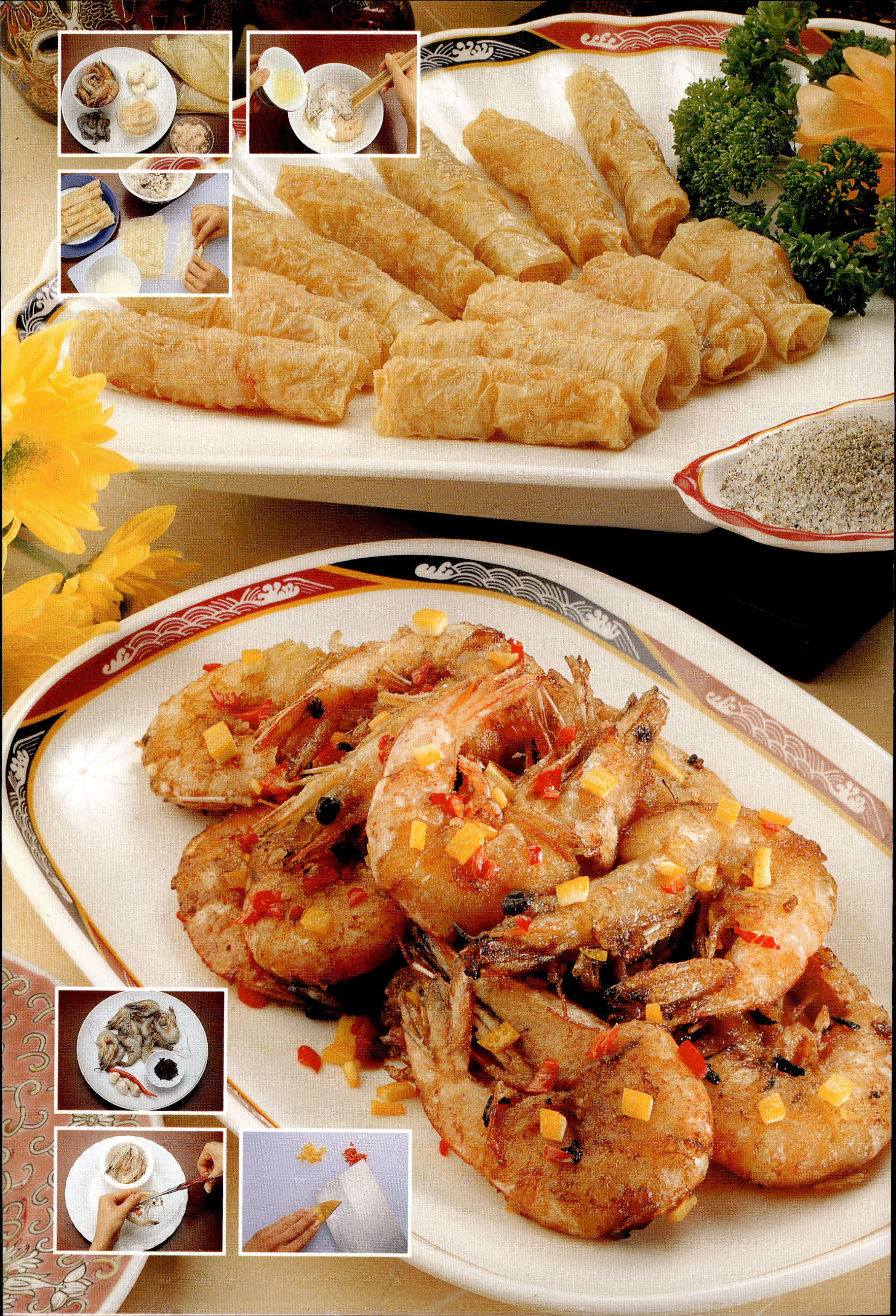

香酥小蝦捲

材料
小蝦仁4兩　魚漿2兩　荸薺4個　肥肉少許　蔥屑½湯匙　豆腐衣2張

醃蝦料
鹽¼茶匙　蛋白半個　太白粉1茶匙

調味料
鹽½茶匙　糖¼茶匙　麻油½茶匙　五香粉少許

作法
1. 小蝦仁用少許鹽抓洗過後，沖水並瀝乾，每隻切為二，加入醃蝦料拌醃。荸薺切小粒，肥肉煮熟冷後切小粒。
2. 將1.項材料置碗中，加入魚漿及調味料拌勻，豆腐衣切成3寸寬長方形，每張包入蝦料，捲成如中指般長條（豆腐衣上塗少許麵粉糊），收口處用麵粉糊黏住。
3. 蝦捲用熱油小火炸熟至外皮酥脆為止，撈出裝盤，可附花椒鹽或番茄醬沾食。

Crispy Shrimp Rolls

Ingredients:
150g Shrimp (shelled), 75g Fish paste, 4pcs Waterchestnuts, Pork fat, 1/2T Green onion chopped, 2pcs Dried bean curd sheet

Seasonings:
1. 1/4t Salt, 1/2 Egg white, 1t Cornstarch.
2. 1/2t Salt, 1/4t Sugar, 1/2t Sesame oil, Five-spicy powder.

Methods:
1. Rinse and clean the shrimp, drain and cut each into two pieces, marinate with ❶ for a while. Cut waterchestnuts into small pieces Boil the pork fat and cut into small pieces.
2. Mix shrimp, waterchestruts, pork fat, fish paste and ❷, mix well. Cut dried bean curd sheet into 3" wide rectangles to wrap in the shrimp mixture, roll into a thumb-size cylinder. Seal edges with flour paste.
3. Deep fry shrimp rolls over medium heat to crispy. Serve with sweet & sour pickle, ketchup or brown peppercorn powder

醬燒蝦

材料
大草蝦或蘆蝦10隻　太白粉1湯匙　大蒜片15片　陳皮屑1茶匙　紅椒屑、柳橙皮屑各少許

綜合調味料
蠔油、醬油各½湯匙　酒1湯匙　水2湯匙　糖、醋各1茶匙　麻油½茶匙　胡椒粉少許

作法
1. 每隻蝦剪除鬚與腳後，由腹部剖開一刀，並用刀面拍平一點，撒下太白粉，用熱油炸熟撈起。
2. 用1湯匙油爆香大蒜片，淋綜合調味料煮滾，放入陳皮屑與蝦，燒煮至汁乾，裝盤後撒下紅椒屑及柳橙屑即可。

Stewed Shrimps with Brown Sauce

Ingredients:
10pcs prawns, 1T Cornstarch, 15pcs Garlic slices 1t Dried tangerine peel, 1t Red pepper, chopped, 1t Fresh orange peel, chopped.

Seasonings:
1/2T Oyster sauce, 1/2T Soysauce, 1T Wine, 2T Water, 1t Sugar, 1t Vinegar, 1/2t Sesame oil. Pepper.

Methods:
1. Trim the shrimp, score a cut on the belly part pat with the side of a cleaver, coat with cornstarch and deep fry in hot oil to done. drain.
2. Heat 1T oil to stir fry garlic slices, add seasonings, bring to a boil, add tangerine peel & shrimp, stew until sauce reduced. Sprinkle the fresh orange peel & red pepper. Serve

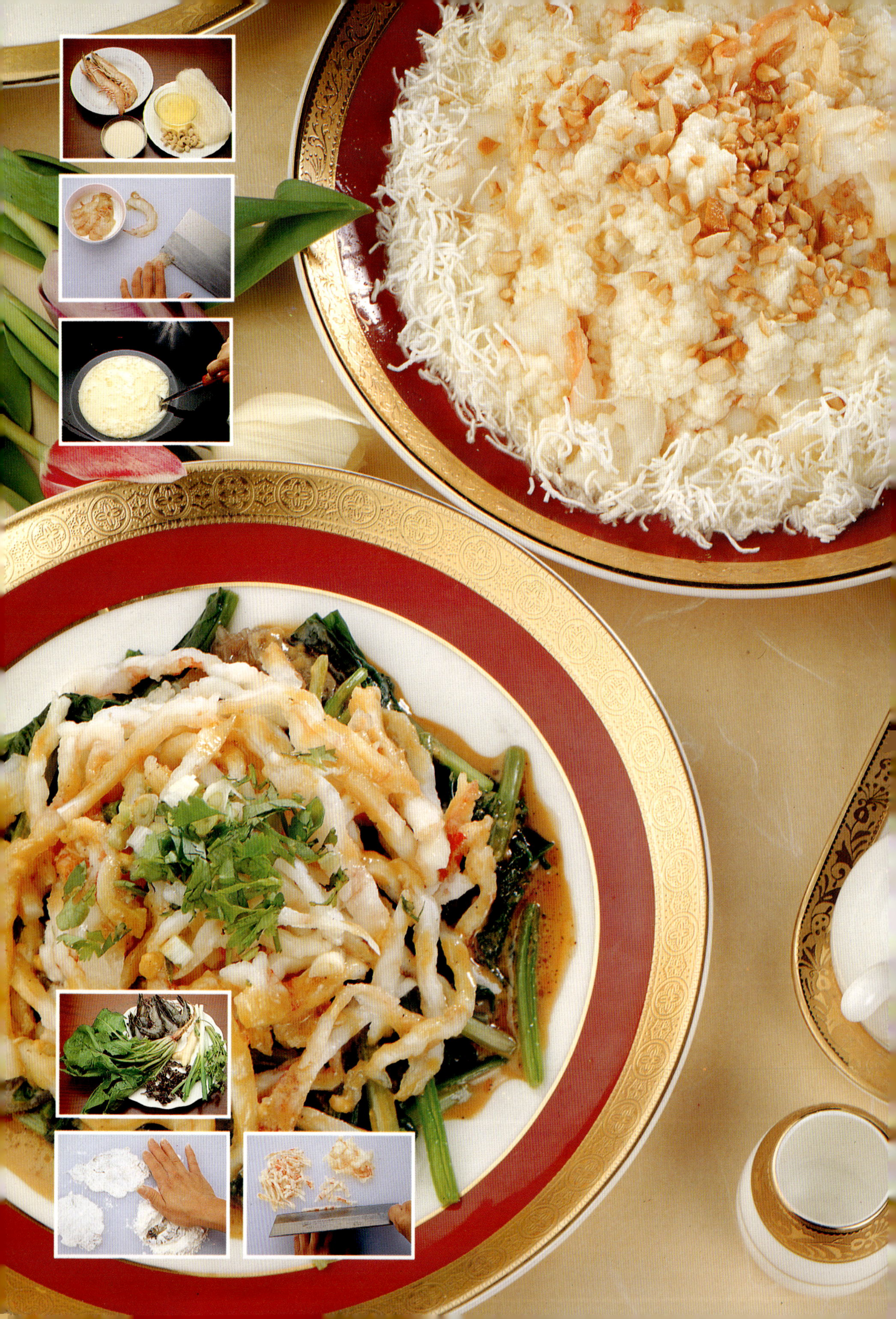

蝦片炒鮮奶

材料
草蝦5隻　米粉1片（約1兩）　腰果屑1湯匙

醃蝦料
蛋白1湯匙　鹽¼茶匙　太白粉½茶匙

奶糊料
蛋白5個　鹽、糖各¼茶匙　胡椒粉少許　濕太白粉1½茶匙　鮮奶1杯

作法
1. 草蝦去殼，抽砂後洗淨，用紙巾吸乾水分，切成薄片，用醃蝦料醃10分鐘以上。
2. 大碗中將5個蛋白打鬆，加入其他奶糊料拌勻。
3. 鍋中燒熱½杯油，倒入蝦片泡熟瀝出。另用5湯匙油炒奶糊料，炒至大部分已凝固時，放入蝦片續炒至全熟，盛入盤內，撒下炸過之腰果屑即可（盤底用炸泡之米粉墊底）。

Stir Fried Prawn with Milk Sauce

Ingredients:
5 Prawns, 37.5g Dried rice noodle, 1T Cashewnut chopped.

Seasonings:
1T Egg white, 1/4t Salt, 1/2t Cornstarch.

Batter:
5 Egg white, 1/4t Salt, 1/4t Sugar, Pepper, 1-1/2t Cornstarch paste, 1C Milk.

Methods:
1. Shell the prawn, slice thinly, marinate with seasonings for 10 minutes.
2. Beat egg white, mix with batter, deep fry rice noodle to pop crispy, put on a plate.
3. Heat 1/2C oil to deep fry prawns to done. Heat 5T oil to stir fry the egg mixture. When solidify, add in prawns, pour on the rice noodle, sprinkle the nuts. Serve.

芥辣鮮蝦絲

材料
草蝦6隻　菠菜或青梗菜4兩　水發木耳½杯　太白粉1杯　蛋白半個

綜合調味料
蔥屑、香菜屑各1湯匙　芥末醬（調稀）1湯匙　芝麻醬（調稀）1湯匙　醬油、麻油各½湯匙　鹽¼茶匙　糖½茶匙　味精、胡椒粉各少許

作法
1. 蝦去殼後洗淨，每隻橫切成2片，並劃一刀口在蝦肉上，全部用蛋白半個和鹽少許拌勻，再在太白粉中沾裹，用力壓成一大片。
2. 將菠菜切短，木耳切寬絲在開水中川燙一下，瀝乾後放盤中，倒入一半已調勻之綜合調味料拌合。
3. 蝦片也投入開水中川燙至熟，瀝乾後切成絲狀，用剩餘之綜合調味料拌勻，堆放在菜料上即可。

Shrimp Shreds with Mustard Sauce

Ingredients:
6 Prawns, 150g Green vegetable, 1/2C Wood ear, 1C Cornstarch, 1/2 Egg white.

Seasonings:
1T Green onion, 1T Chinese parsey, 1T Mustard paste, 1T Sesame seed paste, 1/2T Soysauce, 1/2T Sesame oil, 1/4t Salt, 1/2t Sugar, MSG, Pepper.

Methods:
1. Shell the prawns, slice each into 2 slices, score one cut on each half, mix with egg white & salt, then coat with cornstarch. Press into a large flat piece.
2. Mix the seasonings.
3. Blanch vegetable and wood ear, drain and mix with 1/2 seasonings. Put on a plate.
4. Blanch prawns in boiling water, drain and cut into shreds, mix with the other half seasonings put on top of the wood ear. Serve.

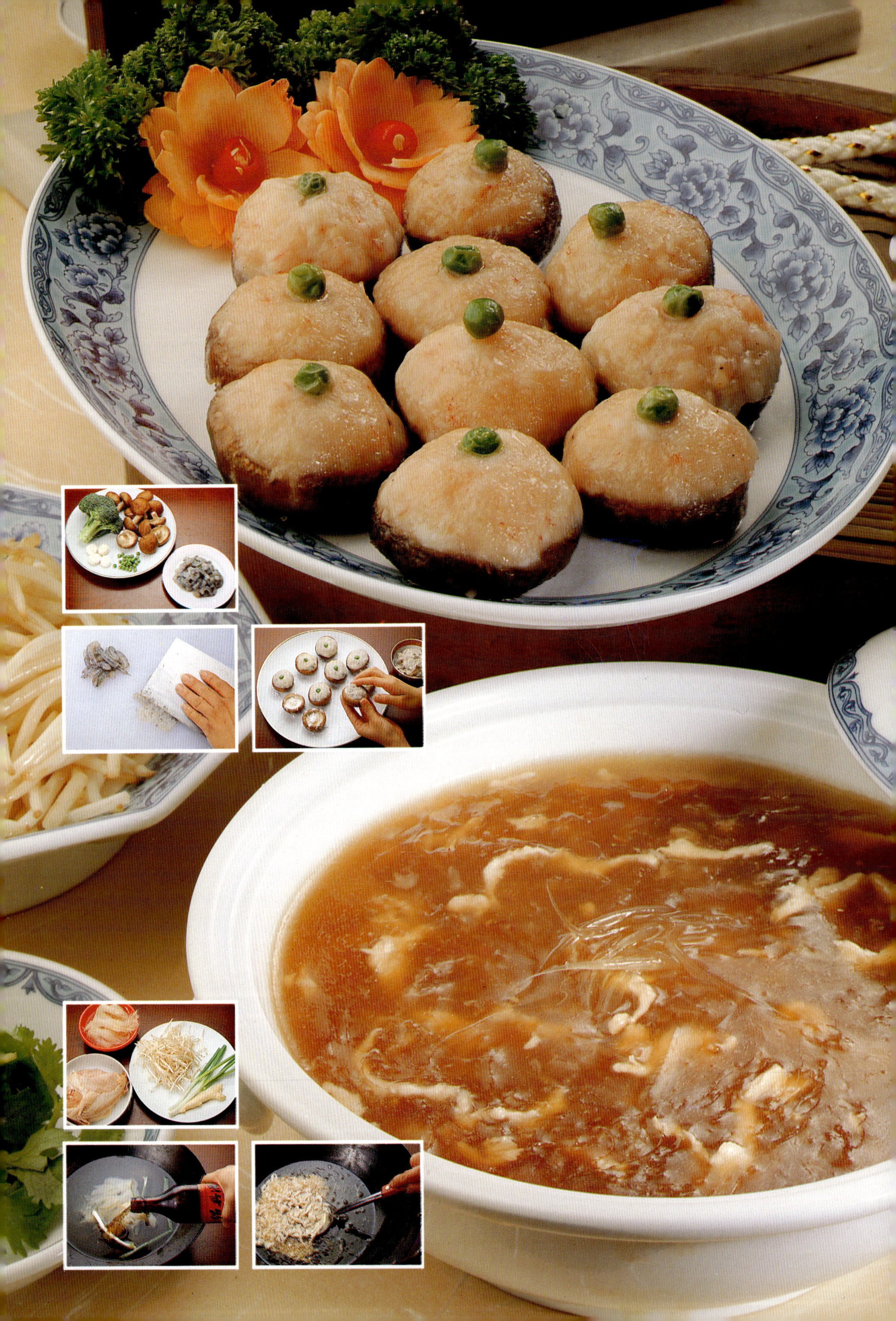

百花鮮菇盒

材料
新鮮香菇10朵　荸薺4粒　蝦仁6兩　青花菜1小棵　青豆10粒

拌蝦料
絞肥肉少許（約1湯匙）　蛋白1湯匙　酒1茶匙　鹽1/3茶匙　白胡椒粉、麻油各少許　太白粉2茶匙

作法
1. 鮮菇去蒂洗淨，用鹽水略泡一下，擦乾備用，荸薺切碎。
2. 蝦仁洗淨擦乾，壓成蝦泥，加入荸薺及拌蝦料，順同一方向攪拌均勻，使蝦肉有彈性。
3. 香菇內撒上太白粉，將蝦泥釀在裡面，手指沾水抹光蝦泥表面，放一粒青豆裝飾之，排入大盤中蒸12分鐘。
4. 青花菜分成小朵，用熱水燙熟（水中加油及鹽少許）排入餐盤中，鮮菇盒蒸好後亦排入盤中。

＊也可用上好高湯煮滾勾芡，淋在鮮菇盒上，以增光亮。
　釀好之鮮菇盒也可用烤箱烤熟，直接上桌別有風味。

Stuffed Mushrooms with Shrimps

Ingredients:
10pcs Fresh mushrooms, 4pcs Water chestnuts 225g Shrimp, 1 Broccoli, 10pcs Snow peas.

Seasonings:
1T Egg white, 1t Wine, 1/3t Salt, 1/4t Pepper Sesame oil, 2t Cornstarch.

Methods:
1. Cut off stems from fresh mushroom, soak in water with 1T of salt, drain.
2. Rinse clean the shrimp, smash and mix with seasonings, stir to very sticky.
3. Sprinkle some cornstarch on inside of mushrooms, stuff the shrimp mixture inside of mushroom, insert a snow pea on top, steam for 12 minutes.
4. Blanch separated broccoli in hot water with some oil and salt. Arrange on a plate together with mushrooms.

♣ This dish can be baked

雞絲燴翅

材料
水發魚翅4兩　雞胸肉3兩　綠豆芽1小碟　蔥2支　薑3片　高湯6杯　香菜少許

醃雞料
蛋白1湯匙　太白粉1茶匙　水2茶匙　鹽1/4茶匙

調味料
酒、醬油各1湯匙　鹽1/2茶匙　濕太白粉1½湯匙

作法
1. 魚翅用冷水及蔥、薑、酒煮10分鐘，去除腥味，另換高湯1½杯煨煮至軟。
2. 雞肉順紋切細絲，用醃雞料醃15分鐘，過油泡熟。
3. 豆芽摘去頭尾，用少量油炒熟，香菜洗淨切短。
4. 用1湯匙油煎香蔥、薑，淋入調味料中之酒及高湯，煮3分鐘，挑出蔥、薑，將魚翅下鍋，用醬油及鹽調味，勾芡後將雞絲拌入即熄火，分裝小碗或盅內，附銀芽及香菜上桌。

Stewed Shark's Fin with Chicken Shreds

Ingredients:
150g Shark's fin, 112.5g Chicken breast, 1C Mung bean sprouts, 2 Green onion, 3pcs Ginger slices. 6C Soup stock, Chinese Parsley.

Seasonings:
❶ 1T Egg white, 1t Cornstarch, 2t Water, 1/4t Salt
❷ 1T Wine, 1T Soysauce, 1/2t Salt, 1-1/2T Cornstarch paste.

Methods:
1. Cook shark's fin in cold water with green onion, ginger and wine for 10 minutes, drain and cook with 1-1/2C soup stock until soft.
2. Shred the chicken, marinate with sauce ❶. Fry in warm oil to done, drain.
3. Peel off 2 ends from bean sprouts, stir fry in hot oil. Rinse parsley, cut into small sections.
4. Heat 1T oil to fry green onion and ginger, add wine & soup stock, cook for 3 minutes, add shark's fin and seasonings ❷. Pour in a soup bowl, serve with sprouts & parsley

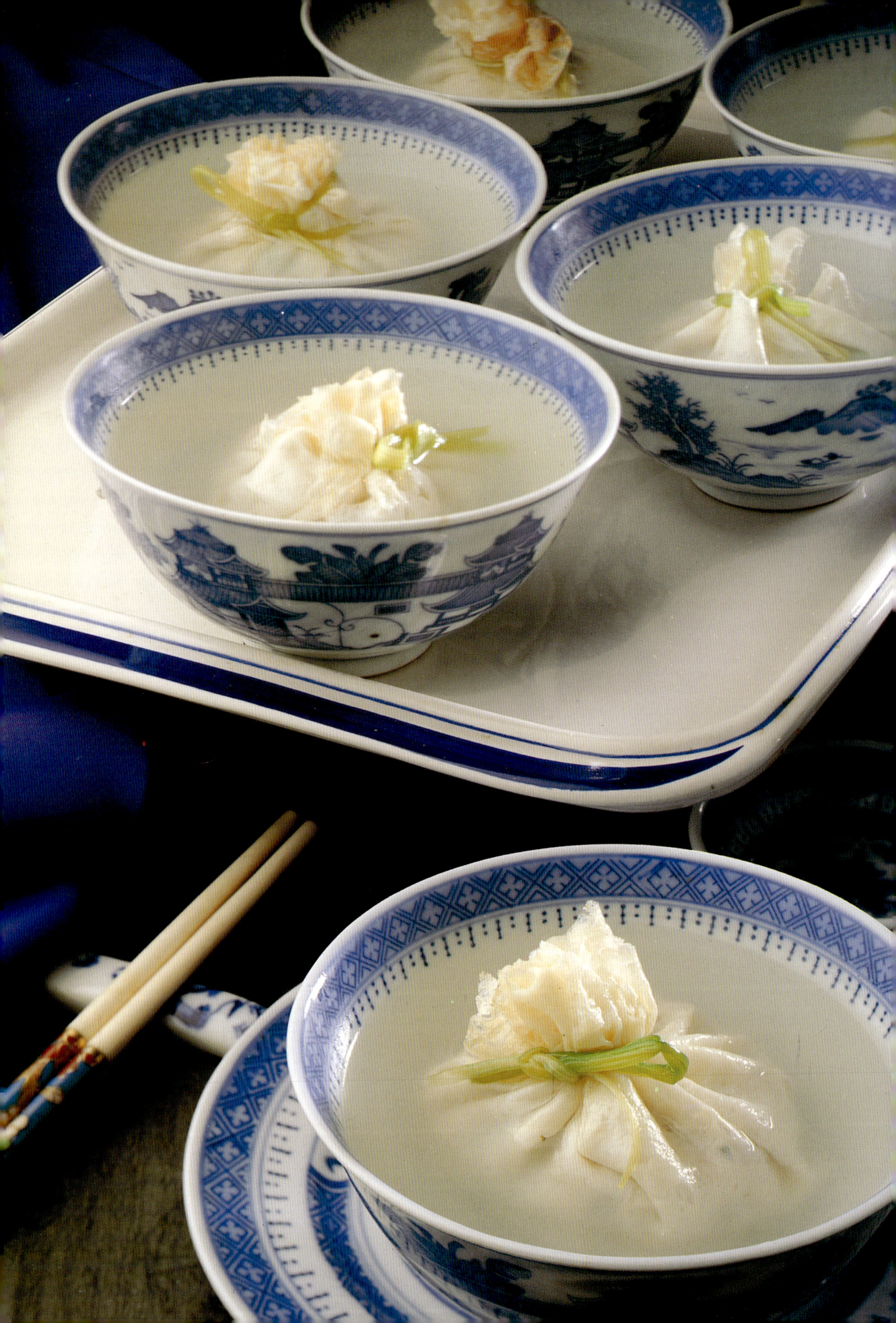

魚翅石榴包

材料
水發散翅3兩　雞胸肉半個　香菇4朵　芹菜數支　金菇半把　豌豆少許　嫩薑末、蔥末各少量　濕太白粉少許　高湯4杯

蛋白皮料
蛋白4個　太白粉1茶匙　水1湯匙　鹽少許

調味料
酒1茶匙　鹽¼茶匙　糖、胡椒粉各少許　濕太白粉酌量

作法
1. 魚翅放鍋中加水、蔥、薑及酒，小火煮10分鐘，去腥味後撈出，另用1杯高湯煨煮至軟。雞胸肉切細絲，用少許濕太白粉拌醃一下；香菇泡軟切絲；金菇去除尾端切短；芹菜燙軟。
2. 熱油2湯匙爆香蔥、薑，並將雞絲炒散，再放1.項中各種絲料，並加調味料及魚翅炒勻。
3. 蛋白打散，加入其他蛋白皮料，打勻後再用小網過濾一次，鍋中刷少許油，將蛋白分別煎成約6片4寸大小的圓薄皮。
4. 用蛋白皮來包魚翅料，收口用燙軟之細芹菜紮好，分別裝入小碗中，入鍋蒸4分鐘即可，每碗中加煮滾且調味之高湯即可供食。

Sharks Fin in Pomegranate Package

Ingredients:
112.5g Shark's fin, 1/2 Chicken breast, 4pcs Black mushroom, Celery, 50g Needle mushroom, Snow peas, Ginger, Green onion, chopped. (each a little).

Egg skin:
4 Egg white, 1t Cornstarch, 1T Water, 1/4t Salt.

Seasonings:
1t Wine, 1/4t Salt, Sugar, Pepper, Cornstarch paste.

Methods:
1. Cook shank's fin in water with ginger, green onion and wine for 10 minutes, drain. Shred the chicken breast, marinate with cornstarch and salt. Shred the soaked black mushroom. Blanch the Chinese celery.
2. Heat 2T oil, stir fry green onion, ginger, chicken and all vegetables, add seasonings and mix well with shark's fin.
3. Beat egg white and mix all egg skin materials, brush, oil on wok, fry 6 round thin egg sheets (about 4" diameter round).
4. Use egg sheet to wrap shark's fin mixture, fasten with blanched celery string. Put each in a bowl. Steam for 4 minutes. Add boiling soup stock (seasoned). Serve.

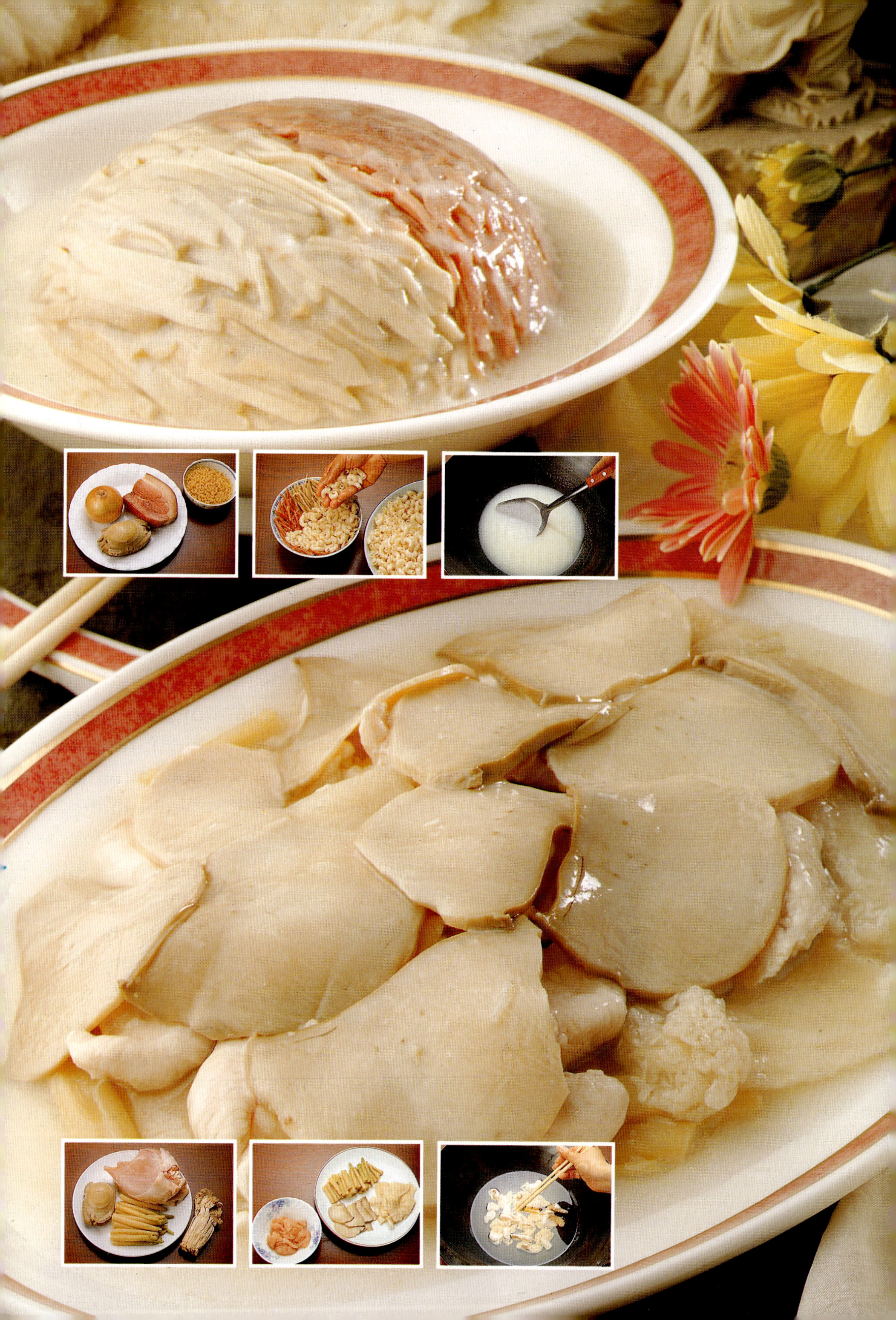

鮑魚火腿扣通粉

材料
罐頭鮑魚半罐　火腿絲半杯　洋葱丁2湯匙　通心粉1½杯　麵粉2湯匙　高湯3杯

調味料
鹽½茶匙　胡椒粉少許　奶水2湯匙

作法
1. 鮑魚、火腿均切絲（如用中國火腿需蒸熟後切絲）；通心粉用滾水中火煮熟
2. 取一只蒸碗，底層排入鮑魚及火腿絲，中間填入通心粉，撒¼茶匙鹽及半杯水，蒸15分鐘，扣在大盤中。
3. 用3湯匙油將洋葱丁炒軟，加入麵粉同炒，慢慢淋入高湯攪勻，煮滾後撈棄洋葱，加鹽調味，熄火後加入奶水及胡椒粉，拌勻後淋到鮑魚通心粉上。

＊可將鮑魚、火腿、通心粉與麵糊拌勻後裝入烤碗中，撒少許起司粉烤熟，唯烤的麵粉糊要做的濃稠些

Mold Abalone and Ham

Ingredients:
1/2 Can Abalone, 1/2C Chinese ham, shredded, 2T Onion, Chopped, 1-1/2C Macaronni, 2T Flour, 3C Soup.

Seasonings:
1/2t Salt, Pepper, 2T Milk.

Methods:
1. Shred the abalone, steam the Chinese ham, cut into shreds.
2. Boil the macaroni.
3. Put abalone and ham strings on bottom of a bowl, stuff center with macaronni, add 1/4t salt & 1/2C water. Steam for 15 minutes, reverse the bowl and let stand on a plate.
4. Heat 3T oil to stir fry onion and flour add in soup stock and mix evenly, discard onion, season with salt, milk, pepper. Pour on abalone.

✤ You may mix the ingredients with cream sauce and bake.

鮑魚燴三白

材料
鮑魚半罐　白蘆筍12支　雞胸肉半個　竹笙10條　高湯4杯　鹽酌量　濕太白粉2茶匙　雞油少許

作法
1. 將雞胸肉切薄片，用1茶匙太白粉及鹽少許拌勻醃十餘分鐘，用1杯油將雞肉過油泡熟後瀝出。
2. 蘆筍對切為二，蒸熟排入盤中墊底。
3. 竹笙泡軟，用開水燙一下，再用1杯高湯蒸10分鐘，鮑魚切薄片留用。
4. 將高湯煮滾後加鹽調味，放下雞片、竹笙一滾即勾芡盛入大盤中，鍋中留半量湯汁，放入鮑魚片再一滾即全部倒入大盤內，淋少許雞油便成。

＊罐頭中之鮑魚湯汁可包括在高湯中使用之。

Braised Abalone Slices with Bamboo Skirt Mushroom

Ingredients:
1/2 can Abalone, 12pcs Asparagus, 1/2 Chicken breast, 10pcs Bamboo skirt mushroom, 4 C Soupstock, Salt, Cornstarch paste.

Methods:
1. Slice chicken breast, marinate with cornstarch paste & salt for 10 minutes, then deep fry in 1C warm oil to done, drain immediately.
2. Cut asparagus into 2 sections, steam to done and put on a plate.
3. Soak the dried bamboo skirt mushroom, blanch in boiling water, add 1C soup stock and steam for 10 minutes. Slice abalone thinly
4. Cook 3C soup stock, add salt, chicken, bamboo skirt mushroom, bring to a boil, thicken with cornstarch paste. Finally add abalone, splash chicken grease.

✤ The canned abalone soup can be included in 3C soup stock.

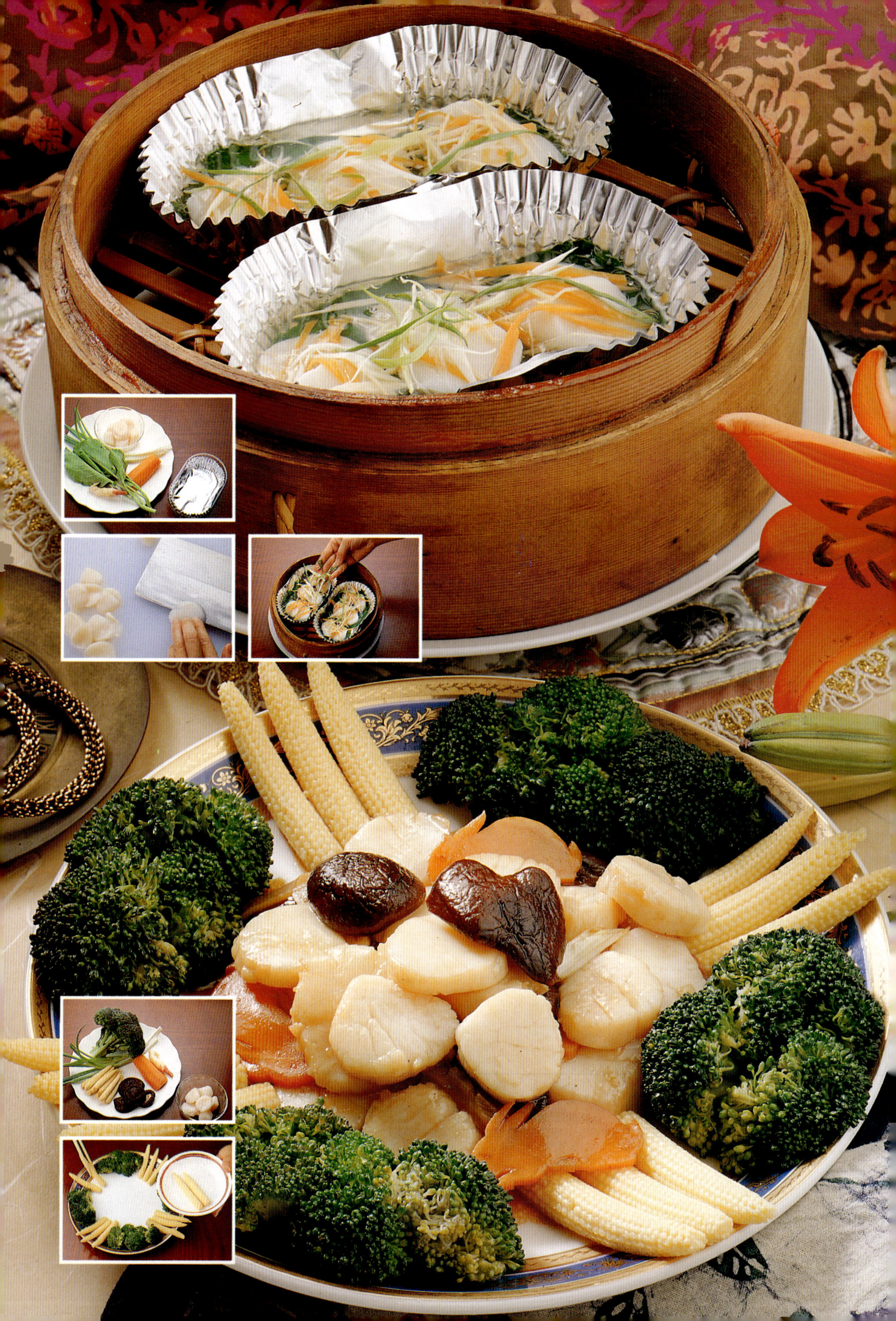

銀紙蒸鮮貝

材料
新鮮干貝6粒　葱、薑絲、胡蘿蔔絲酌量
鋁箔紙盒2張　橄欖菜葉3片

調味料
水¾杯　酒½湯匙　鹽¼茶匙　油½湯匙　胡椒粉少許

作法
1. 干貝橫剖為二，鋁箔紙盒內（可用鋁箔紙折疊）鋪上燙過的橄欖菜葉，每個中間放入鮮貝6片，再在上面撒下葱、薑絲及胡蘿蔔絲各少許。
2. 調味料調妥注入干貝中，再放入蒸籠中蒸3分鐘即成，也可放在烤箱中烤熟。

＊可用蛤蜊、明蝦、螃蟹、蚵等其他海鮮類來代替鮮貝。

Steamed Scallop

Ingredients:
6pcs Fresh scallop, 1/3C Green onion, shredded, 1/3C Ginger, shredded, 1/3C Carrot, shredded, Aluminum foil.

Seasonings:
3/4C Water, 1/2T Wine, 1/4t Salt, 1/2T Oil, 1/4t Pepper.

Methods:
1. Slice scallop into 2 slices. Place the blanched mastard green leaves on inside of the aliminum foil box. Put scallop slices in and cover with ginger, green onion, carrot each a little bit.
2. Mix the seasoning and pour on scallop.
3. Arrange on a steamer and steam over high heat for 3 minutes. Serve. (You may bake also, in the oven.)

♣ The crab, clam, prawns or other sea food can be also cooked this way.

碧綠玉筍帶子

材料
新鮮干貝(即帶子)6粒　葱支、薑片酌量
香菇4朵　青花菜1小棵　玉米筍10支
熟胡蘿蔔片15片

醃料
鹽⅓茶匙　酒½湯匙　白胡椒粉少許
太白粉1湯匙

綜合調味料
酒、淡色醬油各½湯匙　鹽¼茶匙
糖、胡椒粉各少許　麻油¼茶匙

作法
1. 將干貝片切成0.3公分厚的片狀，全部用醃料拌醃半小時，香菇泡軟切成小片。
2. 將青花菜割成小朵，和玉米筍全部用滾水燙熟（水中需加油1湯匙及鹽半茶匙），撈出排在盤中。
3. 將水燒至四分熱，放下干貝片小火泡至熟，撈出。
4. 起油鍋爆香葱、薑及香菇片，放入胡蘿蔔片及干貝，淋下綜合調味料，大火拌炒均勻即裝入盤中。

Fresh Scallop & Baby Corn

Ingredients:
6pcs Fresh scallop, 1 Green onion, 2 Ginger slices, 4 Black mushroom, 1 Broccoli, 10 Baby corn, 15pcs Carrot slices.

Sauce:
❶ 1/3t Salt, 1/2T Wine, Pepper, 1T Cornstarch.
❷ 1/2T Wine, 1/2T Soysauce, 1/4t Salt, Sugar, Pepper, 1/4T Sesame oil.

Methods:
1. Cut fresh scallop into 0.3 cm thick slices, marinate with ❶ for 1/2 hour. Soak the black mushroom and cut into small pieces.
2. Split the broccoli into small pieces. Cut the baby corn into two pieces. Blanch these two in boiling water (add 1T oil & 1/2t salt in water), drain and arrange on the plate.
3. Blanch scallop in warm water over low heat for 2 minutes, drain.
4. Heat 2T oil to fry green onion, ginger and black mushroom, then add carrot & scallop, pour ❷ in, stir well over high heat and serve.

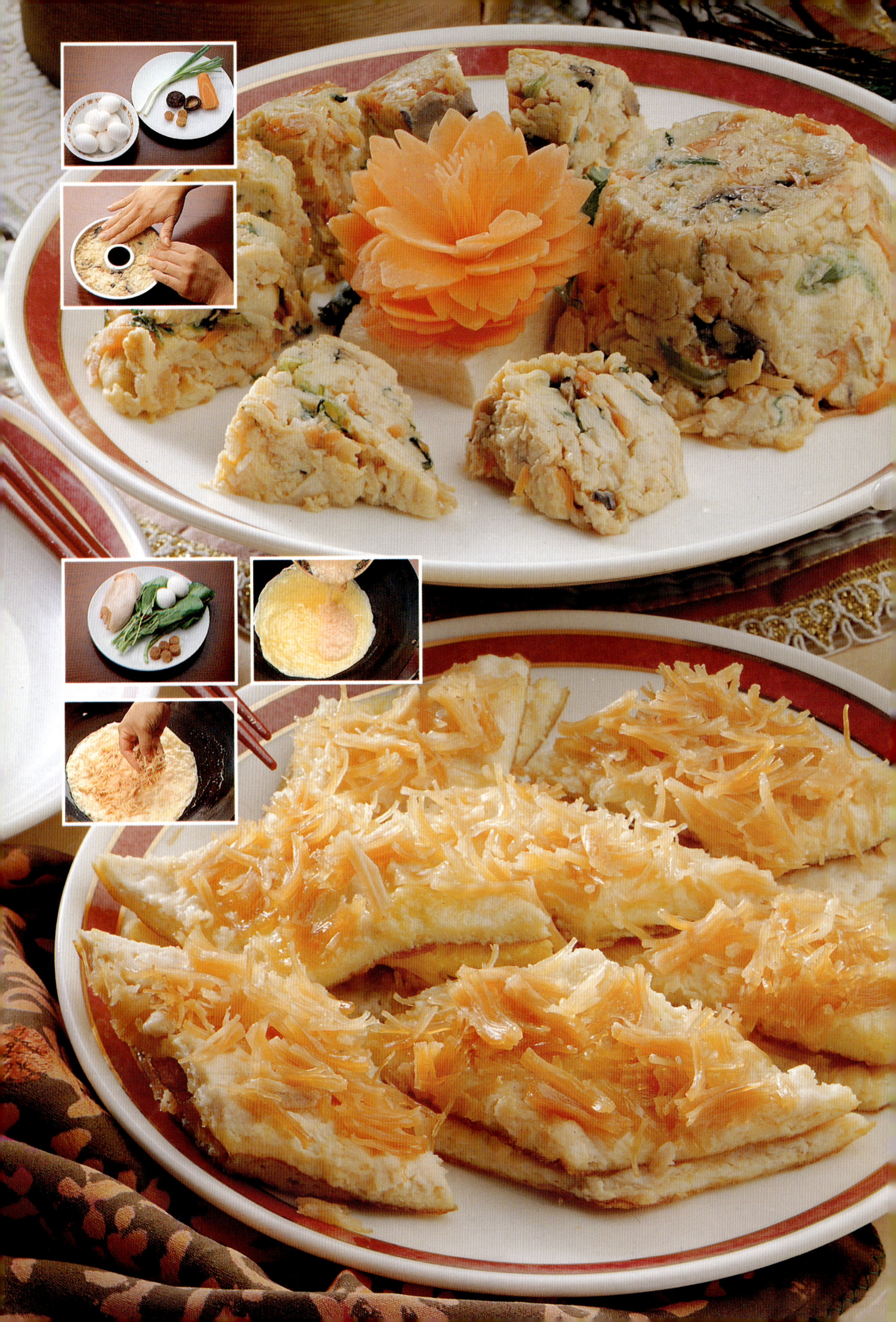

炒干貝蛋糕

材料
蛋8個　葱絲1湯匙　熟胡蘿蔔絲2湯匙
干貝3粒　香菇絲2湯匙

調味料
鹽¼茶匙　胡椒粉少許　麻油1茶匙

作法
1. 蛋中加鹽½茶匙打勻。干貝加水蒸軟，撕成絲。
2. 用1湯匙油炒香葱絲、香菇絲及胡蘿蔔絲，加調味料調味，放下干貝絲拌勻，盛出。
3. 用熱油4湯匙炒蛋汁，同時放下干貝料同炒，見蛋汁均勻凝固便熄火。
4. 將干貝蛋盛入模型或便當盒中，壓以重物，使蛋固定成型，約2小時以上，食前扣出切厚片，如喜歡熱食可重蒸片刻。

Stir-Fried Scallop Egg Cake

Ingredients:
8 Eggs, 1T Green onion, shredded, 2T Cooked carrot, shredded, 3pcs Scallop, 2T Black mushroom, shredded.

Seasonings:
1/4t Salt, Pepper, 1t Sesame oil.

Methods:
1. Mix eggs and 1/2t salt. Steam scallop in water to soft, tear into shreds.
2. Heat 1T oil to stir fry green onion, mushroom & carrot, add seasonings, mix well with scallop.
3. Heat 4T oil to stir fry beaten egg, mix with scallop mixture, when solidified, turn off heat
4. Put egg scallop into a box, cover & press tightly for 2 hours. Turn over, pour out and cut into thick slices. Serve.

鍋貼干貝酥

材料
雞胸肉或雞柳3兩　干貝3粒　芥蘭菜葉酌量

拌雞料
葱薑水2湯匙　蛋白2個

蛋汁料
蛋2個　鹽¼茶匙　太白粉1茶匙　水1茶匙

作法
1. 雞肉用刀刮成泥狀，加入葱薑水調開，將蛋白分別加入調成糊狀。干貝蒸軟撕成絲。
2. 蛋汁料打散調勻，鍋中塗油將蛋汁倒下，攤煎成15公分左右的蛋皮，在蛋汁半凝固時即將雞茸糊均勻淋在蛋皮上，再將干貝絲撒下。
3. 沿鍋邊淋入油半湯匙，小火慢煎至凝固狀態時，小心翻面再略煎一下即可，切塊排盤（芥蘭菜葉可切絲墊在盤底）。

Fried Scallop Cake

Ingredients:
112.5g Chicken breast, 3pcs Scallop.

Sauce:
❶ 2T Green onion & Ginger juice, 2 Egg white
❷ 2 Eggs, 1/4t Salt, 1t Cornstarch, 1t Water.

Methods:
1. Smash the chicken, mix with ❶. Steam the scallop with water and tear into strings.
2. Mix ❷, Heat 1/2C oil to fry the egg mixture, spread into a 15 cm diameter round cake, spread chicken on and arrange scallop on top.
3. Add 1T oil around the edge of wok. Fry over low heat until egg solidified. Turn over and fry to done. Cut scallop cake into 6 pieces, arrange on a plate.

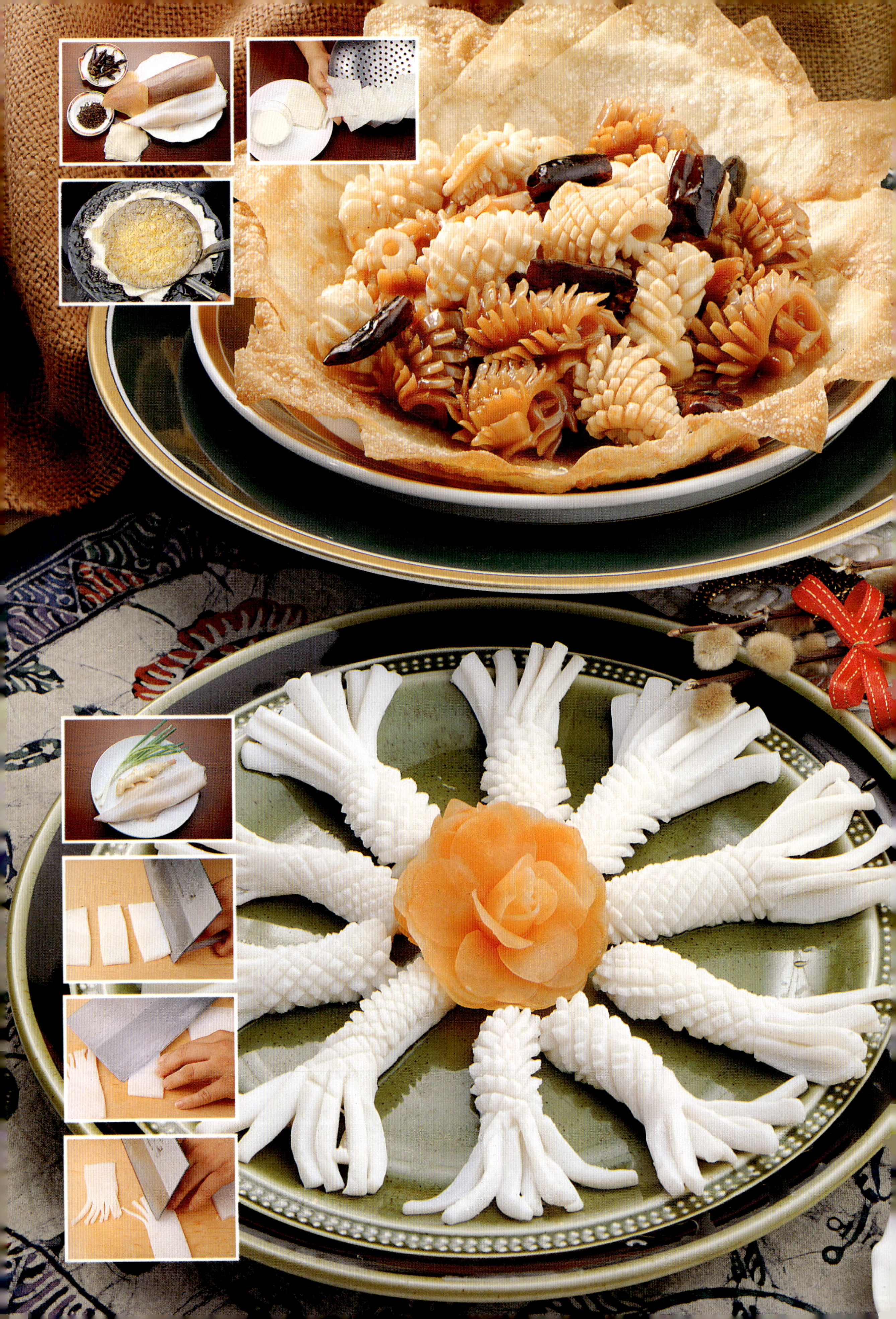

金盤雙魷

材料

餛飩皮20張　鮮魷及水發魷魚各1條　花椒粒½湯匙　乾辣椒10支

綜合調味料

醬油1湯匙　糖½湯匙　酒1湯匙　鹽¼茶匙　醋2茶匙　太白粉1茶匙　麻油1茶匙

作法

1. 分別在鮮魷及水發魷魚內部切交叉切口，再分割成1寸多大小，用滾水川燙過瀝出。
2. 將20張餛飩皮鋪排在漏勺上(漏勺需先在油中沾一下，以免黏住取不下來)，每張皮交接處需塗少許麵糊，使其黏住，用另一漏勺沾油壓住，放入熱油中炸熟，小心取下，放在盤中。
3. 用2湯匙油將花椒粒煎香後撈棄，放入乾辣椒段(切1寸長)炸香，放下雙魷花及綜合調味料，大火拌炒均勻，盛到金盤中。

Double Squid in Golden Plate

Ingredients:
20pcs Won-Ton skin, 1 Squid (Dried), 1 Fresh squid, 1/2T Brown pepper corn, 10pcs Dried red chili.

Seasonings:
1T Soysauce, 1/2T Sugar, 1T Wine, 1/4t Salt, 2t Vinegar, 1t Cornstarch, 1t Sesame oil.

Methods:

1. Slice crisscross on inside of fresh squid and soaked dried squid, then cut each into 1" squares, blanch in boiling water.
2. Brush oil on a round frying strainer. Place the Won-Ton skin one by one on the strainer, stick on each other with flour paste, then press down the strainer with another strainer (brush some oil too), deep fry in hot oil for 1 minute, take out the golden plate carefully, put on a plate.
3. Heat 2T oil to fry brown pepper corn for a while, discard, use this oil to fry dry hot red chili, (cut into 1" long), then add 2 squids and seasonings, stir over high heat, mix evenly and pour on the golden plate.

白灼鮮魷

材料

新鮮魷魚2條　蔥1支　薑2片　酒1湯匙

薑醋汁

薑末½湯匙　白醋、醬油、麻油各1湯匙

芥末汁

芝麻醬、醬油各1湯匙　糖½茶匙　芥末粉、麻油各1茶匙

麻辣汁

蔥、蒜屑各½湯匙　辣豆瓣醬、醬油各½湯匙　糖、麻油各1茶匙

作法

1. 將魷魚外皮剝除洗淨，先橫切成1½寸寬段，每段再取3寸長，使每一塊均為1½寸×3寸大小，每一塊前一半切交叉刀紋，後一半切直條刀口。
2. 燒半鍋水，加蔥、薑及酒，滾過片刻後將切花之魷魚放下，川燙10秒鐘即撈起，瀝乾排入盤中。
3. 備3只小碗內分別或選擇自己喜愛的口味調好佐料，和鮮魷一起上桌。

Blanched Fresh Squid

Ingredients:
2 Fresh squids, 1 Green onion, 2 Ginger slices, 1T Wine.

Ginger vinegar sauce:
1/2T Smashed ginger, 1T Vinegar, 1T Soysauce, 1T Sesame oil.

Mustard sauce :
1T Sesame seed paste, 1T Soysauce 1/2t Sugar, 1t Mustard powder, 1t Sesame oil.

Hot spicy sauce:
1/2T Green onion, 1/2T Garlic, 1/2T Hot bean paste, 1/2T Soysauce, 1t Sugar, 1t Sesame oil.

Methods:

1. Trim the squid, cut (along the grain) into 1-1/2" wide sections, then cut each section into 1-1/2" x 3" rectangles. Cut half part of each rectangle crisscross, then cut the other half part into strings.
2. Add ginger, green onion, wine in boiling water. Blanch squid till the squid shrink into a roll, drain and arrange on a plate.
3. Serve with three kinds of sauces.

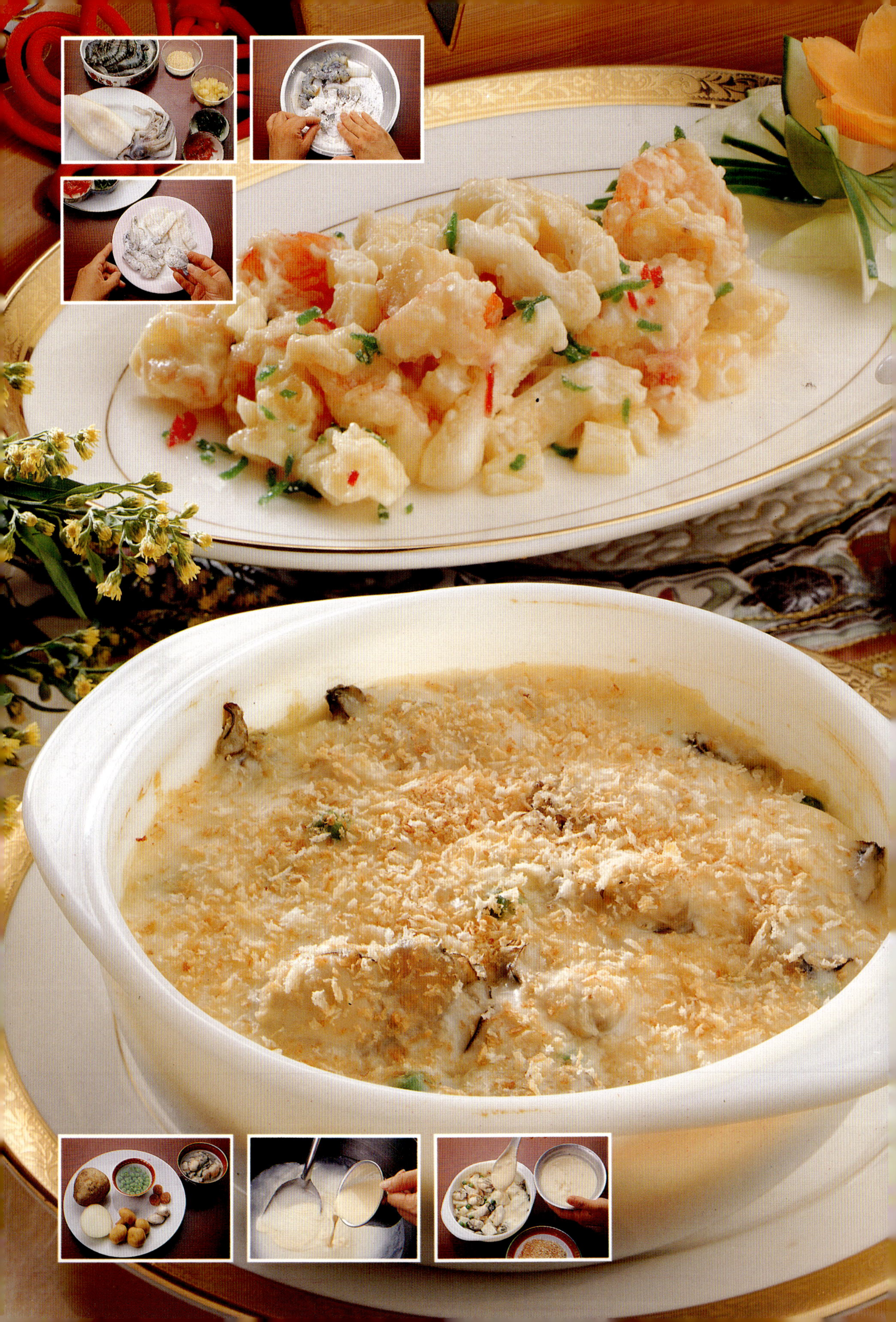

果粒溜雙鮮

材料
新鮮墨魚（即花枝）1隻　小型草蝦8隻　鳳梨丁、青、紅絲各少許　沙拉醬½杯　鮮奶1湯匙　白芝麻½湯匙　玉米粉半杯

醃料
鹽¼茶匙　酒½茶匙　胡椒粉¼茶匙　蛋白1湯匙　太白粉½茶匙

作法
1. 墨魚剝去外皮後切成8寸長的粗條，草蝦剝殼，洗淨擦乾，背部劃一刀口，兩者一起用醃料醃10分鐘，沾上玉米粉。
2. 沙拉醬放大碗中，加入鮮奶調勻，放下鳳梨丁、青、紅絲備用。
3. 燒熱炸油，放入花枝及草蝦，大火炸酥，瀝出後裝入2.項的大碗中，輕輕翻動拌勻，裝入盤中，撒下炒香的白芝麻

Squid, Shrimp with Fruits

Ingredients:
1 Cuttlefish, 8 Prawns, Pineapple, shreds, Dried candied papaya shreds, 1/2C Mayonnaise, 1T Milk, 1/2T Sesame seeds, 1/2C Cornstarch.

Seasonings:
1/4t Salt, 1/2t Wine, 1/4t Pepper, 1T Egg white, 1/2t Cornstarch.

Methods:
1. Clean and cut cuttlefish into 1" long strips. Shell the prawns, marinate with seasonings for 10 minutes, coated with cornstarch.
2. Mix mayonnaise and milk, add pineapple and candied papaya.
3. Deep-fry cuttlefish and prawns with high heat to crispy. Mix with ❷. Remove to a plate and sprinkle the sesame seeds. Serve.

奶油焗鮮蚵

材料
鮮蠔（蚵）6兩　馬鈴薯1個　洋菇片¼杯　青豆少許　大蒜屑1茶匙　洋蔥屑2湯匙　油4湯匙　麵粉3湯匙　清湯2杯　牛奶½杯　麵包粉2湯匙

調味料
鹽½茶匙　胡椒粉少許

作法
1. 鮮蠔用鹽抓洗乾淨，放入滾水中（水中放蔥、薑及酒各少許）川燙5秒鐘撈出，馬鈴薯煮熟剝皮切厚片，乾鍋中將麵包粉炒黃。
2. 用4湯匙油炒香大蒜屑及洋蔥屑，加入麵粉繼續炒勻，再加入清湯攪勻，調味後再加入牛奶調成糊狀，盛出一半。
3. 將馬鈴薯片、洋菇片及青豆倒入糊中拌勻，盛入烤碗中，將鮮蠔散放其上，再蓋上另一半麵糊料，撒下麵包粉，大火烤12～15分鐘。

Oyster with Cream Sauce

Ingredients:
225g Oyster, 1 Potato, 1/4C Mushroom, slices. Snow peas, 1t Garlic, chopped, 2T Onion, chopped, 4T Oil, 3T Flour, 2C Soup stock, 1/2C Milk, 2T Bread crumb.

Seasonings:
1/2t Salt, Pepper.

Methods:
1. Rinse oyster with salt and water, blanch in boiling water together with green onion, ginger & wine, drain.
2. Boil potato and peel the skin, cut into 0.5 cm slices.
3. Heat 4T oil to stir fry garlic and onion, add flour and stir until it turns brown, add soup stock gradually and stir evenly, season and mix with milk to a smooth paste. Take out half of the paste.
4. Mix the potato, mushroom, snow peas with flour paste, pour into a bake ware, put oyster on top, then pour the other half of flour paste on top. Sprinkle the bread crumb. Bake for 12-15 minutes. Serve.

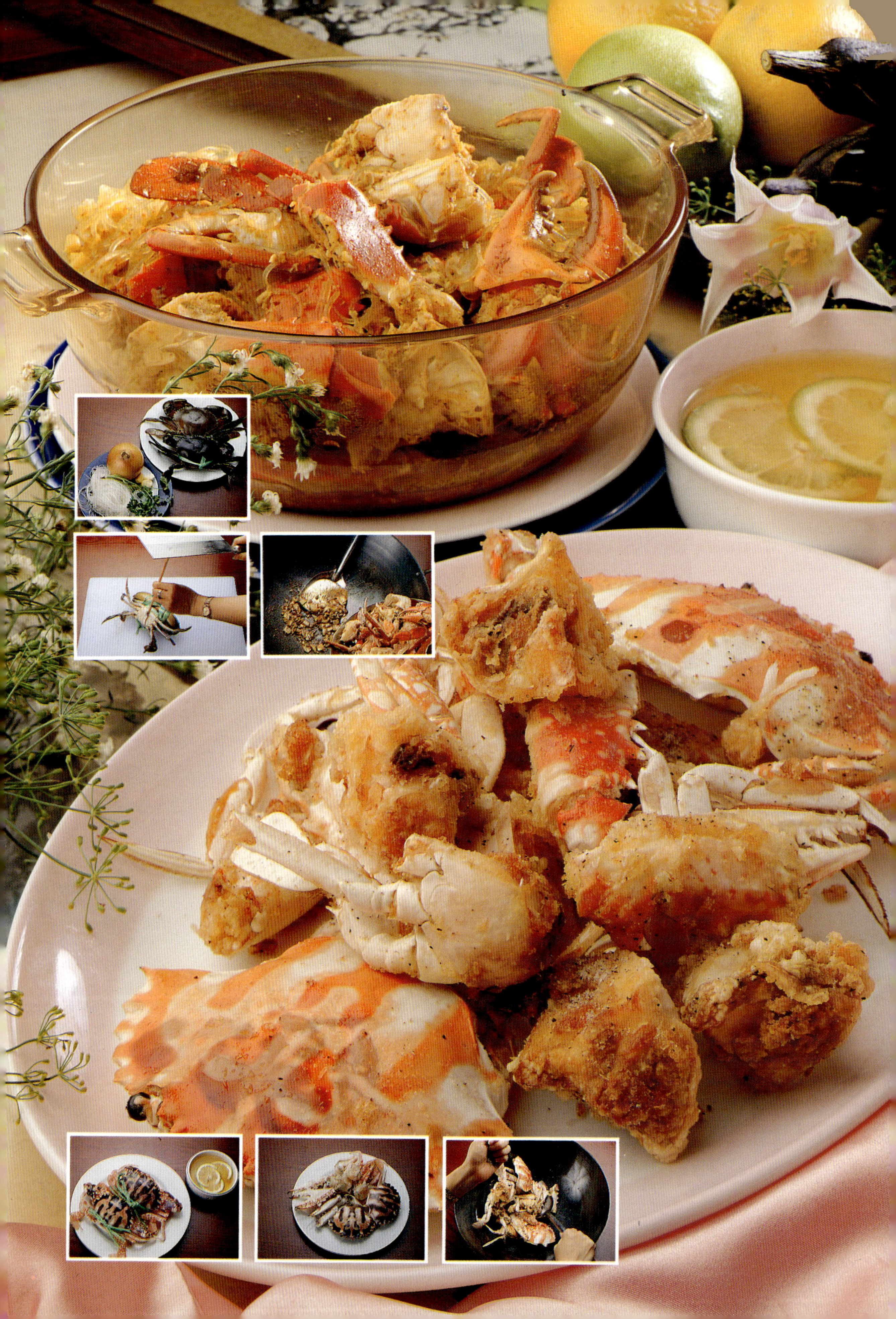

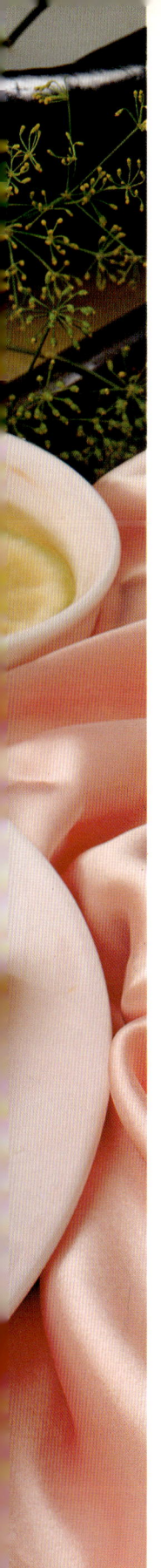

咖哩鮮蟹煲

材料
青蟹或其他鮮蟹2隻　粉絲1把　大蒜屑1湯匙　洋蔥丁½杯　青蒜絲少許

調味料
咖哩粉1½湯匙　酒1湯匙　鹽¼茶匙　糖¼茶匙　清湯或水2杯

作法
1. 將蟹切成小塊，用4湯匙熱油炒熟。
2. 另用2湯匙油炒香大蒜屑及洋蔥丁，並加入咖哩粉小火炒香，淋下酒，加入蟹塊拌炒片刻，調味後注入清湯，大火燒煮至滾。
3. 砂鍋內放下泡軟之粉絲，倒入2.項之湯汁，中火燒透粉絲，再將蟹全部放進（水若太少可酌量增加）蓋妥繼續燒一下，撒下青蒜絲或蔥花，淋少許油即可上桌分食。

Curry Sauce Crab in Casserole

Ingredients:
2 Crabs, 2 Mung bean shreds, 1T Garlic, chopped, 1/2C Onion, chopped, Green garlic.

Seasonings:
1-1/2T Curry powder, 1T Wine, 1/4t Salt, 1/4t Sugar, 2C Soup stock.

Methods:
1. Cut crab into small pieces, stir fry with 4T hot oil.
2. Heat 2T oil to stir fry garlic & onion, add in curry powder, wine and crab, cook over low heat, finally pour the soup, bring to a boil.
3. Put soaked mung bean shred in a casserole, pour the crab and sauce in the casserole, cover and cook for 5 minutes, sprinkle green garlic or green onion. Serve.

椒鹽焗花蟹

材料
花蟹或海蟹2隻　太白粉2湯匙　檸檬片3片　茶水1杯

調味料
鹽¼茶匙　五香粉、胡椒粉、味精各少許

作法
1. 將蟹蓋打開，除去腮等，分割成小塊，用太白粉拌勻，投入熱油中炸熟。
2. 乾淨鍋子燒熱後，放下炸蟹塊，緩緩撒下混合之調味料，不停拌炒至均勻為止。
3. 裝盤後與泡了檸檬片的茶水（食後洗手用）同時上桌。
* 也可將炸過之蟹塊用蔥、薑、蒜末烹過，口味較重。

Salt & Pepper Crab

Ingredients:
2 Crabs, 2T Cornstarch, 2-3pcs Lemon slices, 1C Tea.

Seasonings:
1/4t Salt, Pinches of Five-spicy powder, Pepper, MSG.

Methods:
1. Open the crab lid, remove dirt, cut into 4 pieces, mix with cornstarch. Deep fry in hot oil till done.
2. Heat the wok, add crabs and seasonings, stir evenly.
3. Serve with Tea (with lemon added) for hand washing.
✤ You may stir fry the frying crabs with garlic, green onion & ginger.

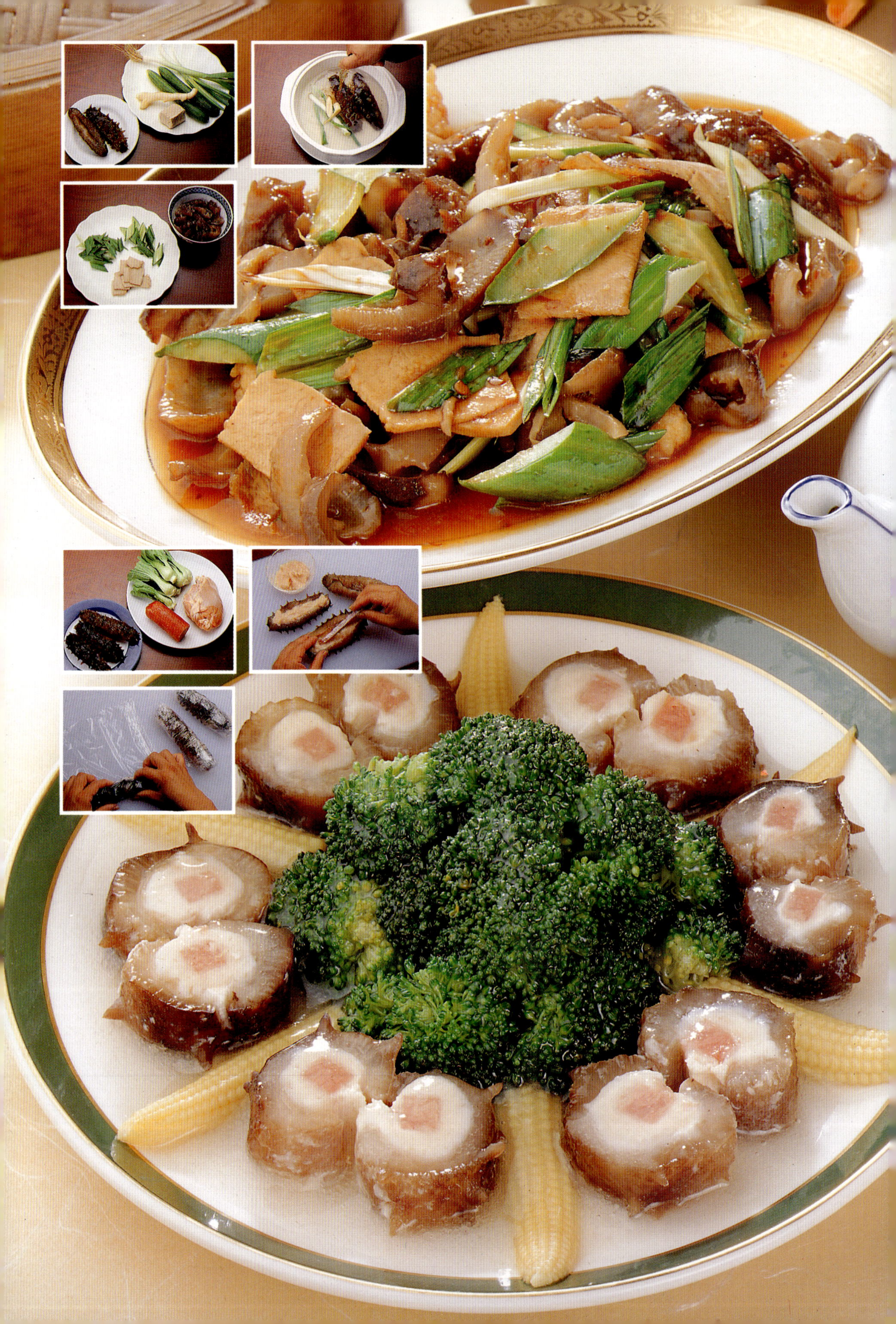

麻辣海參

材料
海參2條　熟豬肉3兩　黃瓜1條　青蒜1支

調味料
辣豆瓣醬1湯匙　清湯(或水)1杯　醬油½湯匙　糖、酒各1茶匙　濕太白粉酌量　麻油1茶匙　花椒粉少許

作法
1. 海參先出水去腥(鍋中放海參加蔥2支、薑2片、酒1湯匙及冷水3杯,煮至適軟),切成半寸多厚斜片。
2. 熟豬肉切小厚片,青蒜切斜段,黃瓜剖成四半,切斜段備用。
3. 用1湯匙油炒透肉片,加入辣豆瓣醬同炒,並加水、醬油、糖、酒等調味料,放入海參及黃瓜片,燒煮3～4分鐘。
4. 加入青蒜段拌合後勾芡,淋下麻油、花椒粉即可裝盤。

Spicy Sea Cucumber

Ingredients:
2 Sea Cucumber, 112.5g Boiled pork, 1 Cucumber, 1 Green garlic.
Seasonings:
1T Hot bean paste, 1C Soup stock, 1/2T Soysauce, 1t Sugar, 1t Wine, 1T Cornstarch paste 1t Sesame oil, 1/4t Brown pepper corn powder
Methods:
1. Put sea cucumber in a wok, add water, 1 green onion, 2 slices ginger & 1T wine, cook over medium heat to moderate soft, drain and cut diagonally each into 4 slices.
2. Cut boiled pork into slices, shred the green garlic, cut cucumber into slices.
3. Heat 1T oil, stir fry pork, add hot bean paste and all seasonings, finally add sea cucumber and cucumber slices, cook for 3~4 minutes.
4. Mix with green garlic shreds, thicken with cornstarch paste, splash sesame oil, sprinkle brown pepper corn powder. Serve.

如意海參

材料
海參3條　雞胸肉3兩　洋火腿3條　玉米筍、青花菜少量　玻璃紙3張

雞茸料
酒1茶匙　蔥薑水1茶匙　鹽¼茶匙　太白粉2茶匙

調味料
清湯1½杯　醬油、酒各½湯匙　鹽、胡椒粉各少許　濕太白粉2茶匙　麻油½茶匙

作法
1. 雞胸肉用刀剁成雞茸,加入雞茸料拌勻。
2. 海參洗淨腸砂,放入鍋中出水(參考麻辣海參)至軟。擦乾內部,撒入乾太白粉,釀入雞茸,雞茸中央放1條火腿條(火腿要先沾上太白粉),用玻璃紙包住,蒸10分鐘左右。
3. 取出海參包,待冷卻後,拆除玻璃紙,切成薄圓片,排入盤中。
4. 用1湯匙油煎香蔥、薑,注入清湯並調味,勾芡後淋入麻油,再淋到海參片上(用燙過之玉米筍及青花菜圍飾)。

＊海參夠大時,可完全包裹住雞茸,切片後即成金錢狀,名為「金錢海參」。

Stuffed Sea Cucumber with Chicken

Ingredients:
3pcs Sea cucumber, 112.5g Chicken breast meat, 3pcs Ham (cut into chopstick size stick), 1C Baby corn, Broccoli, 3pcs Cellophane paper
Sauce:
❶ 1t Wine, 1t Green onion & Ginger juice, 1/4t Salt, 2t Cornstarch.
❷ 1-1/2C Soupstock, 1/2T Wine, 1/2T Soysauce, Salt, Pepper, 2t Cornstarch paste, 1/2t Sesame oil.
Methods:
1. Cut and smash the chicken, mix with ❶.
2. Rinse and clean the sea cucumber, discard the intestine, cook with water, ginger, green onion and wine over medium heat for 3~5 minutes, drain, pat dry by a towel, sprinkle cornstarch, stuff with the chicken meat, insert a stick of ham, wrap and roll tightly with cellophane paper. Steam for 10 minutes.
3. Take out the sea cucumber, discard cellophane paper, cut into 1" slices, arrange on a plate.
4. Heat 1T oil to stir fry green onion & ginger, add soup stock, season with salt, thicken with cornstarch paste, splash sesame oil, pour on sea cucumber, decorate with baby corn & broccoli.

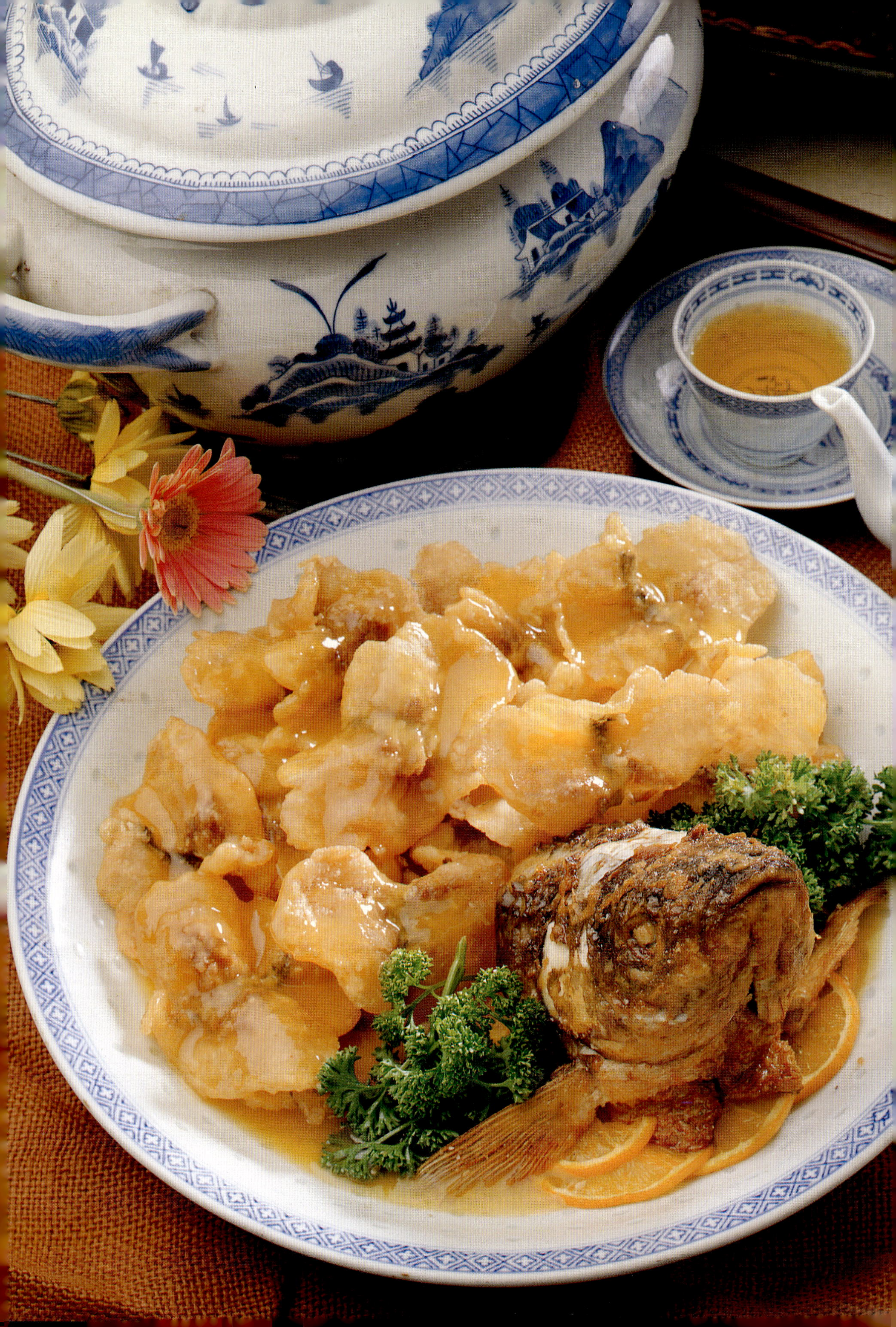

香汁蝴蝶魚

材料
小草魚1條　葱、薑絲各1湯匙　玉米粉½杯　麵粉少許

醃魚料
鹽⅓茶匙　酒½湯匙　胡椒粉少許　蛋白半個　太白粉1茶匙

綜合調味料
糖2湯匙　醋1湯匙　水2湯匙　淡色醬油1湯匙　鹽¼茶匙　桔子汁3湯匙　太白粉½湯匙　麻油1茶匙

作法
1. 魚頭及尾部切下，用少許鹽、酒抹一下，裹上麵粉。
2. 魚肉去骨後，切成蝴蝶薄片(連皮第一刀不切斷，第二刀才切斷)，用醃魚料醃10分鐘，用玉米粉沾裹魚片，並用木棒敲打成薄片。
3. 炸油燒至九分熱，先將魚頭及尾炸酥，再將魚一片片翻開下鍋，大火炸至熟且酥脆撈出。
4. 用少許油爆香葱、薑絲，放下綜合調味料煮滾，放入魚片，快速溜一下便盛盤。

＊除桔子汁外也可用鳳梨汁或檸檬汁等代替以增香氣。

Butterfly Fish

Ingredients:
1 Fish, 1T Green onion, shredded, 1T Ginger, shredded, 1/2C Cornstarch.

Sauce:
❶ 1/3t Salt, 1/2T Wine, Pepper, 1/2 Egg white, 1t Cornstarch.
❷ 2T Sugar, 1T Vinegar, 2T Water, 1T Soysauce, 1/4t Salt, 3T Orange juice, 1/2T Corstarch, 1t Sesame oil.

Methods:
1. Cut off head and tail from fish, marinate with salt & wine, coat with flour and deep fry in hot oil to crispy, put on two sides of a plate.
2. Debone the fish spine, slive the fish (skin-side down), every two slice of meat connected by the skin, so it looks like the wings of a butterfly, marinate with ❶ for 10 minutes, coat with cornstarch.
3. Deep fry the fish slices to cispy, drain.
4. Heat 1T oil to fry ginger, green onion, add ❷ sauce, bring to a boil, mix with fish quickly, remove to the plate.

♣ The orange juice can be replaced by pineapple or lemon juice.

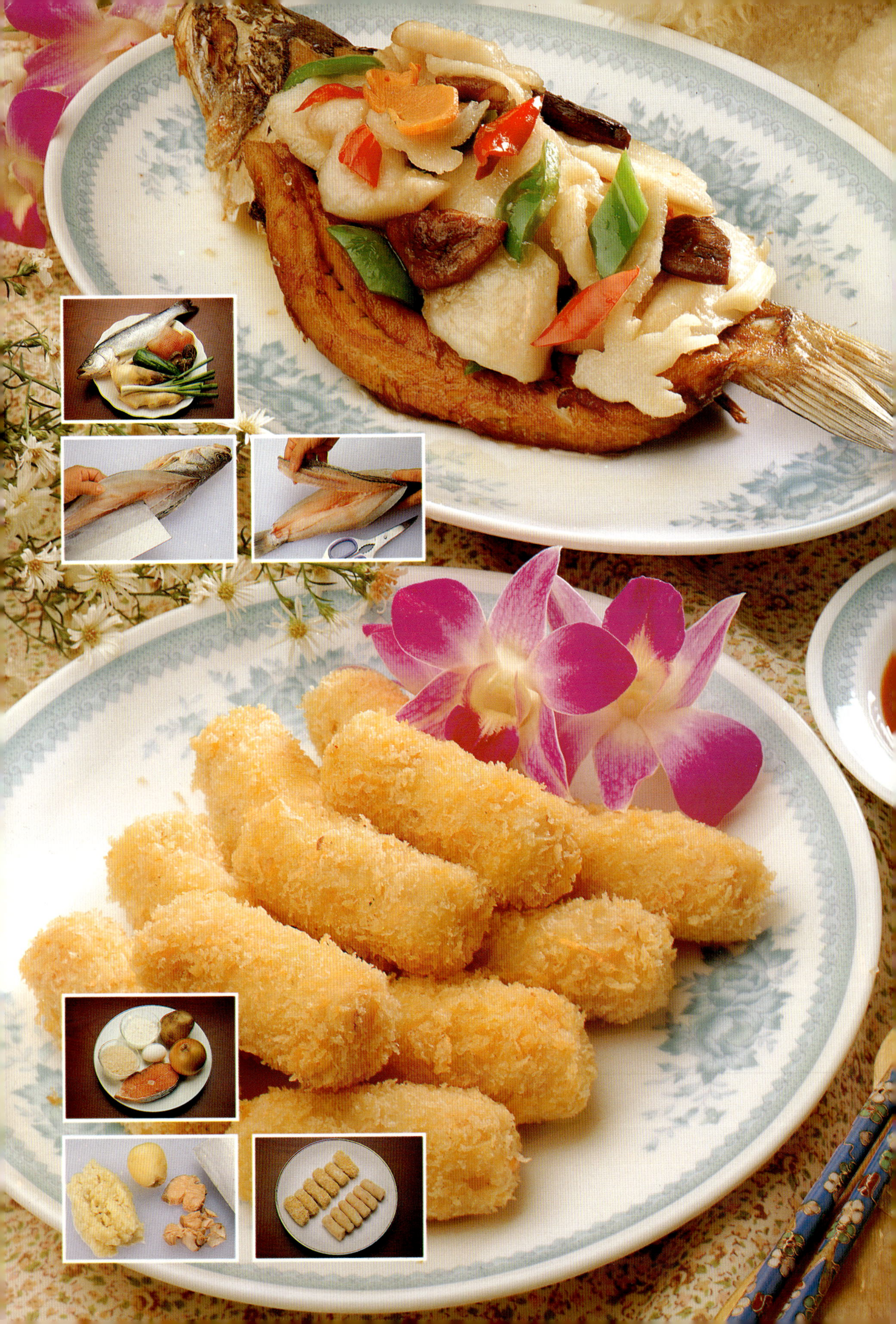

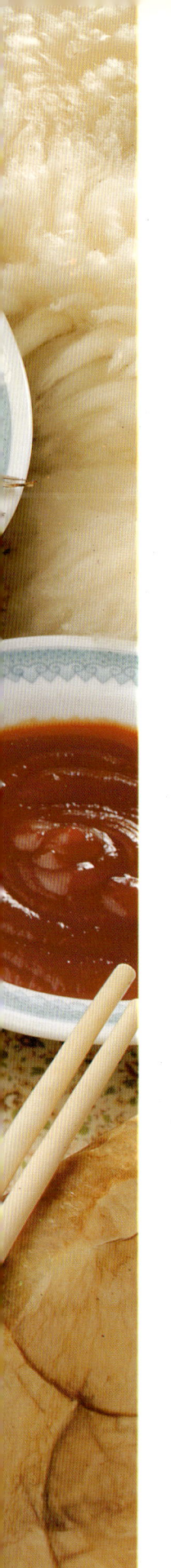

魚中有餘

材料

鮮魚1條（約25公分長） 魚肉10兩 香菇3朵 熟筍片½杯 青、紅椒片各少許 蔥段、薑片酌量

醃魚料

鹽½茶匙 酒½湯匙 胡椒粉少許

醃魚肉料

鹽½茶匙 酒½湯匙 太白粉½湯匙

調味料

酒1茶匙 鹽¼茶匙 胡椒粉、麻油少許

作法

1. 整條魚洗淨後由背部貼著大骨，兩面劃開，取出大骨，魚肉及尾部保持完整，用醃魚料抹勻醃10分鐘，再投入熱油中炸酥。
2. 另一魚肉順紋切厚片，用醃魚肉料醃片刻，香菇泡軟再切片。
3. 將2杯油燒至八分熱，放下魚片泡熟，瀝出。另用1湯匙油爆香蔥段及薑片，放下香菇、筍片、青、紅椒片及魚片，撒下酒及調味料，大火拌炒均勻，淋少許熱油便可盛入已炸好之整條魚中間

Fish in Fish's Pocket

Ingredients:

1 Fish (25cm), 375g Fish fillet, 3pcs Black mushroom, 1/2C Bamboo shoot (cooked), Green bell pepper, Red bell pepper, Green onion, Ginger.

Sauce:

❶ 1/2t Salt, 1/2T Wine, 1/4t Pepper.
❷ 1/2t Salt, 1/2T Wine, 1/2T Cornstarch.
❸ 1t Wine, 1/4t Salt, Pepper, Sesame oil.

Methods:

1. Trim the fish, split the fish meat and debone the spine, make the fish meat into a large flat piece with the head and tail still attached, marinate with sauce ❶ for 10 minutes, deep fry in hot oil to crispy, drain. Then put on a plate as a fish pocket.
2. Slice the fish fillet, marinate with sauce ❷ for 10 minutes, deep fry in warm oil for 5 seconds, drain. Soak black mushroom to soft and slice.
3. Heat 1T oil to stir fry green onion and ginger, add all other ingredient slices and fish fillet, add sauce ❸ and stir over high heat, mix evenly and place in the fish pocket. Serve

西炸鮭魚球

材料

新鮮鮭魚3兩 馬鈴薯1斤 洋蔥屑½杯

調味料

鹽½茶匙 胡椒粉少許

西炸料

麵粉3湯匙 蛋1個 麵包粉1½杯

作法

1. 馬鈴薯煮軟（筷子可插透即可）取出，待稍涼後剝去外皮，用刀背壓成泥，放在大碗中。
2. 鮭魚抹少許鹽後入鍋蒸熟，剝成小粒。用2湯匙油將洋蔥屑炒軟，連魚肉一起放入大碗中，加調味料仔細拌勻，再分成小粒，並搓成橢圓形。
3. 鮭魚球先沾一層麵粉，再沾上蛋汁，最後滾滿麵包粉，投入熱油中炸黃，瀝乾油裝入盤中，另附沙拉醬沾食

Deep-Fried Salmon Balls

Ingredients:

112.5g Fresh salmon, 600g Potato, 1/2C Onion minced.

Sauce:

❶ 1/2t Salt, Pepper.
❷ 3T Flour, 1 Egg, 1-1/2C Bread crumb.

Methods:

1. Boil potato, peel and smash.
2. Rub some salt on salmon, steam to done & tear into small pieces. Heat 2T oil to stir fry onion, add salmon & ❶, mix well, divide into small oval balls.
3. Sprinkle flour on salmon balls, dip in beaten egg then coat with bread crumb. Deep fry in hot oil to golden brown, drain and serve with mayonnaise.

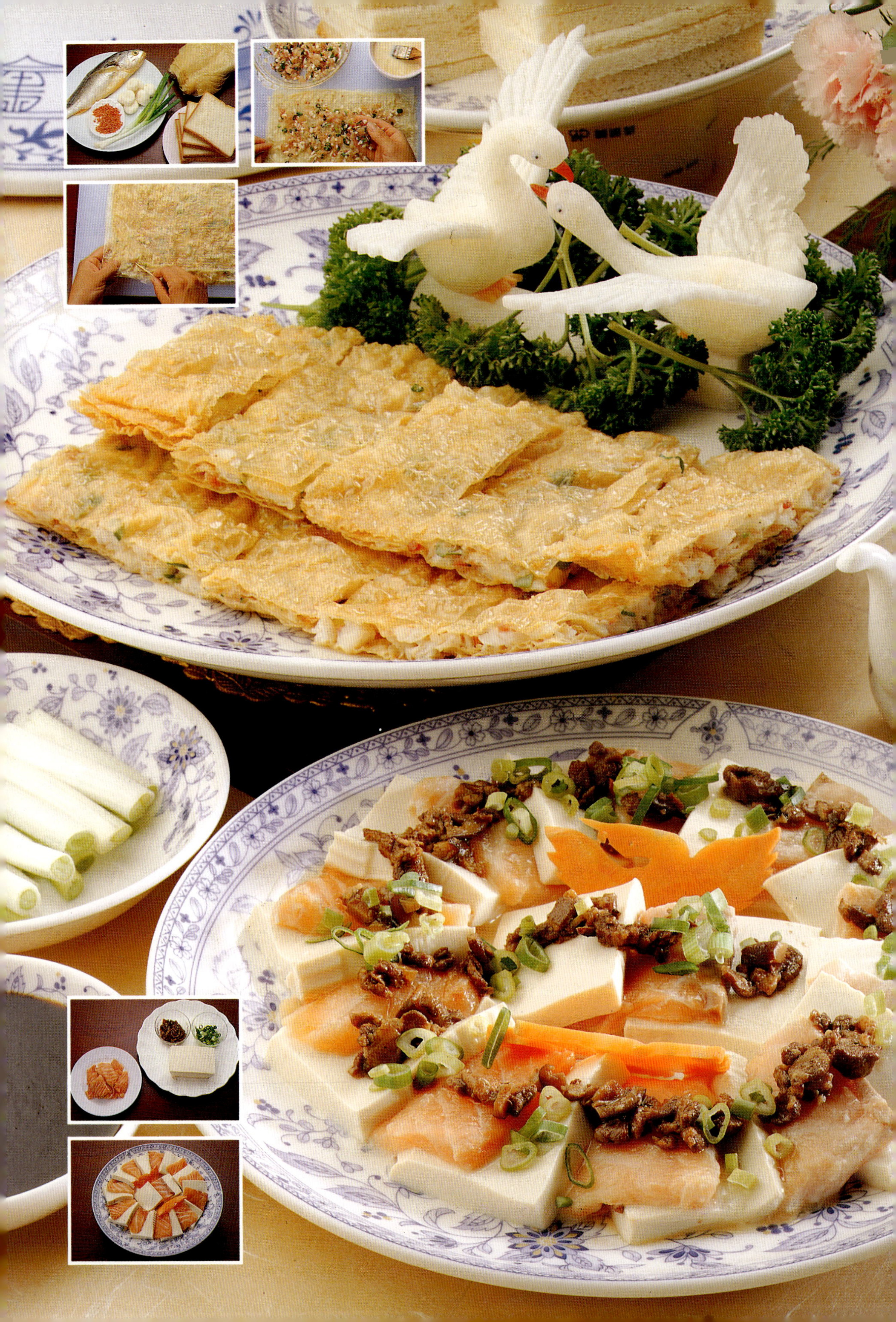

黃魚酥方

材料
豆腐衣6張　黃魚1條（約12兩）或白色魚肉6兩　荸薺6粒　蔥屑½杯　火腿屑2湯匙　土司麵包6片　甜麵醬2湯匙　蔥段酌量　牙籤數支

醃魚料
蛋白半個　鹽¼茶匙　酒少許　胡椒粉少許

蛋麵糊
蛋1個　麵粉⅓杯　水⅔杯　鹽少許

作法
1. 剔下黃魚肉或白色魚肉切粗絲，用醃魚料醃一會兒。
2. 荸薺切絲擠乾和蔥屑、火腿屑一起加入魚肉中拌勻。
3. 豆腐衣裁去兩邊成長方形，在第1張塗一層蛋麵糊，再鋪上1張豆腐衣，然後塗糊並撒上魚肉料，另覆蓋2張豆腐衣（每張都要塗麵糊）及撒魚料，再蓋2張豆腐衣，用牙籤別住四邊。
4. 放入熱油中，小火慢炸至酥，切成長方小塊排盤，附活頁土司麵包(1片土司先對切為2，再片開成活頁狀)上桌，與蔥段沾醬夾食。

＊甜麵醬1湯匙加糖½湯匙、水1湯匙調稀，用少許油炒香。

香菇肉燥蒸鮭魚

材料
新鮮鮭魚4兩　嫩豆腐1盒　肉燥2湯匙　蔥屑1湯匙

作法
1. 將鮭魚切成3公分寬、5公分長、半公分厚的長方片，嫩豆腐也切成相同大小，兩者相間隔鋪排在深盤中。
2. 將2湯匙肉燥撒在鮭魚及豆腐上，入鍋蒸10分鐘端出，撒下蔥屑並淋上熱油即可上桌。

＊除肉燥外還可以用炒過的蝦子（蝦膏）或肉醬來蒸。

＊用油炒香絞肉及香菇屑，加酒、醬油、糖、鹽、五香粉、紅蔥酥及水同煮至肉香汁乾便是肉燥（約1小時）。

Deep-Fried Fish Cake

Ingredients:
6pcs Bean curd sheet (dried), 1 Yellow croker, 6pcs Water chestnuts, 1/2C Green onion, chopped, 2T Ham, minced, 6 slices Toast, 2T Sweet soybean paste, Green onion, sectioned, Tooth picks.

Sauce:
❶ 1/2 Egg white, 1/4t Salt, Wine, Pepper.
❷ 1 Egg, 1/3C Flour, 2/3C Water, Salt.

Methods:
1. Take meat from yellow croker, cut into shreds, marinate with ❶ for a while.
2. Shred the water chestnuts, mix with fish together with green onion, ham.
3. Rub ❷ on a dried bean curd sheet, cover with another sheet, rub ❷ again, add some fish mixture and spread, cover 2 slices bean curd sheet, seal with tooth picks.
4. Deep fry in hot oil over low heat to crispy, cut into rectangles, serve with toast, sweet soybean paste, green onion.

♣ Mix 1T Soybean paste with 1/2T Sugar, 1T water, then stir fry with 1T hot oil. This is the sauce.

Steamed Salmon with Meat Sauce

Ingredients:
140g Salmon, 1pack Bean curd, 2T Meat sauce, 1T Green onion, chopped.

Methods:
1. Cut salmon into 2 cm x 5 cm x 0.5 cm slices. Cut bean curd into same size slices. Place fish and bean curd slice one against the other on a plate.
2. Pour 2T meat sauce on top of fish, steam for 10 minutes, sprinkle green onion and splash 1T boiling oil. Serve.

♣ Fried dried-Shrimp-roe can substitute the meat sauce.

♣ Stir fry minced meat & black mushroom, add wine, soysauce, sugar, salt, five spicy powder, dried red scallion and water, cook over low heat about 1 hour till sauce reduced and becomes fragrant. This is the meat sauce.

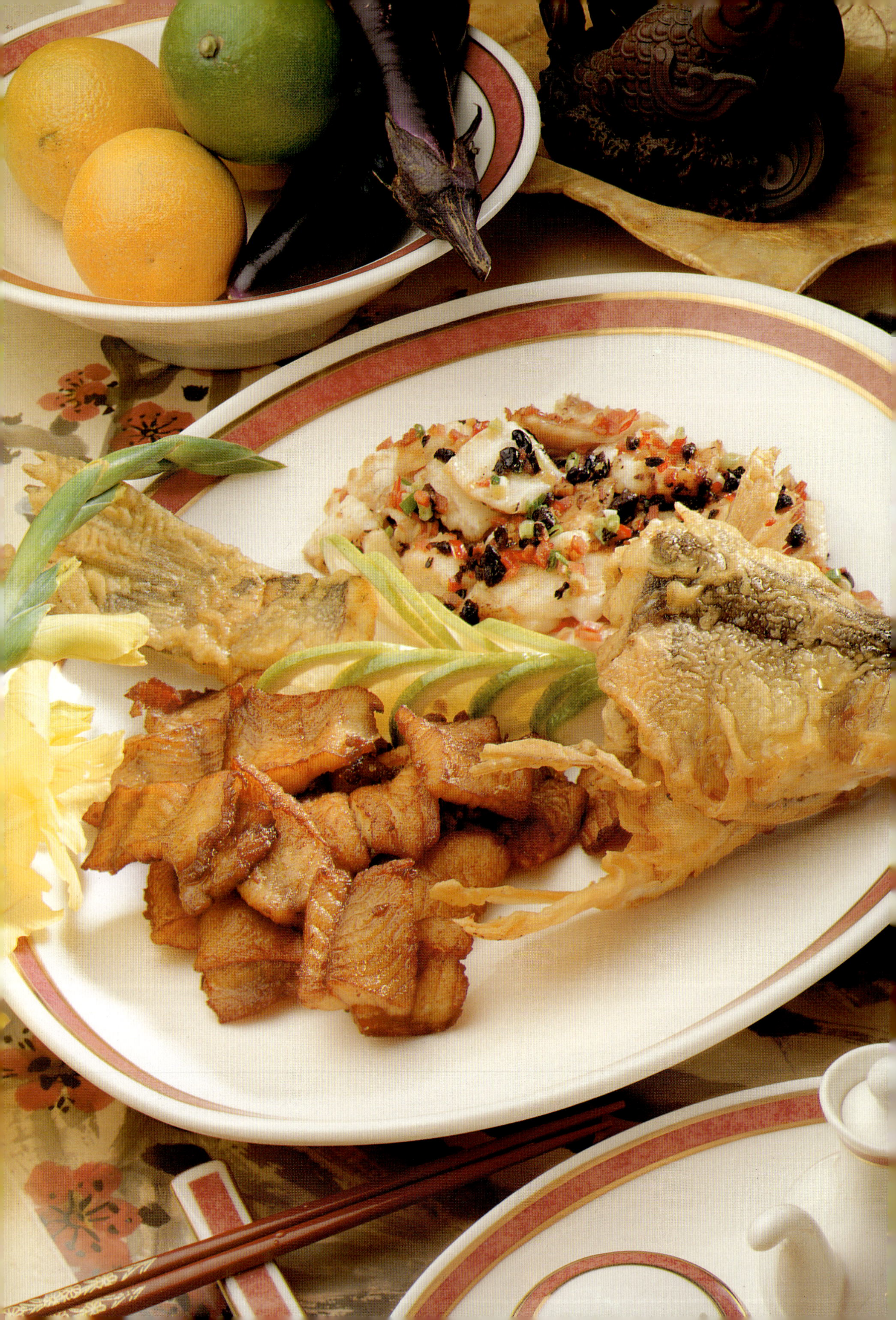

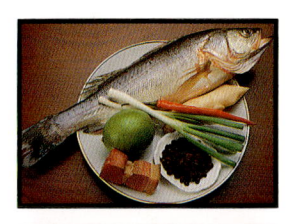

鱸魚雙味

材料
新鮮鱸魚(或其他新鮮魚)1條,約1½公斤　太白粉少許

醃魚料
葱1支　薑1片　酒1湯匙　淡色醬油1湯匙

蒸魚料
豆豉1湯匙　紅辣椒屑½湯匙　火腿屑1湯匙
薑屑½茶匙　葱花1湯匙

作法
1. 切下魚頭及魚尾,再將半邊魚肉片切下來魚肉斜刀切大片,用醃魚料醃10分鐘以上,用熱油炸酥,撒上少許五香花椒鹽,排列在大盤中之一邊。
2. 另一邊的魚肉也切下來,切成大片,拌少許太白粉及鹽,放在蒸盤內,撒上蒸魚料,大火蒸10分鐘,取出後排在另一邊。(中間排一列檸檬片間隔)

＊此係椒鹽魚片與豆豉辣椒蒸魚兩種口味,也可改用酥炸魚捲、蠔油魚片或麵拖魚條等其他口味之魚的菜式。

Two Ways Fish

Ingredients:
1 Fish (about 900g).

Sauce:
❶ 1 Ginger slice, 1 Green onion, 1T Soysauce.
❷ 1T Fermented black bean, 1/2T Red pepper (chopped), 1T Ham (chopped), 1/2t Ginger (chopped), 1T Green onion (chopped).

Methods:
1. Cut off head & tail from fish. Remove one side of fish meat from the spine, slice and marinate with ❶ for 10 minutes, deep fry in hot oil till crispy. Arrange on one side of plate, sprinkle brown peppercorn salt.
2. Slice another half fish meat, arrange on a plate sprinkle a little salt and cornstarch, pour ❷ on, steam for 10 minutes, arrange on the other side of the plate. (Divided by lemon slices as decoration)

✤ The flavor can be changed to oyster flavor or deep fried fish rolls.

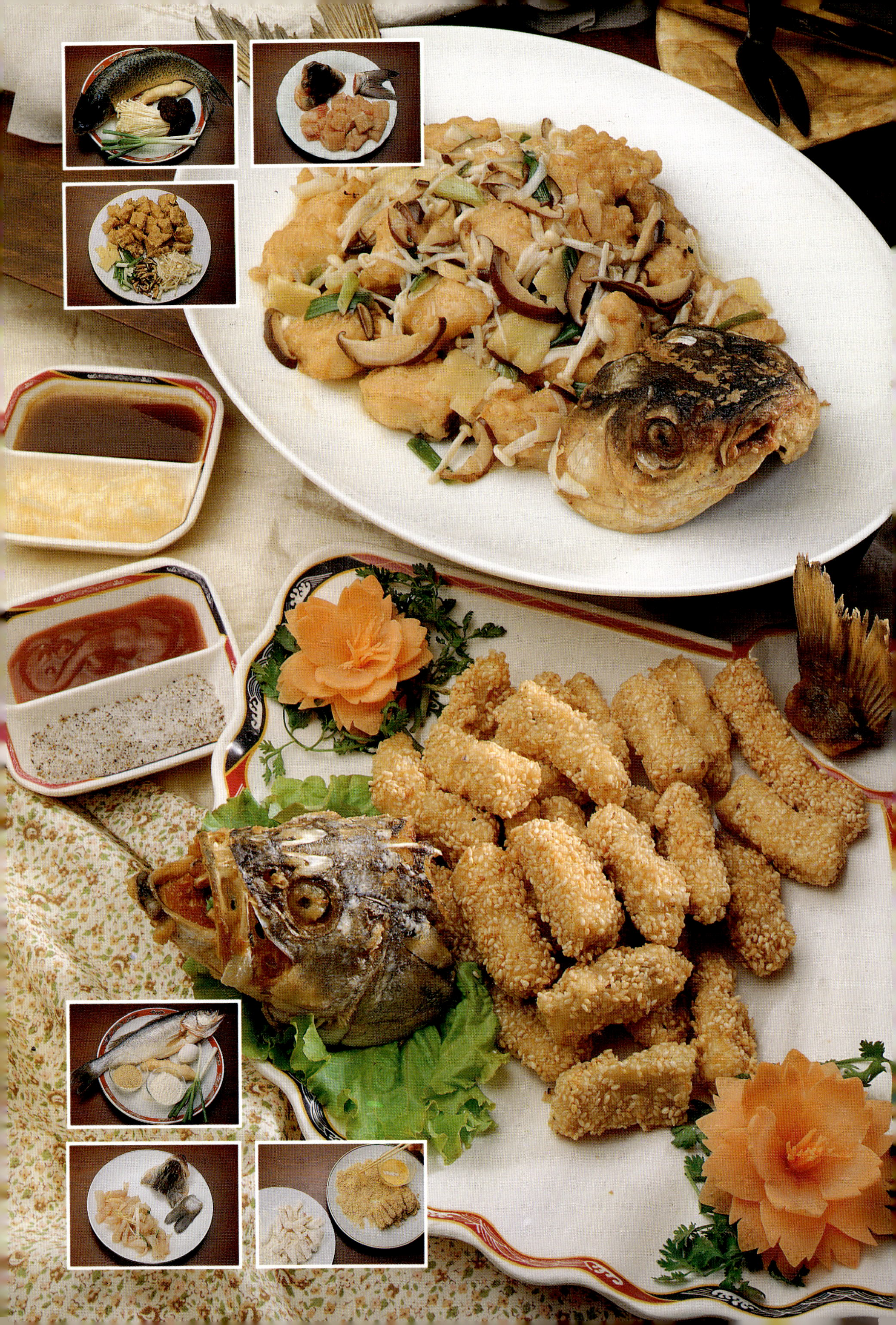

雙菇燜鮮魚

材料
小鱸魚或石斑魚、鮸魚、大的金線魚1條
香菇3朵　金菇半把　蔥段、薑片酌量
高湯½杯

醃魚料
酒½湯匙　鹽¼茶匙　胡椒粉少許

蛋糊
蛋1個　麵粉4湯匙　水酌量

調味料
醬油½湯匙　鹽½茶匙

作法
1. 將魚頭及尾切下，由背部剖開，取下兩邊之魚肉，魚頭、尾沾上乾麵粉，用熱油炸黃，放在大盤兩端裝飾，另外魚之大骨亦沾乾粉炸黃，墊底用。
2. 魚肉切1½寸大小，用醃魚料拌醃，約5分鐘。沾上一層乾麵粉後再裹上蛋糊，炸黃。
3. 用1湯匙熱油爆香蔥段、薑片，淋下清湯(或水)，放下魚塊及調味料，小火煮3分鐘。
4. 撈出魚塊堆放在魚骨上，湯汁中加入香菇絲(泡軟切絲)和金菇(切段)，大火煮滾片刻，勾成薄芡，淋到魚面上即成。

Fish with Mushrooms

Ingredients:
1 Grouper (or other fish), 3 Black mushrooms, 100g Needle mushrooms, Green onion, Ginger, 1/2C Soup stock.

Sauce:
❶ 1/2T Wine, 1/4t Salt, Pepper.
❷ 1 Egg, 4T Flour, Water (moderate amount).
❸ 1/2T Soysauce, 1/2t Salt.

Methods:
1. Cut off head & tail from fish, debone fish spine, leave fish meat for later use. Coat fish head, tail and spine with flour, deep fry in hot oil to golden brown. Arrange on a plate.
2. Cut fish meat into 1-1/2" long sticks, marinate with sauce ❶ for 5 minutes, coat with flour and dip in ❷ batter, then deep-fry in hot oil to golden brown.
3. Heat 1T oil to stir fry green onion & ginger, add soup stock, ❸ and fish sticks, cook over low heat for 3 minutes.
4. Take fish sticks out from wok and arrange on top of bones of the plate. Add soaked black mushroom (shredded) & needle mushroom. When done, thicken and pour on fish.

四味芝麻魚

材料
新鮮鱸魚1條(或魚肉1斤)　麵粉3湯匙
蛋1個　白芝麻½杯

醃魚料
蔥1支　薑2片　鹽½茶匙　胡椒粉¼茶匙　麻油1茶匙

四味料
沙拉醬、蕃茄醬、五香花椒鹽各酌量　蠔油醬(油½湯匙　蠔油1湯匙　水2湯匙煮滾)

作法
1. 取下兩邊之魚肉後，將魚頭及魚尾切下，沾上麵粉炸黃，排在大盤中。
2. 魚肉去皮，順紋切成姆指般粗條，用醃魚料拌醃片刻。
3. 魚條上撒少許麵粉，再沾上蛋汁，最後沾裹上白芝麻，全部沾好，投入七分熱的溫油中，小火慢炸至熟，撈出瀝乾油。
4. 將魚條排列在魚骨上，並將四小碟不同之調味料附上，以供沾食。

Four Flavors Fish

Ingredients:
1 Fresh fish, 3T Flour, 1 Egg, 1/2C Sesame seeds.

Sauce:
❶ 1 Green onion, 2 Slices ginger, 1/2t Salt, 1/4t Pepper, 1t Sesame oil.
❷ Mayonnaise.
❸ Ketchup.
❹ Brown pepper corn salt.
❺ Oyster sauce: 1/2T Hot oil, 1T Oyster sauce, 2T Water.

Methods:
1. Cut off head & tail from fish, coat with flour and deep fry in hot oil to golden brown. Arrange on two sides of a plate. Debone the spine, cook the same way, place on the plate too.
2. Cut the fish meat into thumb size sticks, marinate with ❶ for a while.
3. Sprinkle flour on fish, coat with egg batter, and sesame seeds. Deep fry with 150°C oil to golden brown. Drain. Arrange on the plate.
4. Serve with ❷ ❸ ❹ ❺ four kinds of dipping sauce.

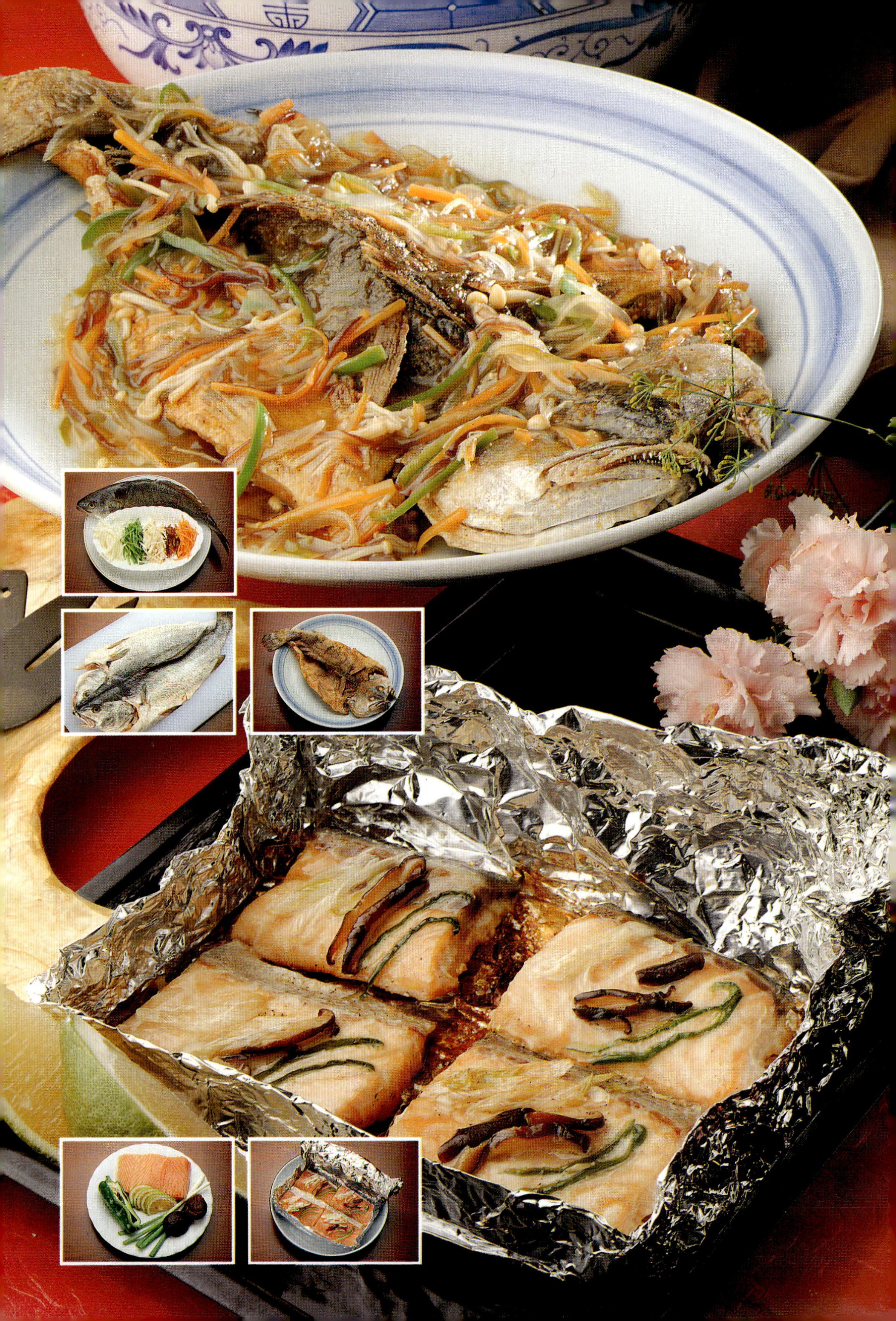

脆皮五柳魚

材料
新鮮魚1條　洋蔥絲、青椒絲、胡蘿蔔絲、金菇絲、木耳絲各酌量　油炸粉半杯

調味料
鹽¼茶匙　淡色醬油1湯匙　糖1湯匙　醋1湯匙　水4湯匙　麻油、胡椒粉各少許　濕太白粉酌量

作法
1. 魚清理乾淨之後，由腹部下刀片切開，但背部仍需連著，剪除大骨，撒下鹽及胡椒粉醃片刻，沾上油炸粉，用熱油炸脆撈出，放入盤中。
2. 用1湯匙油炒香洋蔥絲及胡蘿蔔絲，加入鹽、醬油、糖、醋及水調味，煮滾後，放下青椒、金菇及木耳絲，再用濕太白粉勾芡，淋下麻油及胡椒粉，全部淋到魚上即可。

Crispy Fish with Assorted Strings

Ingredients:
1 Fish (any kind), Onion, Green pepper, Carrot, Wood dear, Needle mushroom, each a little amount (shredded).

Batter:
❶ 1 Egg, 2T Flour, 2T Cornstarch, 1/4t Salt, 1/2T Oil, Water.

Sauce:
❷ 1/4t Salt, 1T Soysauce, 1T Sugar, 1T Vinegar, 4T Water, Sesame oil, Pepper, Cornstarch paste

Methods:
1. Trim the fish. Slice from the belly part to make a large flat sheet, remove the spine. Marinate with salt & pepper for a while.
2. Sprinkle flour on fish, coat with batter ❶, deep fry in hot oil to crispy, drain and put on a plate.
3. Heat 1T oil to stir fry onion & carrot, add sauce ❷, bring to a boil, add green pepper, needle mushroom and wood ear, then thicken and pour on fish.

銀紙烤鮭魚

材料
新鮮鮭魚12兩　香菇1朵　青椒¼個　蔥絲1湯匙　鋁箔紙（6寸四方）2張　檸檬片2～3片

醃魚料
酒1湯匙　淡色醬油2湯匙　糖¼茶匙　胡椒粉少許　水2湯匙

作法
1. 新鮮鮭魚切成4片，用醃魚料拌醃10分鐘。
2. 香菇泡軟切絲，青椒也切絲。
3. 鋁箔紙上塗上油後，放入魚肉，再將香菇、青椒、蔥絲，分別撒在魚肉上，淋下醃魚汁，折角包妥。
4. 放入烤箱中大火烤熟（約8～10分鐘）。也可用平底鍋採蒸烤方式（平底鍋中放水1杯，放下鋁箔包，蓋上鍋蓋，約10分鐘）。附檸檬片上桌。

＊也可1片鮭魚包成1包，包成4小包。

Baked Salmon in Silver Package

Ingredients:
300g Fresh salmon fillet, 2 Black mushroom, 1/4 Green pepper, 1 Green onion, shredded, 2pcs Aluminum foil (6" x 6"), 3pcs Lemon piece.

Sauce:
❶ 1T Wine, 2T Soysauce, 1/4t Sugar, Pepper.

Methods:
1. Marinate salmon with ❶ for 10 minutes.
2. Soak black mushroom to soft and slice. Shred the green pepper.
3. Rub some oil on center of aluminum foil, put the fish on, arrange black mushroom, green pepper and green onion on fish, then add sauce ❶, fold and wrap into package.
4. Bake in oven over high heat for 12~15 minutes Serve with lemon slices.

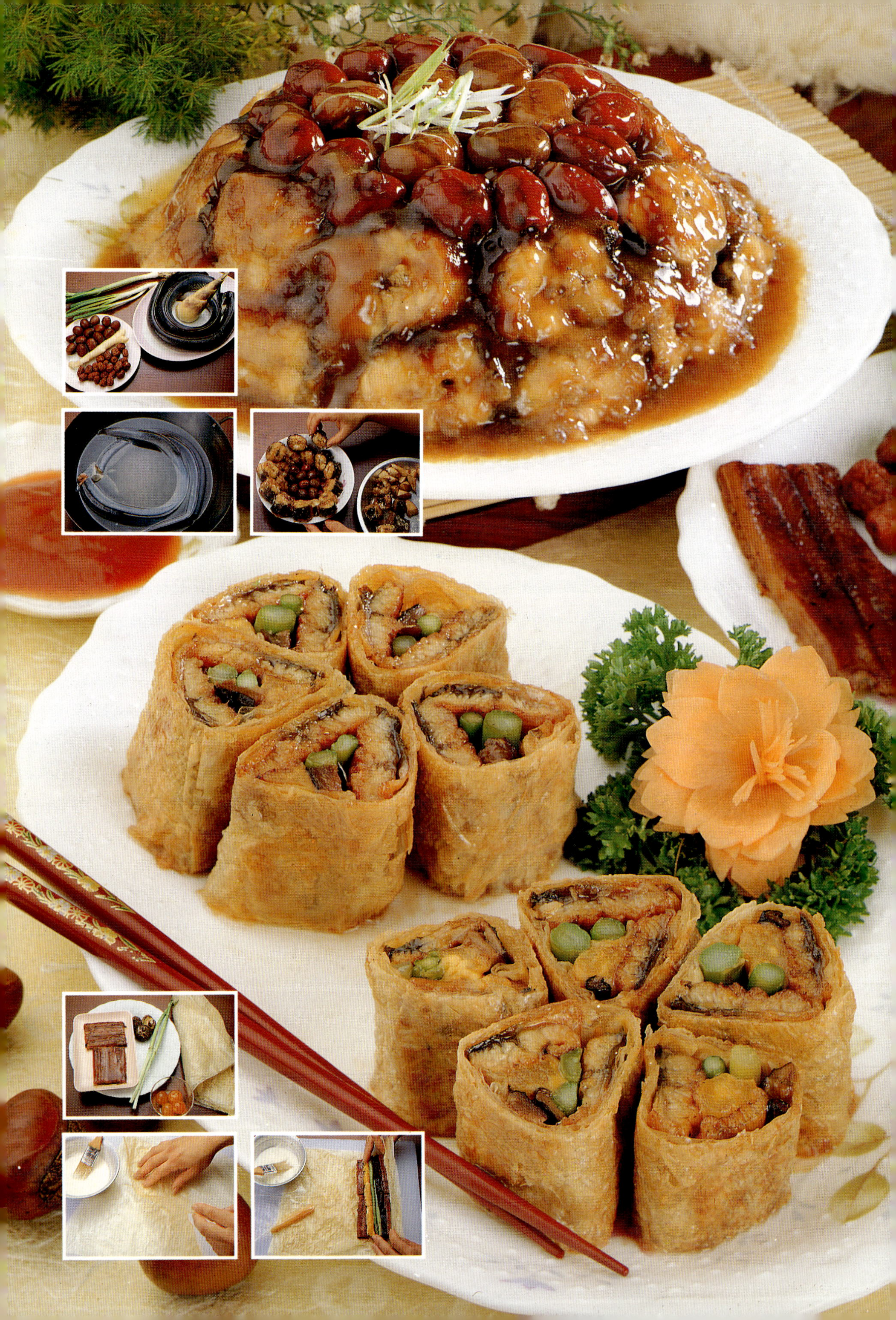

栗棗扣河鰻

材料

河鰻1條　乾栗子30粒　紅棗15粒　筍1支　蔥末1湯匙　薑末1茶匙　青蒜絲1湯匙

調味料

酒1湯匙　醬油4湯匙　冰糖1湯匙　胡椒粉少許　水3杯　濕太白粉酌量　麻油1茶匙

作法

1. 將鰻魚放入七分熱的水中燙3秒鐘，撈出後將白色黏膜刷洗乾淨，切成1寸長段，拌上醬油，沾滿太白粉，投入熱油中炸黃。
2. 筍切塊也拌醬油，炸黃。乾栗子泡軟，剔除澀衣，燙一下；紅棗亦泡軟。
3. 用2湯匙油爆香蔥、薑末，放下調味料煮滾後，加入鰻魚、栗子、紅棗及筍塊，燒煮8分鐘。
4. 將湯汁過濾出來，另用一只蒸碗，將鰻魚等料排入碗中（筍塊填塞中間），淋下湯汁再蒸15分鐘。
5. 泌出湯汁，鰻魚扣在盤中，湯汁勾芡淋下麻油，澆在鰻魚上，撒青蒜絲即可食。

Mold Eel & Walnut

Ingredients:

1 Eel, 30 Walnut, shelled, 15 Red dates, 1 Bamboo shoot, 1T Green onion, chopped, 1t Ginger chopped, 1T Green garlic, shredded.

Sauce:

❶ 1T Wine, 4T Soysauce, 1T Rock sugar, Pepper, 3C Water, 1t Sesame oil, Cornstarch paste.

Methods:

1. Blanch eel in 140°C water over medium heat for 3 seconds, brush and clean the liquid skin off eel, cut into sections 1/2" long. Dip in soysauce, coat the cornstarch and deep fry in hot oil to golden brown.
2. Cut bamboo shoot (shelled) into cubes, brush some soysauce and deep fry to brown, drain. Soak walnut to soft, blanch in boiling water, soak the red dates to soft.
3. Heat 2T oil to stir fry green onion & ginger, add seasoning sauce ❶, bring to a boil, add in eel, walnut, red dates and bamboo shoot, cook for 8 minutes.
4. Arrange eel in the bottom of a large bowl, stuff all other ingredients in center, pour the soup in the bowl, steam for 15 minutes. Reverse the bowl up side down to remove eel on a plate.
5. Pour the eel soup in wok, thicken and pour on eel. Sprinkle green garlic. Serve.

酥炸鰻魚捲

材料

豆腐衣4張　蒲燒鰻（即烤鰻）1條　香菇3朵　蘆筍2支　鹹蛋黃4個

麵糊

麵粉2湯匙　水3湯匙

作法

1. 香菇泡軟後，加醬油（連泡香菇之水）入鍋蒸10分鐘，切條。蘆筍撕去老皮，燙熟。烤鰻去頭尾後一切為二。鹹蛋黃蒸熟搓成15公分長條狀。
2. 將豆腐衣一切為二，在1張上面抹一些麵糊，另1張反方向對放在上面，連成方型，再將2張同樣重疊放在上面（共4張），最上面一張再刷一層麵糊，中間放1塊烤鰻，上面再放蛋黃，1支蘆筍及香菇條，包捲成筒狀，用麵糊封口。
3. 用熱油小火慢慢將鰻魚捲炸酥黃，趁熱切成1寸長小段，排盤上桌。

Crispy Eel Rolls

Ingredients:

4 pcs Bean curd sheets, 1 Eel (Roasted), 3 pcs Black mushroom, 2 Asparagus, 4 Salty egg yolk.

Batter:

2T Flour, 3T Water.

Methods:

1. Soak black mushroom, add soysauce, steam for 10 minutes. Cut into shreds, peel asparagus, blanch and cut into sections. Cut off head & tail from eel, cut into 2 pieces. Steam the salty egg yolk, roll into two cylinders about 15cm long.
2. Cut each bean curd sheet into halves, rub some batter on top, placing the second piece with the angle on opposite direction, rub batter again and cover the bean curd sheet again (total 4 pcs of bean curd sheet layers). Brush batter then put a piece of eel. Finally arrange egg yolk roll, asparagus, black mushrooms, roll and wrap into a cylinder roll, seal with batter.
3. Deep fry in hot oil over low heat till golden brown, cut into sections 1" long. Serve.

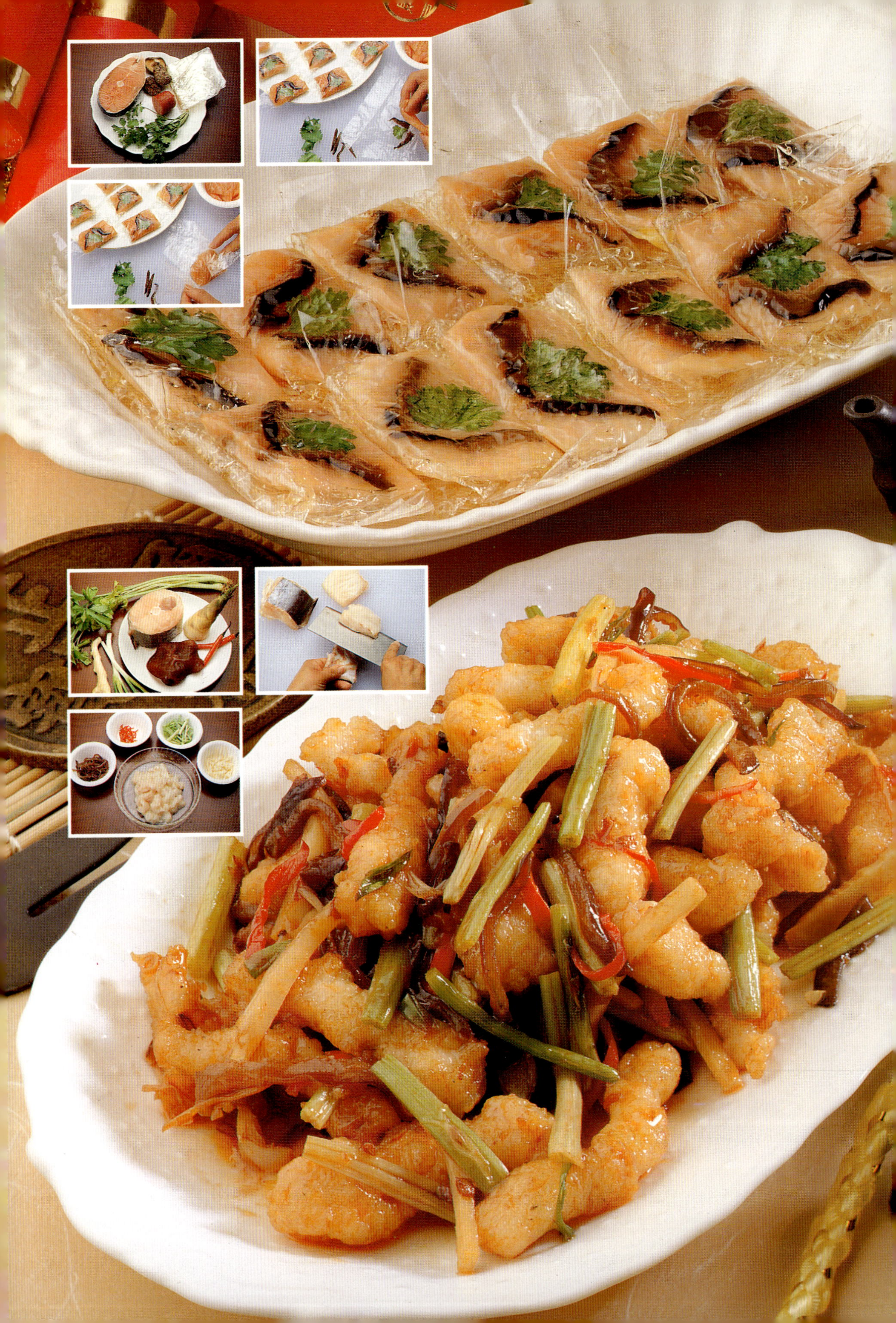

玻璃鮭魚片

材料

新鮮鮭魚6兩　玻璃紙1大張　香菇絲1/3杯　香菜酌量

醃魚料

蔥1支　薑1片　鹽1茶匙　酒2茶匙

作法

1. 將魚順紋切成1寸多寬、2寸長之厚片，用醃魚料拌醃10分鐘。
2. 玻璃紙剪成6寸四方大小，每張分別塗上油，中間放上香菇絲3~4條及香菜葉1~2片，上面蓋上一片鮭魚片。玻璃紙先對折成三角形，再將兩邊折向中間，再反折露出紙角，收口塞入紙包中。
3. 將乾淨的油燒至八分熱，放下紙包魚小火炸熟，瀝乾油排盤。

＊這種包法，吃時只要輕拉兩邊露出的紙角，便可打開紙包

Transparent Package Fish

Ingredients:
225g Fish, 1 pce Cellophane paper, 1/3C Ham. shredded, 1/3C Black mushroom, shredded, Parsley.

Sauce :
❶ 1 Green onion, 1 slice Ginger, 2t Wine.

Methods:
1. Cut fish into 1" x 2" thick slices, marinate with sauce ❶ for 10 minutes.
2. Cut cellophane paper into squares 6" x 6", rub oil on center, put a little amount of ham, black mushroom, parsley, cover with a slice of fish. Fold paper to a triangle, fold two-sides-angles to the center, fold out again to let two angles left outside, finally fold the top angle down and insert to inside of the middle.
3. Deep fry in 160°C hot oil over low heat until done, drain & serve.

❖ When serving, pull out two sides angles. It's easy to open.

家常海鰻絲

材料

海鰻半斤　芹菜段、木耳絲各半杯　熟筍絲1/3杯　紅椒絲1湯匙　蔥、薑絲各少許　太白粉1/2杯

醃魚料

酒1茶匙　蛋白半個　鹽1/4茶匙　胡椒粉少許　太白粉2茶匙

調味料

辣豆瓣醬1/2湯匙　醬油2茶匙　糖1茶匙　酒1茶匙　清水1/3杯　麻油1/2茶匙　醋1茶匙

作法

1. 鰻魚去除大骨及魚皮後，順紋切成粗絲，全部用醃魚料拌勻醃10分鐘，再裹上一層太白粉。用熱油將海鰻絲炸酥撈起。
2. 起油鍋炒香蔥、薑絲，加入辣豆瓣醬同炒，並加入醬油、糖、酒及水，放入鰻魚絲及木耳絲及筍絲拌炒，燒煮一下，見汁將吸乾，放下芹菜段、紅椒絲與麻油，沿鍋邊淋醋，拌勻即可裝盤。

Shredded Eel Home Style

Ingredients:
300g Eel, 1/2C Celery, sectioned, 1/2C Wood ear, shredded, 1/3C Bamboo shoot, shredded, 1T Red pepper, shredded, Green onion, shredded, Ginger, shredded, 1/2C Cornstarch.

Sauce:
❶ 1t Wine, 1/2 Egg white, 1/4t Salt, Pepper, 2t Cornstarch.
❷ 1/2T Hot bean paste, 2t Soysauce, 1t Sugar, 1t Wine, 1/3C Water, 1/2t Sesame oil, 1t Vinegar.

Methods:
1. Debone the eel and remove the skin off, cut into strings along the grain, marinate with ❶ for 10 minutes. Coat with cornstarch, deep fry in hot oil to crispy.
2. Heat 2T oil to stir fry green onion, ginger, add hot bean paste and ❷ sauce, then add eel, wood ear, bamboo shoot, cook over low heat until liquid dissolved, add celery, red pepper, sesame oil, finally, add vinegar, mix well. remove to a plate. Serve.

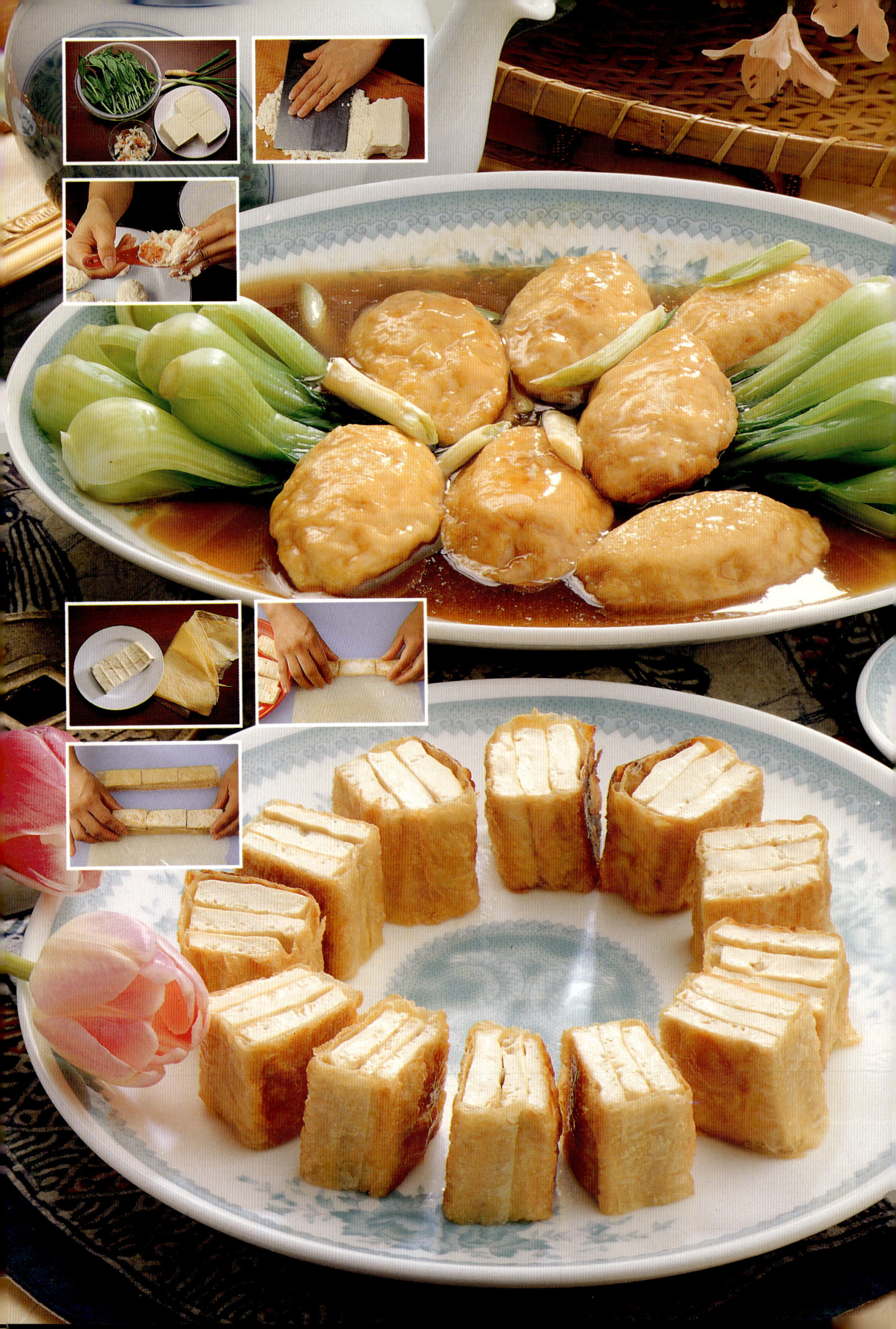

蟹肉荷包豆腐

材料
豆腐3塊　蟹肉½杯　蔥末1湯匙　蔥段5小段　薑片3小片　青菜隨意

豆腐料
鹽½茶匙　蛋白1個　太白粉1湯匙　胡椒粉、味精各少許

調味料
酒1茶匙　清湯1½杯　醬油1½湯匙　糖½茶匙　鹽¼茶匙　胡椒粉少許　濕太白粉少許

作法
1. 將豆腐壓成泥，加入豆腐料拌勻。
2. 爆香少許蔥末，將蟹肉炒過。
3. 湯匙中塗上油，將豆腐餡料鋪在湯匙上，放少許蟹肉再加蓋一些豆腐餡，做成橢圓形，全部蒸熟（約5～6分鐘），取下豆腐片，沾上太白粉，用熱油炸黃。
4. 用1湯匙油炒香蔥段、薑片，淋下酒及清湯，調味後放入豆腐同煮，約3分鐘後即可勾芡盛盤。

Bean Curd Balls Stuffed with Crab

Ingredients:
3pcs Bean curd, 1/2C Crab meat, 1T Green onion, chopped, 5pcs Green onion, sectioned. 3pcs Ginger, sliced, Green vegetables.

Seasonings:
❶ 1/2t Salt, 1 Egg white, 1T Corstarch, Pepper, MSG.
❷ 1t Wine,1-1/2C Soupstock, 1-1/2T soysauce. 1/2t Sugar, 1/4t Salt, Pepper, Cornstarch paste

Methods:
1. Smash bean curd and mix with ❶.
2. Heat 2T oil to stir fry green onion then add crab meat, mix thoroughly.
3. Brush oil on the spoon, put 1/2T bean curd mixture on a spoon, stuff 1t crab meat in, then cover with 1/2T bean curd, make oval balls and steam for 5~6 minutes. Coat with cornstarch. Deep fry in hot oil to golden brown.
4. Heat 1T oil to stir fry green onion and ginger, add wine, soup stock, seasonings and cook with bean curd for 3 minutes. Put on a plate decorate with green vegetables. Serve.

酥皮豆腐捲

材料
老豆腐2方塊　豆腐衣2張　鹽½茶匙　麵粉少許

作法
1. 將豆腐直切成1公分厚而長的片狀，兩面均抹上鹽，再用少量熱油煎黃。
2. 豆腐衣1張切成長方形，先放上一長片豆腐捲一圈，再放第二片再捲，待第三片放上並捲完後，用麵糊黏妥封口處，做好2條，投入熱油中去炸。
3. 待豆腐捲炸至金黃色而外皮酥脆即可撈出，趁熱切成小塊，附花椒鹽或辣醬油沾食。

Crispy Bean Curd Rolls

Ingredients:
2 Bean Curd, 2 Dried bean curd sheet, 1/2t Salt 1T Flour.

Methods:
1. Cut bean curd into thick slices, sprinkle salt, fry with 3T hot oil.
2. Cut bean curd sheet into a rectangle, place the bean curd on, fold and roll once, place the bean curd again, fold and roll again, place the third layer of bean curd, fold and roll again finally stick by flour paste. Deep fry in hot oil to golden brown.
3. Cut the bean curd roll into cubes, serve with brown pepper corn salt and worcester sauce

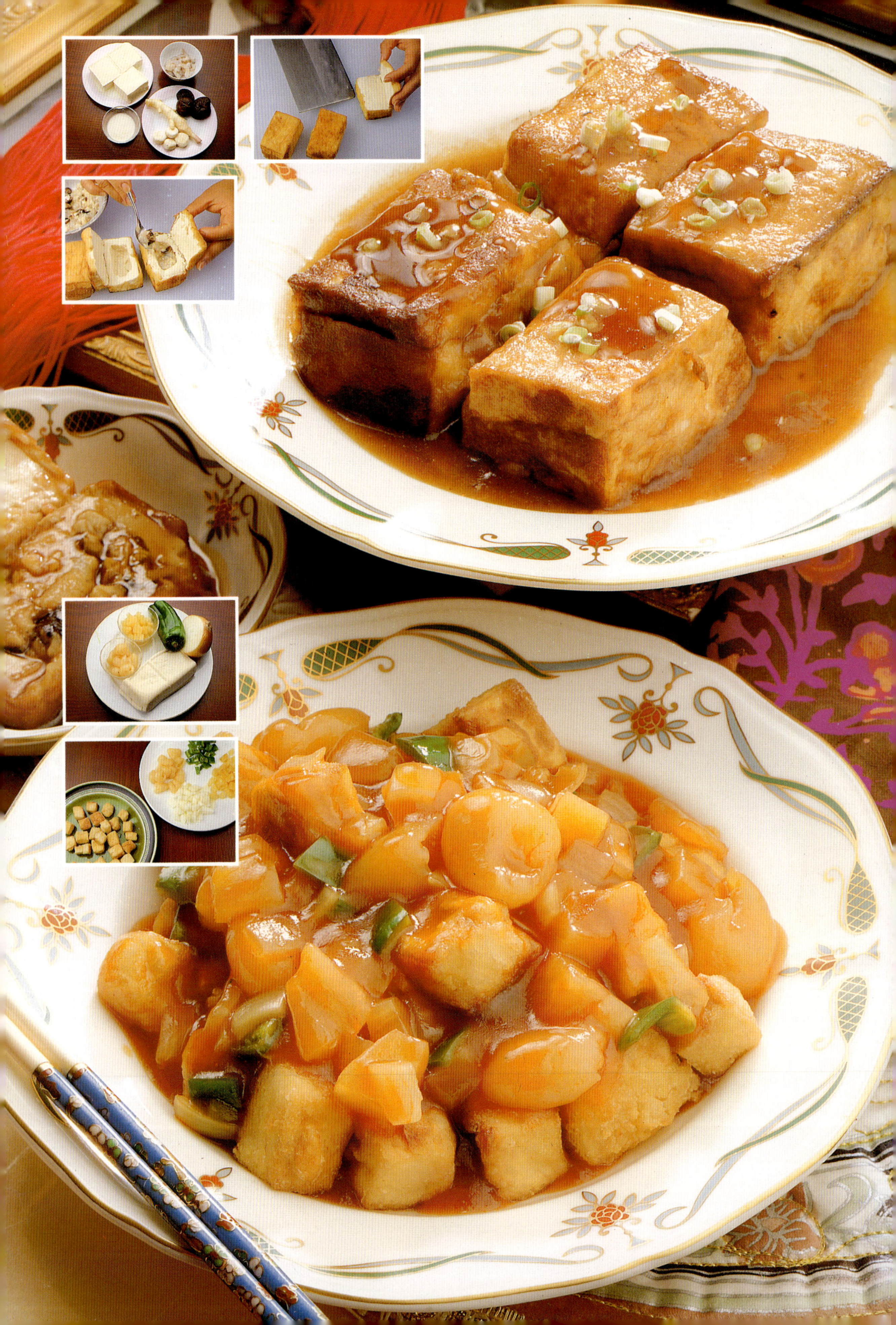

八寶豆腐盒

材料
板豆腐3方塊　蝦仁3兩　香菇3朵　荸薺5粒　薑屑1茶匙　麵糊少許

拌蝦料
葱屑1湯匙　鹽¼茶匙　蛋白½個　太白粉1茶匙

調味料
酒1茶匙　醬油1湯匙　清湯(或水)1杯　濕太白粉酌量　葱花少許

作法
1. 豆腐每方塊切為二，用熱油大火炸透，撈出後，在豆腐⅓厚的部分切一刀口，使成活頁狀，挖出中間少許豆腐。
2. 蝦仁、香菇、荸薺切小丁，加入拌蝦料，填入豆腐中刷少許麵糊，蓋上蓋子。
3. 用2湯匙油來煎豆腐盒(蓋朝下)，加入薑屑及調味料，小火煮5分鐘，盛出豆腐盒，湯汁勾芡，撒少許葱花，淋到豆腐盒上。

＊這道菜也可將餡料炒熟，以盤盛裝上桌，用剛炸透之豆腐自行填塞而食之

Bean Curd Treasure Boxes

Ingredients:
3pcs Bean curd (2" x 2"), 112.5g Shrimp, shelled 3pcs Black mushroom, 5pcs Water chestnuts, 1t Ginger, chopped, Flour paste.

Seasonings:
❶ 1T Green onion, chopped , 1/4t Salt, 1/2 Egg white, 1t Cornstarch.
❷ 1t Wine, 1T Soysauce, 1C Soup stock Cornstarch paste, 1T Green onion, chopped.

Methods:
1. Cut bean curd into 2 rectangles, deep fry in hot oil to golden brown, take out and cut a 1/3" thick slice as a cover lid (do not cut through), scoop out some bean curd.
2. Shred shrimp, black mushroom, water chestnuts, mix with seasoning ❶, stuff in bean curd box, cover the lid and seal with flour paste.
3. Heat 2T oil to fry bean curd box, add in ginger, seasoning ❷, cook over low heat for 5 minutes, take bean curd box out and put on a plate, thicken the soup, pour on the bean curd, sprinkle green onion.

♣ The stuffing can be stir-fried and stuff directly in bean curd.

豆腐咕咾肉

材料
嫩豆腐2方塊　青椒1個　洋葱半個　荔枝(或紅毛丹)10粒(可用罐頭或免用)　鳳梨丁半杯

綜合調味料
番茄醬2湯匙　糖、醋各2湯匙　鹽½茶匙　太白粉2茶匙　水5湯匙　麻油1茶匙

作法
1. 將豆腐切成小方塊後，撒下鹽1茶匙，放置片刻後，拭乾水分，投入熱油，中大火炸至外皮脆硬為止。
2. 青椒去籽切片，洋葱切丁備用。
3. 起油鍋炸香洋葱丁，加入番茄醬炒紅，再加入青椒片及水果同炒，淋下綜合調味料煮滾，倒入豆腐，快速拌合即可。

Kou-Lou Bean Curd

Ingredients:
2 Bean curd, 1 Green pepper,1/2 Onion, 10 Li-Chi (canned), 1/2C Pineapple.

Seasonings:
2T Ketchup, 2T Sugar, 2T Vinegar, 1/2t Salt, 2t Cornstarch, 5T Water, 1t Sesame oil.

Methods:
1. Cut bean curd into cubes, sprinkle 1t salt and leave for 1 minute. Pat dry. Deep fry in hot oil to crispy.
2. Remove seeds from green pepper, cut green pepper and onion into cubes.
3. Heat 2T oil to stir fry onion and ketchup, then add in pepper and fruit, add in seasonings, bring to a boil, mix with bean curd. Arrange on a plate. Serve.

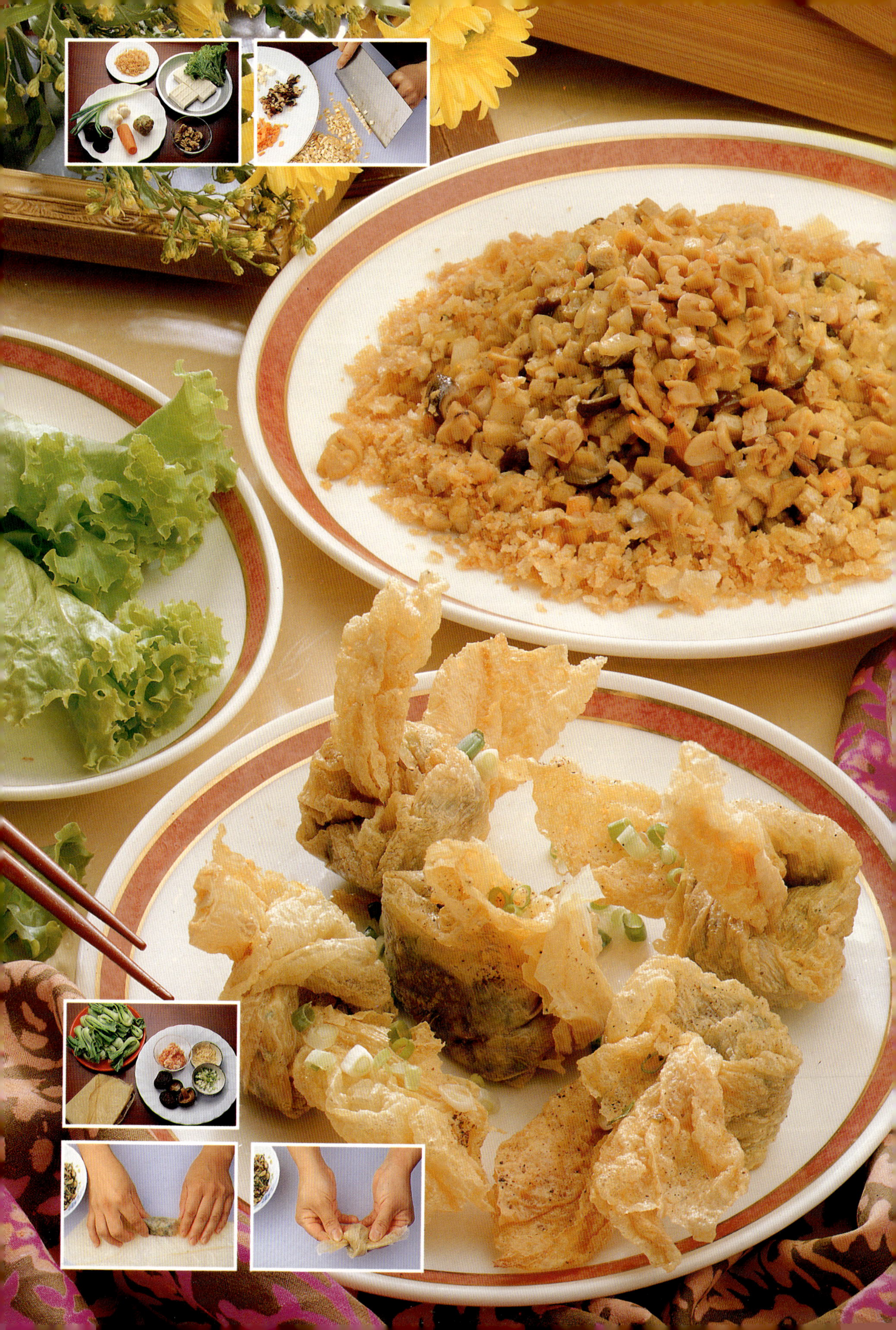

香酥豆腐鬆

材料

老豆腐3方塊　香菇2朵　榨菜丁2湯匙　荸薺4粒或筍丁半杯　熟胡蘿蔔丁2湯匙　油條1根　核桃屑1湯匙　生菜葉12枚　香菜少許

綜合調味料

醬油2湯匙　鹽、糖各½茶匙　胡椒粉少許　水3湯匙　太白粉、麻油各少許

作法

1. 將豆腐切成厚片，先在油中略煎，再切成小丁，其他材料均切成小丁，油條切薄片在油中炸酥，堆放在盤中。
2. 起油鍋炒香香菇，加入豆腐炒乾，再放榨菜、荸薺及胡蘿蔔丁同炒，並淋下綜合調味料拌炒均勻裝盤。
3. 將香菜屑及核桃屑撒在豆腐鬆上，隨生菜上桌包食之。

Crispy Minced Bean Curd

Ingredients:

3pcs Bean curd (2" x 2"), 2pcs Black mushroom, 2T Pickled kale head, 4pcs Water chestnuts, 2T Carrot, cooked, 1 Yiou-Tiau, 1T Walnut, chopped. 12 pcs Lettuce leaves, Chinese parsley.

Seasonings:

2T Soysauce, 1/2t Salt, 1/2t Sugar, Pepper, 3T Water, Cornstarch, Sesame oil.

Methods:

1. Slice the bean curd, fry to hard, cut into small cubes, cut all other ingredients into small cubes, cut Yiou-Tiau into 1" sections, deep fry to crispy, pat on a plate.
2. Heat 2T oil to fry black mushroom, bean curd. kale head, water chestnuts, carrot, add in seasoning, mix well, put in a plate.
3. Sprinkle Chinese parsley and walnut on top Serve with lettuce leaves.

油淋黃雀

材料

豆腐衣5張　絞肉3兩　香菇4朵　青梗菜半斤　蔥、薑屑各少許

調味料

醬油2湯匙　鹽、胡椒粉各少許

油淋料

麻油1½湯匙　蔥花1湯匙　鹽¼茶匙　花椒粉少許

作法

1. 香菇泡軟切片，青梗菜燙軟沖涼後剁碎，擠乾水分。
2. 用2湯匙油炒香蔥、薑屑及絞肉，加入香菇、青梗菜續炒，調味後盛出。
3. 豆腐衣一切為二，包捲 2.項料，從尖角包起，先捲成長條，再打一個結成黃雀狀，用油炸酥。
4. 炸好之黃雀放大碗中，撒下蔥花、鹽和花椒粉，淋下燒熱之麻油，抖動大碗拌勻裝盤。

Fried Crispy Packages

Ingredients:

5pcs Dried bean curd sheet, 112.5g Minced pork 4pcs Black mushroom, 300g Shanghai green cabbage, 1t Green onion, chopped, 1t Ginger. chopped.

Seasonings:

❶ 2T Soysauce, Salt, Pepper.
❷ 1-1/2T Sesame oil, 1T Green onion, 1/4t Salt Brown pepper corn powder.

Methods:

1. Chop soaked black mushroom, blanch shanghai green cabbage, rinse, chop, squeeze dry.
2. Heat 2T oil to stir fry green onion, ginger, minced pork, add in black mushroom, green cabbage. Season with ❶.
3. Cut bean curd sheet, into 2 pieces, wrap item 2 material, roll into a cylinder and tie two ends into a knok. Deep fry to crispy.
4. Put on a plate, sprinkle green onion, salt, brown pepper corn powder, splash sesame oil mix and serve.

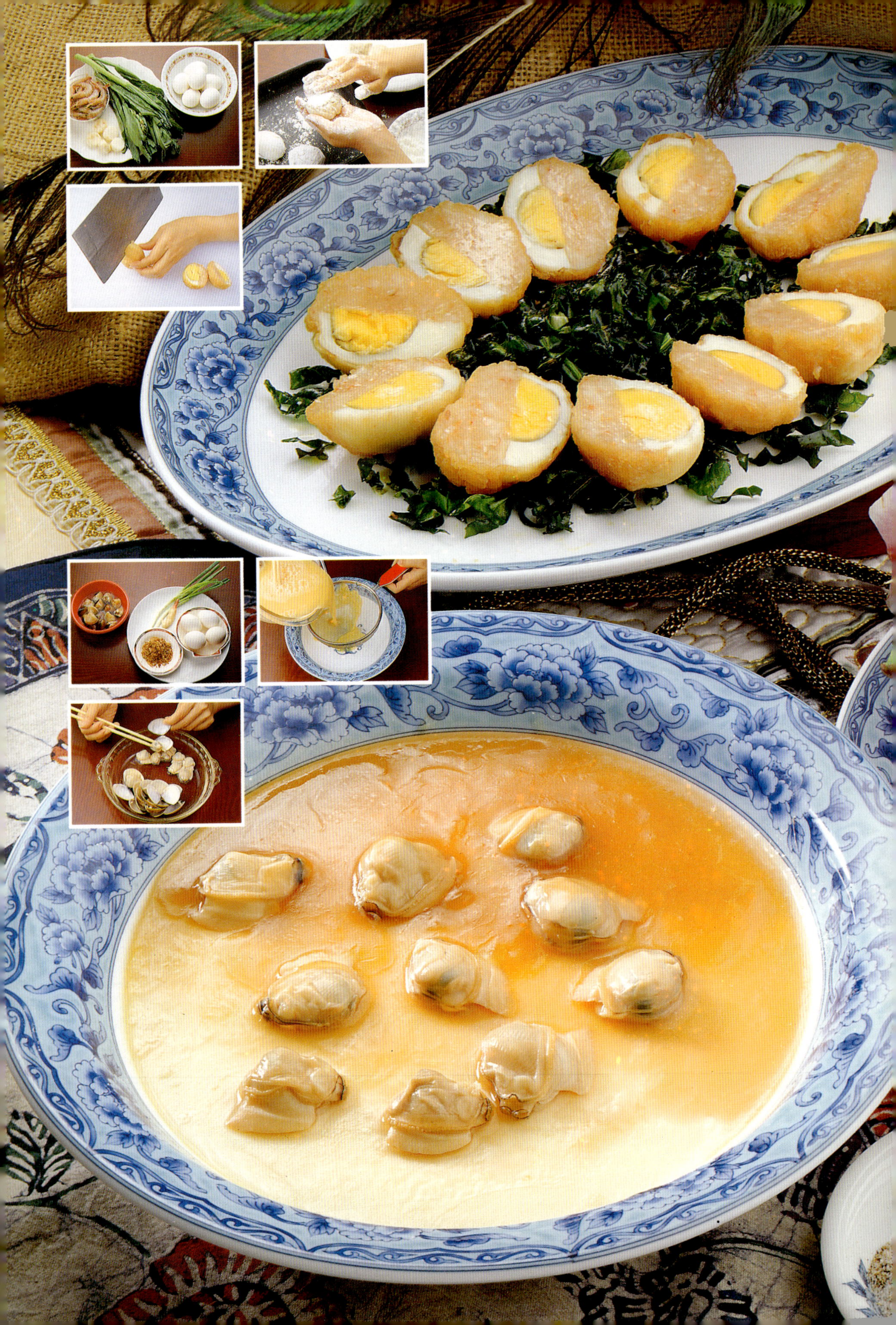

炸百花蛋

材料
雞蛋6個　蝦仁6兩　荸薺5個　米粉或芥蘭菜葉酌量

拌蝦料
蛋白½個　鹽½茶匙　酒1茶匙　太白粉½湯匙　麻油少許

作法
1. 鍋中放水煮蛋，用筷子轉動蛋，以使蛋黃熟後的位置保持在中間部分。蛋煮熟後剝殼，每個對切兩半，撒少許鹽放片刻。
2. 蝦仁壓成泥狀，加入切碎擠乾水分的荸薺，用拌蝦料仔細拌勻，成為有彈性之蝦餡。
3. 灑少許太白粉在蛋面上，再放1湯匙的蝦餡，塗成半凸形狀，沾上一層太白粉。
4. 將炸油燒至七分熱，放下3.項的百花蛋，用慢火炸熟蝦面，使成為黃色為止，每個橫切兩半，排在炸鬆米粉或芥蘭菜葉上即可。

Deep Fried Stuffed Egg

Ingredients:
6 Eggs, 225g Shrimp, shelled, 5pcs Water chestnuts, 5pcs Mustard green leaves.

Seasonings:
1/2 Egg white, 1/2t Salt, 1t Wine, 1/2T Cornstarch Sesame oil.

Methods:
1. Put egg in cold water of a wok, boil and stir with chopsticks tenderly to make every egg yolk in the accurate center. When the egg is done, shell, cut into halves, sprinkle salt.
2. Smash the shrimp, mix with waterchestnuts and seasonings, stir to sticky.
3. Sprinkle cornstarch on the cut surface of eggs put 1T shrimp mixture to form a ball egg, coat with cornstarch.
4. Deep fry in hot oil over low heat till the shrimp is done. Cut each egg balls into halves. (Cut from the middle line from each egg) Decorate with fried vegetable leaves shreds

蠔油蛤蜊蛋

材料
雞蛋4個　冷清湯或水2杯　蛤蜊15粒　蔥1支　薑1片

調味料
酒1茶匙　鹽¼茶匙　胡椒粉少許　蠔油1湯匙　濕太白粉酌量

作法
1. 蛋加鹽少許打散，加入清水調勻，過濾到深盤中，入鍋小火蒸熟。
2. 蛤蜊用清水1¼杯煮至殼微開即撈出，剝肉，汁留用。
3. 用1湯匙油煎香蔥支、薑片，淋酒及蛤蜊湯，煮滾調味並勾芡，加入蛤蜊肉一滾即可淋到蛋面上，可撒下少許香菜或紅蔥酥。

Steamed Egg with Clams

Ingredients:
4 Eggs, 2C Soup stock, 15pcs Clams, 1 Green onion, 1 Ginger, Parsley.

Seasonings:
1t Wine, 1/4t Salt, Pepper, 1T Oyster sauce. Cornstarch paste.

Methods:
1. Beat the eggs, mix with salt, water, sieve into a deep plate, steam to a pudding cake.
2. Cook clams with 1-1/4C water, take clam meat out. Leave the soup for later use.
3. Heat 1T oil to fry green onion & ginger, add wine and clams soup, bring to a boil, thicken and add clams. Pour on egg, sprinkle the parsley.

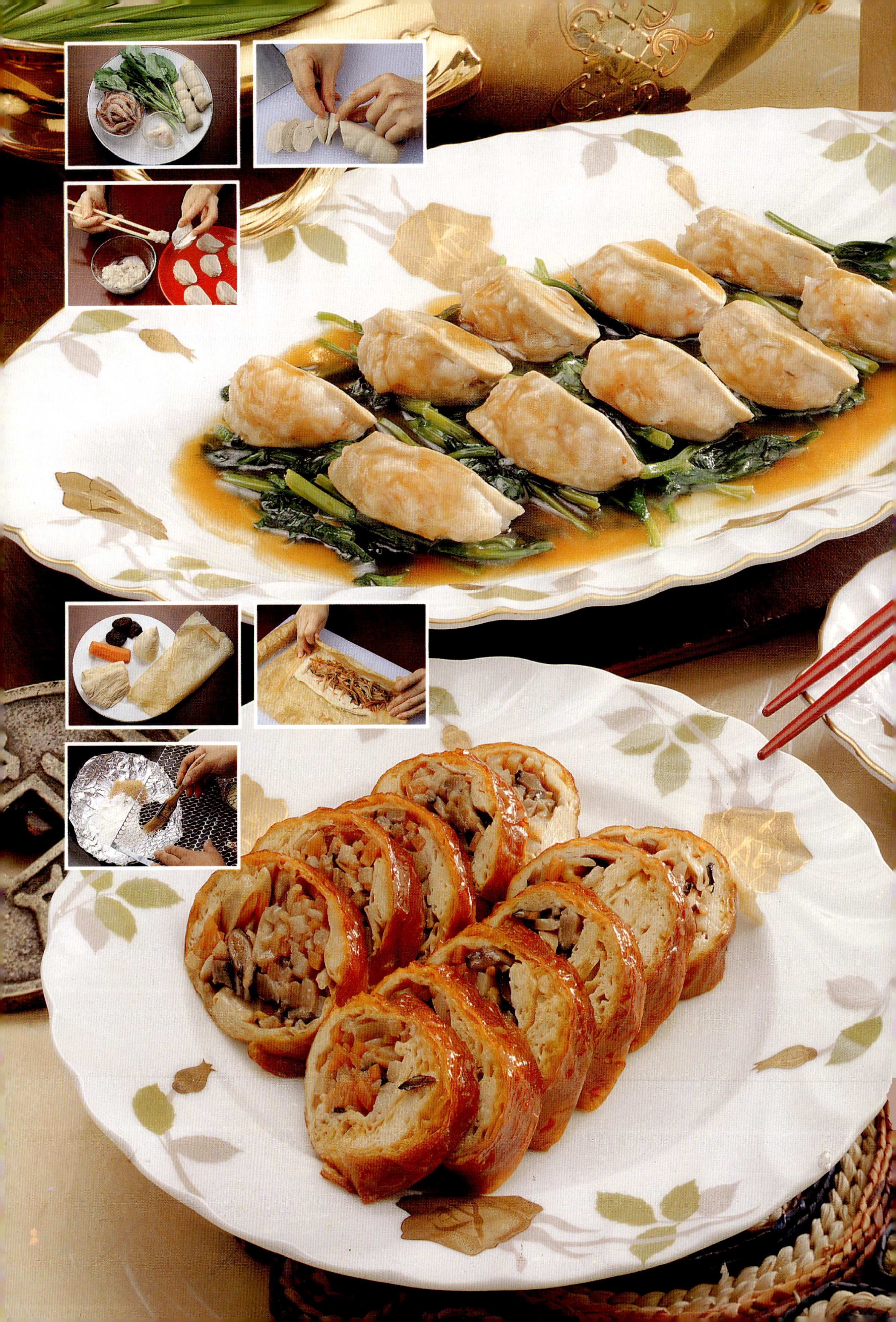

釀百花素雞

材料

蝦仁4兩　絞肥肉少許　大素雞2條　西洋菜或小芥蘭菜數支

拌蝦料

蛋白半個　蔥薑水2湯匙　鹽¼茶匙　麻油½茶匙　太白粉1湯匙

調味料

清湯1杯　蠔油1½湯匙　濕太白粉1茶匙　麻油少許

作法

1. 蝦仁洗淨擦乾，壓成泥狀，放在大碗中，加入絞肥肉及拌蝦料，仔細拌勻。
2. 素雞切成雙飛（活頁）厚片，切口抹少許乾太白粉，夾入蝦泥料，用水將蝦泥抹光滑。
3. 青菜切段在開水中燙軟，放在盤中，上面排放夾好之素雞，滾水大火蒸8分鐘。蒸好後湯汁泌到鍋中，加清湯及調味料，勾芡再淋到百花素雞上。

Stuffed Shrimp in Bean Curd Cake

Ingredients:
150g Shrimp, shelled, 1T Pork fat, minced, 2pcs Bean curd cake, Green vegetables.

Seasonings:
❶ 1/2 Egg white, 2T Green onion & Ginger juice 1/4t Salt, 1/2t Sesame oil, 1T Cornstarch.
❷ 1C Soup stock, 1-1/2T Oyster sauce, 1t Cornstarch paste, Sesame oil.

Methods:
1. Clean the shrimp, smash, mix with pork fat & seasoning ❶.
2. Cut the bean curd cake into butterfly shapes stuff inside with shrimp. (Sprinkle with a little bit of cornstarch first).
3. Blanch vegetables, put on a plate, arrange bean curd cake, steam for 8 minutes. Boil seasoning ❷. Pour on top. Serve.

燻三絲齋鵝

材料

新鮮豆腐包2塊　乾豆腐衣4張　熟筍絲、香菇絲、熟胡蘿蔔絲各½杯

調味料

醬油2湯匙　糖1茶匙　清湯（泡香菇水）½杯　麻油½湯匙

燻料

白糖、米、茶葉各⅓杯

作法

1. 用1湯匙油炒香菇絲、筍絲及胡蘿蔔絲，放入調味料煮透後，瀝出菜料，湯汁留用。
2. 乾豆腐衣2張相對平放，刷上1.項湯汁，再將1塊新鮮豆腐包攤開放在上面，也刷上湯汁，再鋪上一半量之1.項料，捲包成筒狀。做好2個齋鵝。
3. 入鍋大火蒸5分鐘，取出待稍涼即可燻。
4. 鍋中鋪1張鋁箔紙，上放燻料，燻架子塗油後放上齋鵝，先大火待煙冒出後，改小火燻5分鐘，翻面再燻3分鐘，取出切塊上桌。

＊喜燻味重者，可燻久一點，燻的食物宜冷食較香。

Smoked Vegetarian Goose

Ingredients:
2pcs Fresh bean curd package, 4pcs Dried bean curd sheet, 1/2C Cooked bamboo shoot, shredded, 1/2C Black mushroom, shredded, 1/2C Cooked carrot, shredded.

Seasonings:
❶ 2T Soysauce, 1t Sugar, 1/2C Soup stock, 1/2T Sesame oil.

Smoke materials:
1/3C Sugar, 1/3C Rice, 1/3C Tea leaves.

Methods:
1. Heat 1T oil stir fry mushroom, bamboo shoot & carrot shreds add seasonings, bring to a boil, drain. Leave the soup for later use.
2. Place bean curd together, put 1/2 vegetables in center, brush some soup and roll into a cylinder. Make 2 rolls. This is vegetarian goose.
3. Steam for 5 minutes. Take out and let cool.
4. Put a piece of alluminum foil in a wok, put smoke materials on. Brush oil on a rack. Put goose on, cover the lid, smoke over medium heat for 5 minutes, turn over and smoke for 3 more minutes. Cut and serve.

✤ If you like it smell stronger, smoke longer.

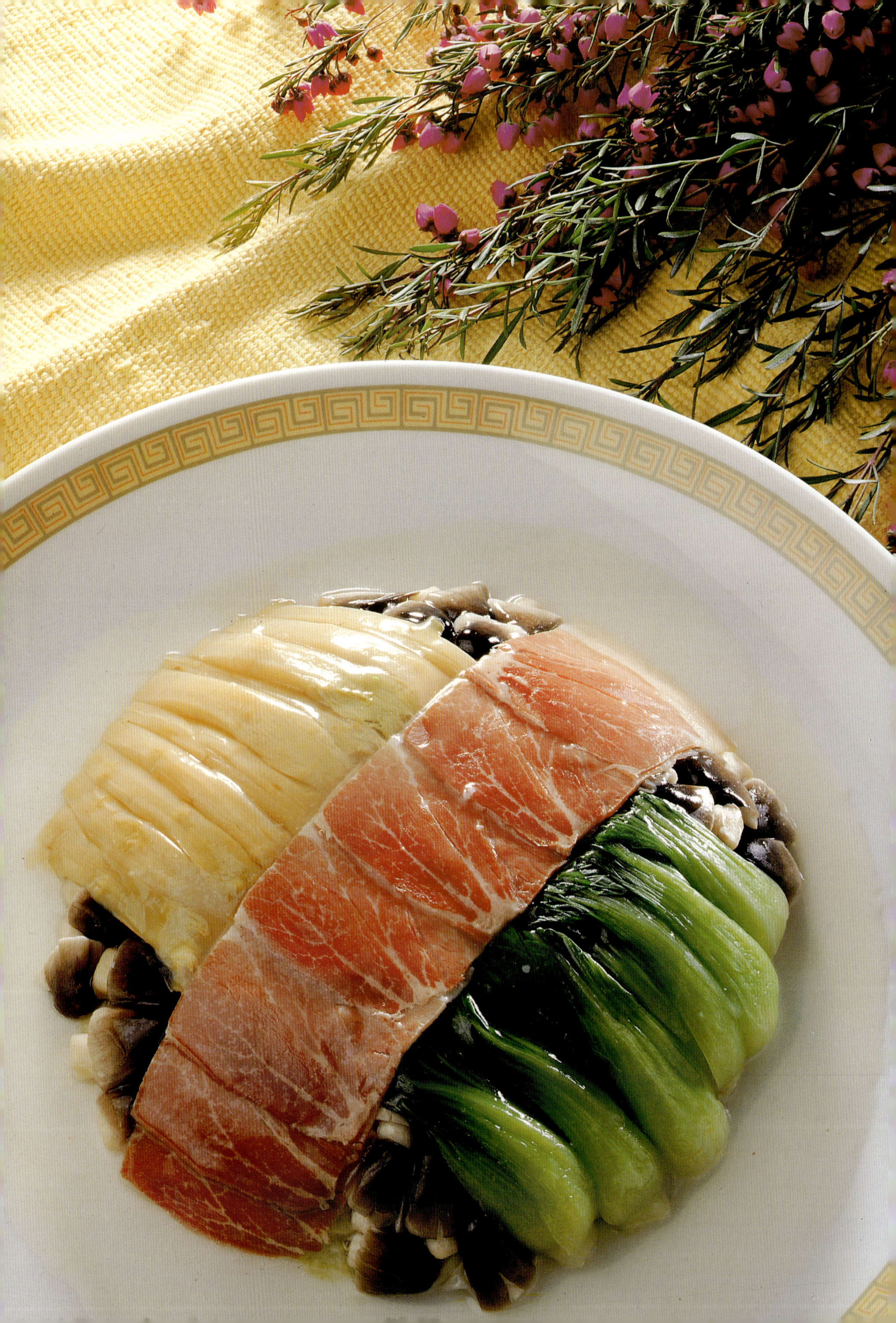

金華扣四蔬

材料
中國火腿10片　白蘆筍罐頭1罐　青梗菜或小芥蘭10支　草菇20粒　大白菜半斤

調味料
高湯2½杯　鹽少許　濕太白粉酌量

作法
1. 中國火腿整塊蒸熟，切成1寸寬2寸長的薄片，青梗菜取中間嫩的部分大約2寸長，用滾水（加少許鹽）燙煮一下，撈出沖涼擠乾。草菇也燙一下撈出。
2. 大白菜切寬條，用高湯1杯煮5分鐘瀝出。
3. 選1只中型淺盒或較深的湯盤，先在中間排火腿片，左右兩邊分別排青梗菜及蘆筍，上下二端排列草菇，中間以大白菜填補凹處，淋入1杯高湯，大火蒸5分鐘。
4. 將3.項之湯汁泌入鍋內，火腿等倒扣在大盤中。湯汁加少許鹽調味後，用濕太白粉勾芡，淋少許雞油，淋在四蔬上即可上桌。

King-Hwa Ham & Vegetables

Ingredients:
10pcs Chinese King-Hwa ham, 1 can Asparagus, 10pcs shanghai green cabbage, 20pcs straw mushroom, 300g Chinese Bok-Choy.

Sauce :
❶ 2-1/2C Soupstock, Salt, Cornstarch.

Methods:
1. Steam the Chinese King-Hua ham to done, cut into thin slices (1" x 2"). Trim the Shanghai cabbage (using the heart part). Blanch in boiling water, season with salt, drain and soak in cold water, squeeze dry. Blanch the straw mushroom in boiling water, too.
2. Cut Bok-Choy to thick sticks, boil with IC soup stock for 5 minutes, drain.
3. Choose a deep plate, arrange ham slices in the middle buttom, put asparagus and Shanghai cabbage on two sides of ham, then put straw mushroom on the left space. Stuff center with Bok-Choy. Add IC soup stock, steam for 5 minutes.
4. Reverse the plate to let the ham & vegetable stand on a large plate. Boil the steamed soup, season with cornstach paste, sprinkle some chicken grease, pour on the vegetables. Serve

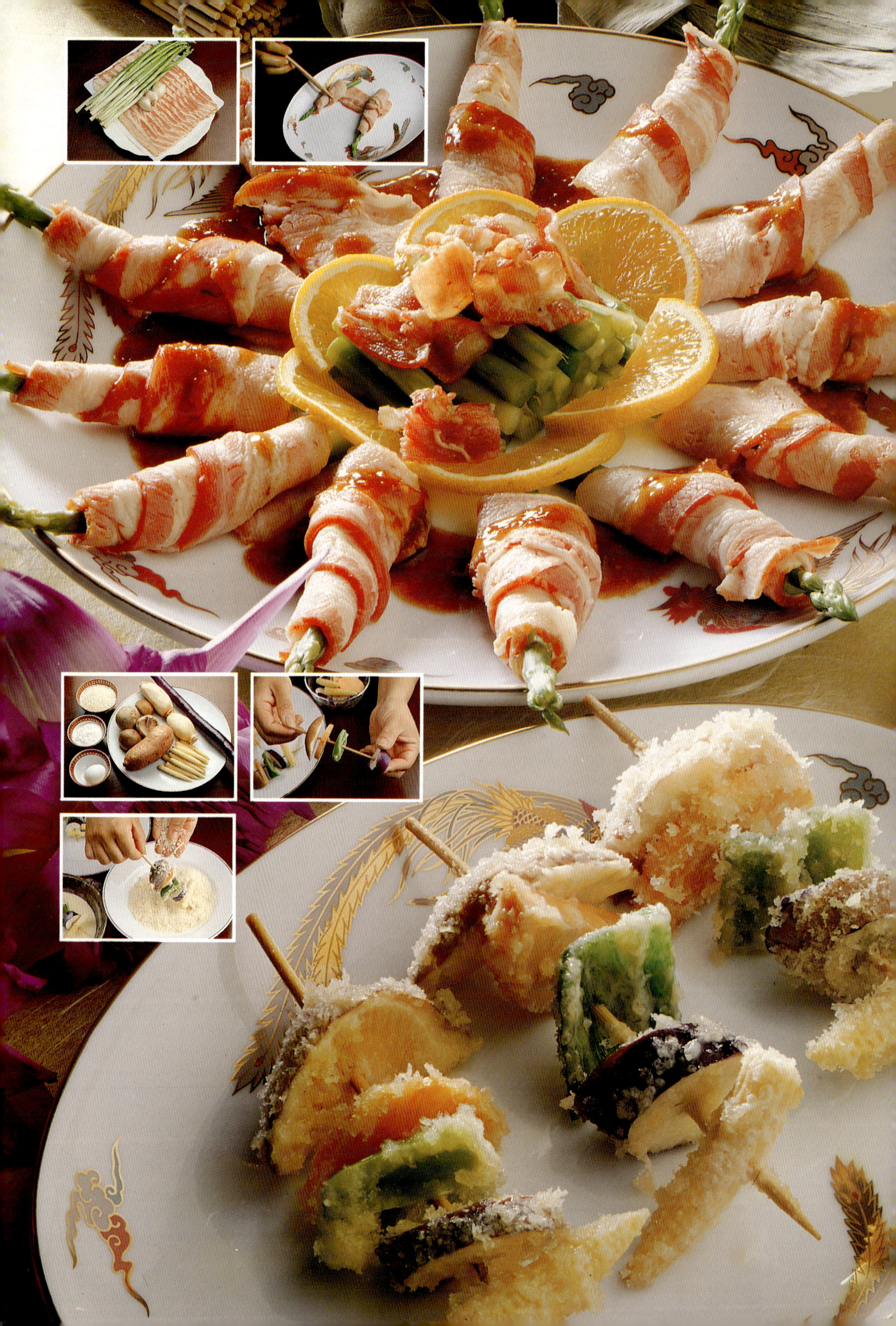

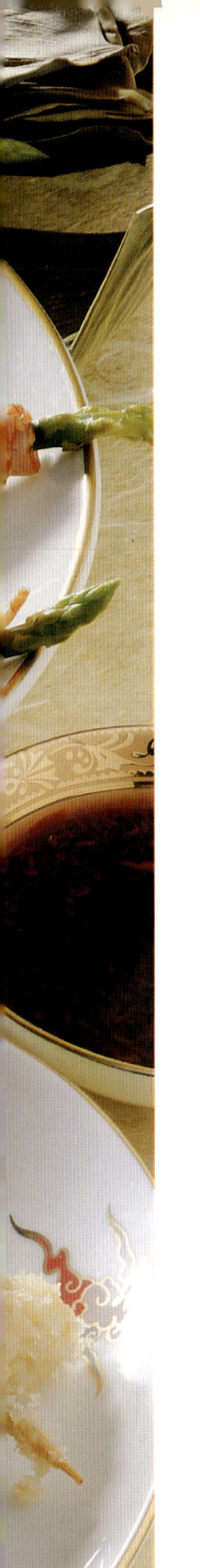

蒜汁肉捲蘆筍

材料
綠蘆筍15支　培根肉15片

調味汁
大蒜泥½湯匙　水1½湯匙　甜醬油1½湯匙　紅油、麻油各1茶匙

作法
1. 蘆筍撕去老皮後切為二段，在滾水中燙熟(水中加鹽)撈出沖冷開水，瀝乾。
2. 培根肉也用滾水燙煮1分鐘，撈起瀝乾
3. 用1片培根肉將尖頭的一半蘆筍捲起(筍尖露出)，另一半則再對切，堆放在盤子中間，肉捲圍放在四周。
4. 調味汁在小碗中調好，上桌後淋在蘆筍捲上。

*可用醬油膏加糖代替甜醬油，甜醬油係醬油2杯加酒3湯匙、糖4湯匙、八角1顆，小火熬煮至濃稠

Asparagus in Bacon Rolls

Ingredients:
15 Asparagus, 15 Bacon slices.

Sauce:
1/2T Garlic (smashed), 1-1/2T Water, 1-1/2T Sweet soysauce, 1t Red pepper oil, 1t Sesame oil.

Methods:
1. Peel asparagus, cut each into halves, blanch in boiling water, season with salt, rinse in cold water, drain.
2. Boil bacon in boiling water for 1 minutes. drain.
3. Roll the asparagus (tip part) with bacon slices. (leave some part of the tip left outside of bacon). Arrange each roll on edge of a plate. Cut the root part sections into two and put on center of the plate.
4. Mix the sauce and pour on rolls.

串炸時蔬

材料
新鮮香菇、茄子、蕃薯、玉米筍、綠蘆筍、青椒隨意　麵粉3湯匙　蛋1個　麵包粉1杯

作法
1. 將各種蔬菜切成1寸長厚塊(香菇對半切)，分別用竹籤串起(四種1串)。
2. 蛋打散，加水成⅔杯後，再放麵粉調成稀糊狀，麵包粉裝在盤子中。
3. 蔬菜串先沾麵粉糊，再輕敷一層麵包粉即可投入七分熱油中，小火慢炸3分鐘左右至呈金黃色便可。

*上桌時可另附個人喜愛之醬料以供沾食，如蘿蔔泥加醬油汁或蕃茄醬或糖醋汁、A1沙士、辣醬油或沙拉醬等。

Deep-Fried Vegetables Skewers

Ingredients:
Fresh black mushroom, Egg plant, Lotus roots, Sweet potato, Aspaaragus, each a little, 3T Flour. 1 Egg, 1C Bread crumb.

Methods:
1. Cut each vegetable into cubes, pierce every four kind into a skewer.
2. Beat the egg, add 1/2C water and flour to a paste.
3. Dip vegetable in egg paste and coat with bread crumb, deep fry in 150°C oil over low heat for about 3 minutes to golden brown.

✤ A1 Sauce, Worcester sauce, Sweet & Sour sauce, Ketchup, Mayonnaise or Japanese sauce with smashed turnip can be dipping sauce.

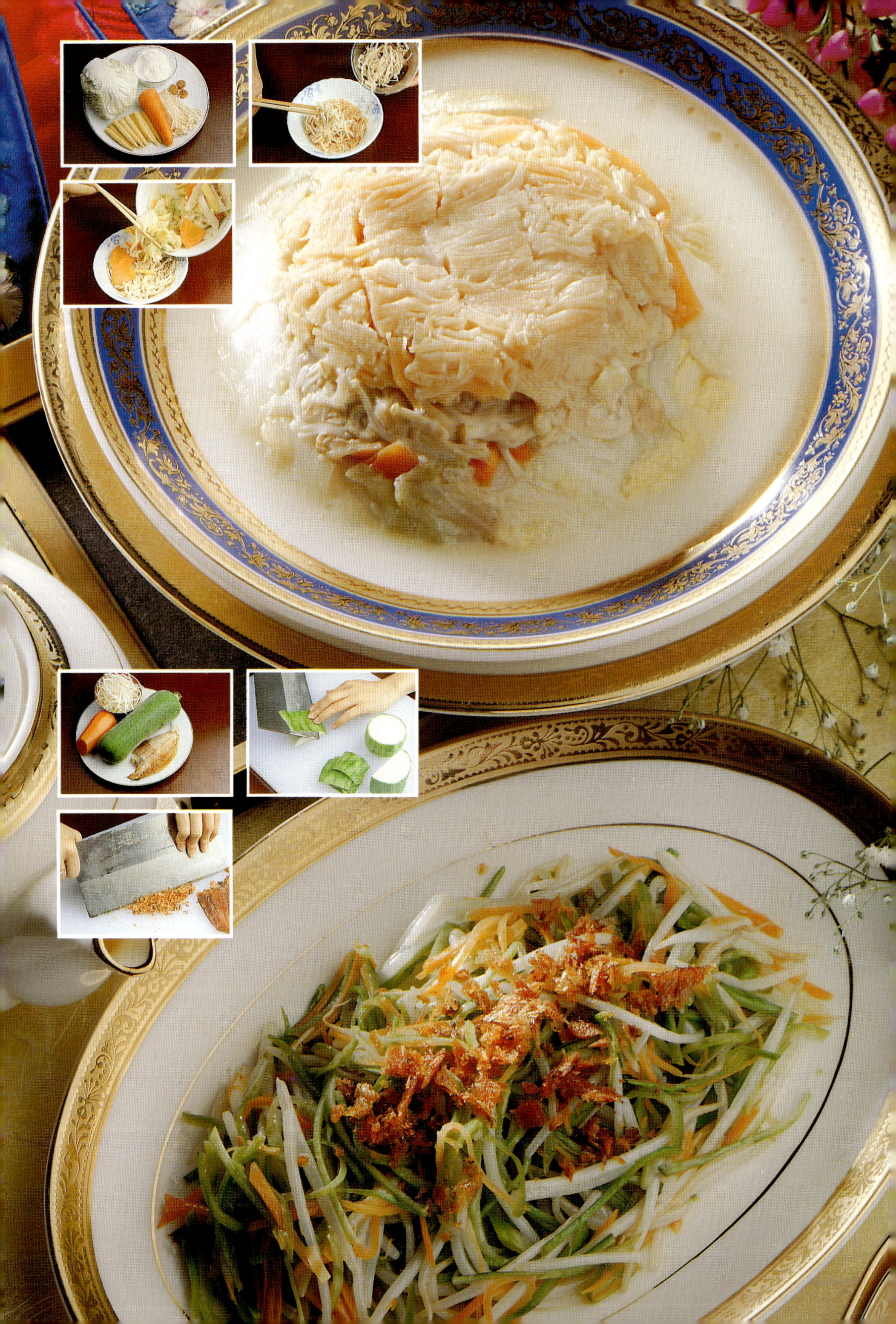

干貝扣四蔬

材料
干貝3粒　金菇1把　白菜1斤　玉米筍10支　胡蘿蔔1小支　油2湯匙　麵粉2湯匙　糖½茶匙　高湯(或水)½杯

調味料
鹽1茶匙　糖½茶匙　胡椒粉少許

作法
1. 干貝置碗內加水⅔杯(蓋過干貝)，蒸半小時至軟，撕成細條，鋪在碗底一層。
2. 金菇切半寸長，用滾水川燙一下撈出，鋪在碗裡干貝上。
3. 用熱油2湯匙炒白菜(切條)，玉米筍(粗者可對剖為二)和已煮過之胡蘿蔔片，加調味料調味。拌合後瀝出，放在干貝碗中，淋下干貝汁及高湯，入鍋蒸20分鐘。
4. 取出干貝，泌出湯汁，倒扣在盤中，用油炒香麵粉，再加入湯汁，攪拌成糊狀，淋下少許油即澆到干貝上供食。

Mold Scallop with Four Kinds of Vegetables

Ingredients:
3 Dried scallops, 100g Needle mushroom, 600g Bok-Choy, 10 Baby corn, 1 Carrot, 2T Oil, 2T Flour, 1/2C Soup stock.

Sauce:
❶ 1t Salt, 1/2t Sugar, Pepper.

Methods:
1. Put scallop in a bowl, add 2/3C water, steam to soft, drain, tear finely, put on the bottom of a large bowl.
2. Cut needle mushroom into 2 sections, blanch in boiling water, drain and place on top of scallop.
3. Cut Bok-Choy into sticks, stir fry with 2T hot oil, add baby corn and cooked carrot slices, season with ❶, drain and stuff in center of bowl, pour steamed scallop soup & soup stock, steam for 20 minutes.
4. Reverse bowl to let scallop & vegetables stand on a plate. Stir fry oil and flour and add the steamed soup, mix into a paste, pour on vegetable, serve.

魚酥翡翠瓜絲

材料
扁魚乾1～2片　絲瓜1條　胡蘿蔔半支　銀芽2兩　蔥花少許

調味料
酒½茶匙　鹽½茶匙　糖¼茶匙　麻油½茶匙　胡椒粉、濕太白粉各少許

作法
1. 將扁魚放在油中小火煎黃，待涼後切碎。
2. 絲瓜刨去外層硬皮後，切成2寸長段，再切下外層較綠色部分(約0.3公分厚)直切成絲，熟胡蘿蔔也切細絲，銀芽用熱油爆炒一下即瀝出。
3. 用1湯匙油爆香蔥花，加入胡蘿蔔及絲瓜，大火拌炒，淋下酒，加鹽等調味料調味，加入銀芽拌合，用少許濕太白粉使汁濃滑即可裝盤，再撒入扁魚酥即可。

Jade Squash with Crispy Sole

Ingredients:
2pcs Dried sole, 1 Squash, 1/2 Carrot, 75g Mung bean sprouts, Green onion, chopped.

Sauce:
❶ 1/2t Wine, 1/2t Salt, 1/4t Sugar, 1/2t Sesame oil, Pepper, Cornstarch paste.

Methods:
1. Fry sole in warm oil over low heat to golden brown, drain and let stand on tissue, when cool, smash.
2. Peel squash, slice thinly the very outside green part, use this green part to shred finely, cut carrot into shreds too.
3. Heat 2T oil to stir fry bean sprouts, drain.
4. Heat 1T oil to stir fry green onion, add in carrot, squash, add sauce ❶ then add bean sprout, remove to a plate, sprinkle smashed sole. Serve.

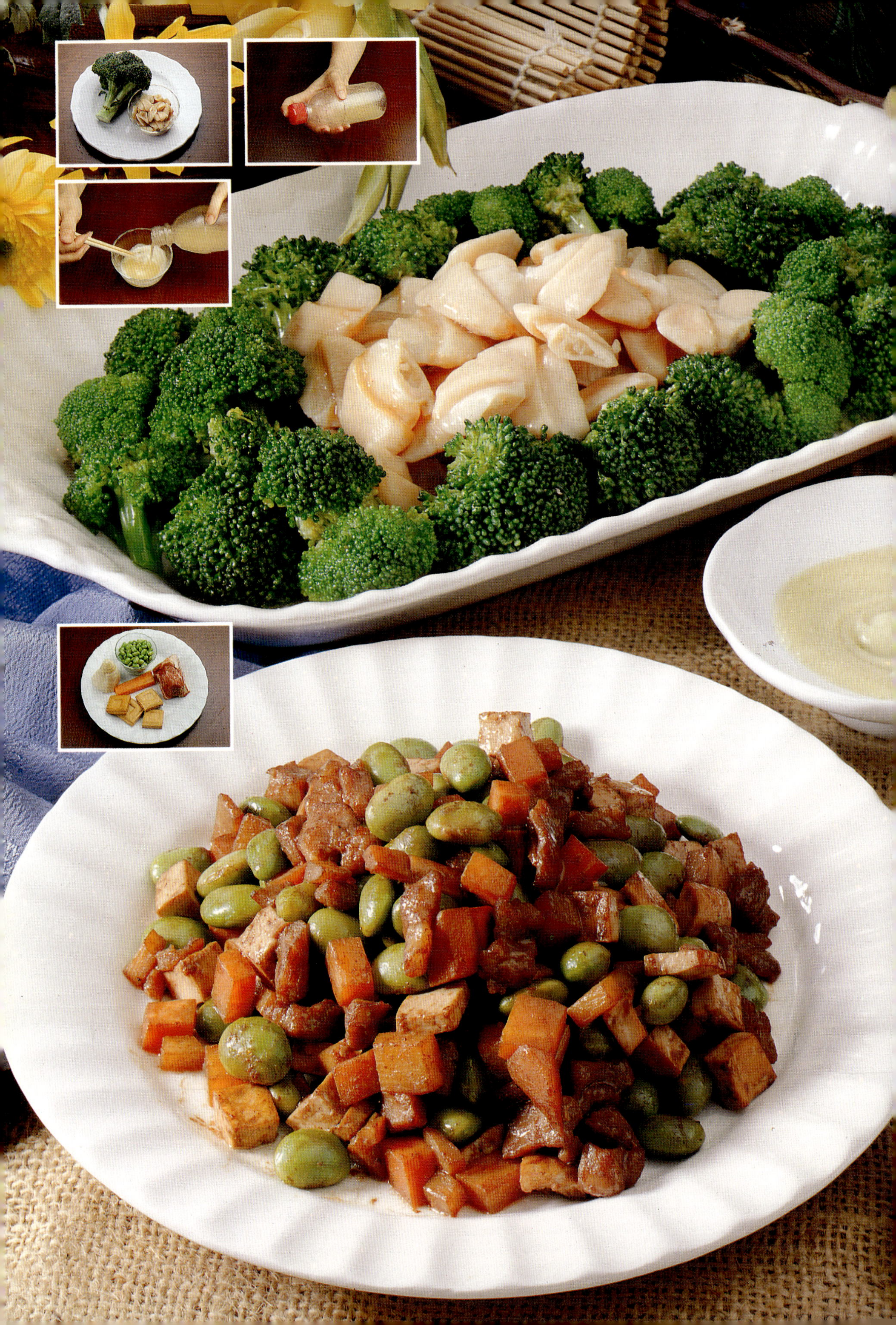

西拌青花菜

材料
青菜花12兩　珍珠貝或任何罐裝貝類半罐

千島醬
沙拉醬2湯匙　蕃茄醬1湯匙

芥辣醬
芥末醬1湯匙　沙拉醬2湯匙

法式汁
油3湯匙　醋1湯匙　鹽1/2茶匙　胡椒粉少許　沙拉醬1湯匙

作法
1. 青花菜分小朵後，投入滾水中燙軟，撈出用冷開水沖涼。
2. 罐頭貝類切成半寸大小，與青花菜混合後裝盤。
3. 法式汁是將調味料（沙拉醬除外）放在瓶中，搖晃均勻後再與沙拉醬混合均勻。另外千島醬、芥辣醬亦分別調好，裝入小碗中上桌。

＊也可挑選一種口味的醬料和青花菜在大碗中拌勻後再上桌。

Broccoli Salad with Assorted Dressing

Ingredients:
450g Broccoli, 1/2 Can Clam (any kind).
Sauce:
❶ Thousand island: 2T Mayonnaise, 1T ketchup
❷ Mustard sauce: 1T Mustard sauce, 2T Mayonnaise.
❸ French style: 3T Oil, 1T Vinegar, 1/2t Salt, Pepper, 1T Mayonnaise.
Methods:
1. Split the broccoli into small pieces, blanch in boiling water, then rinse in cold water, drain.
2. Cut clam into 1/2" cubes, mix with broccoli.
3. Make all dressings respectively, serve as dipping sauce.

毛豆八寶醬

材料
冷凍毛豆1杯　筍丁、豆腐乾丁、豬肉丁各1/2杯　胡蘿蔔丁2湯匙

調味料
甜麵醬、豆瓣醬各1/2湯匙　醬油1/2湯匙　酒1茶匙　水1湯匙　糖1湯匙　麻油1茶匙

作法
1. 豬肉丁用少許醬油和太白粉醃過，筍子和胡蘿蔔煮熟後切丁，毛豆解凍後洗淨（新鮮毛豆用水煮軟）。
2. 燒熱油4湯匙，把肉丁炒熟盛出，用餘油炒香甜麵醬等調味料，加入肉丁及其他材料，大火拌炒均勻，淋下麻油即可。

Eight Treasure Sauce

Ingredients:
1C Frozen Soya bean, 1/2C Bamboo shoot, 1/2cm cubes, 1/2C Dried bean curd, 1/2cm cubes, 1/2C Pork, 1/2cm cubes, 2T Carrot, 1/2cm cubes.
Sauce:
1/2T Sweet soybean paste, 1/2T Hot bean paste, 1/2T Soysauce, 1t Wine, 1T Water, 1T Sugar, 1t Sesame oil.
Methods:
1. Marinate pork with soysauce and cornstarch. Boil carrot & bamboo shoot (shelled) and cut into 1/2 cm cubes.
2. Heat 4T oil, stir fry pork, drain, use the remaining oil to stir fry sauce and all other ingredients, mix evenly. Serve.

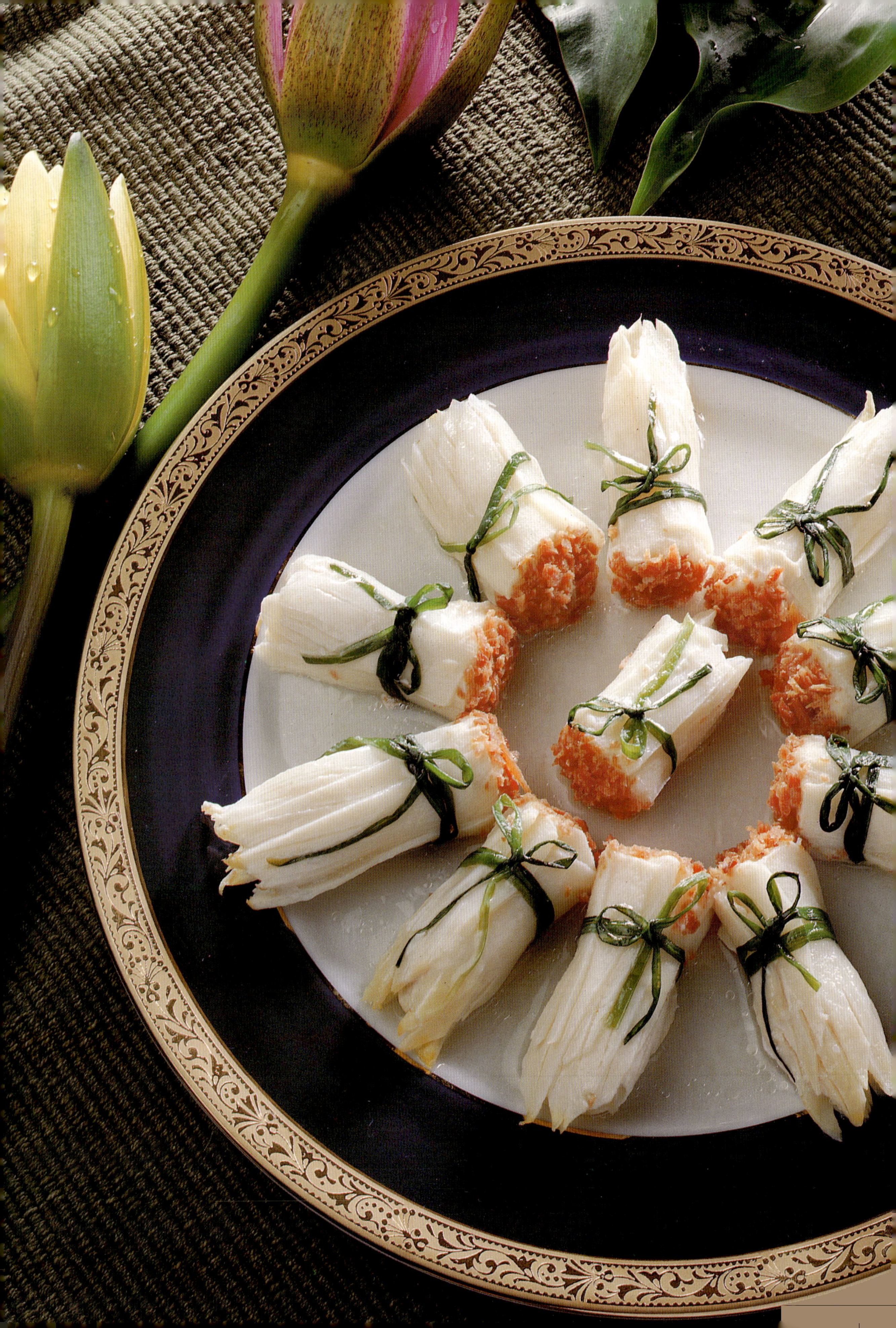

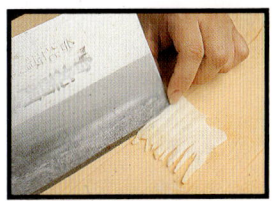

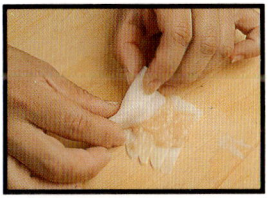

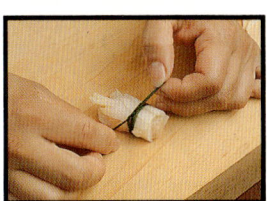

雞茸鮮筍紮

材料
竹筍3支　雞胸肉4兩　火腿屑1湯匙　韭菜數支　高湯1杯

拌雞料
鹽¼茶匙　酒1茶匙　蛋白½個　太白粉1茶匙

調味料
鹽¼茶匙　白胡椒粉少許　濕太白粉酌量

作法
1. 筍去殼煮熟，待冷卻後直剖為四半，分別切薄片，在尖的一邊再加切3～4刀刀口。
2. 雞胸肉絞成肉末，加拌雞料調成雞茸。
3. 每5～6片筍片為1組，攤開後，先撒一層太白粉，再放上雞茸餡，抹平餡後，將筍片捲起成筒狀，用燙軟之韭菜葉紮緊，頂部沾上火腿屑。
4. 將雞茸捲放在塗油的碟中，大火蒸15分鐘至熟，取出排在盤中。
5. 高湯煮滾，調味後用濕太白粉勾成稀芡，淋在筍紮上即可。

Bamboo Shoot Bundles

Ingredients:
3 Bamboo shoot, 150g Chicken breast, 1T Ham, chopped, Leek, 1C Soup stock.

Sauce:
❶ 1/4t Salt, 1t Wine, 1/2 Egg white, 1t Cornstarch
❷ 1/4t Salt, Pepper, Cornstarch paste.

Methods:
1. Boil the bamboo shoot, remove shell, let cool, cut along the grain into 4 parts, then cut into very thin slices. On 2/3 part of the root, cut into thin shreds like a comb.
2. Smash chicken breast, mix with ❶.
3. Connect every 6 pieces of bamboo shoot together into a flat lange sheet, sprinkle cornstarch, spread chicken paste, roll the bamboo shoot into a roll, fasten with a boiled leek. Dip the end with chopped ham.
4. Rub some oil on a plate, put the rolls on, steam over high heat for 15 minutes.
5. Cook the soup stock, season with salt, thicken with cornstarch paste. Bring to a boil, pour on rolls. Serve.

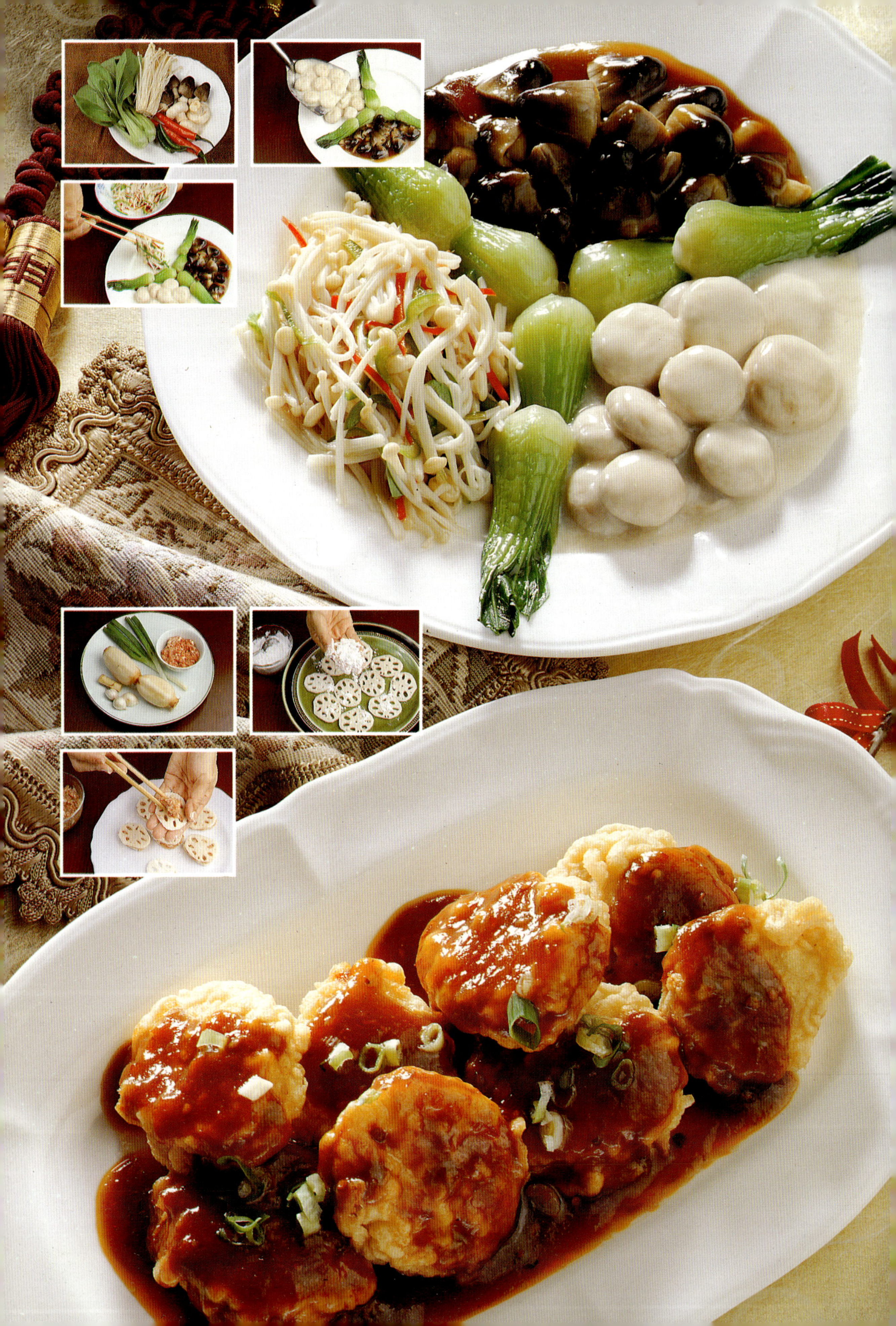

碧綠三色菇

材料

洋菇12粒　草菇12粒　金菇2把(6兩)
青梗菜數支　蔥1支

洋菇料

蔥6小段　清湯1杯　鹽½茶匙　糖少許
濕太白粉酌量　奶水2湯匙

草菇料

蔥6小段　清湯⅔杯　深色醬油1½湯匙
糖½茶匙　濕太白粉酌量

金菇料

蔥絲少許　青、紅椒絲少許　鹽¼茶匙
清湯¼杯　濕太白粉酌量　蠔油½湯匙

作法

1. 青梗菜摘菜心後在水中(加少許鹽)燙熟，排在盤中呈三放射型。
2. 洋菇去蒂洗淨，用1湯匙油爆香蔥段，放下洋菇炒香，淋清湯並調味煮3分鐘，勾芡加奶水調勻，排在盤中⅓處。
3. 另用1湯匙油爆香蔥段，放下草菇炒香，加草菇料煮1分鐘即可勾芡裝盤。
4. 用1湯匙油炒蔥絲及金菇，加蠔油及清湯煮片刻，撒下青、紅椒絲勾芡裝入盤中。

魚香溜藕夾

材料

鮮藕2節　絞肉4兩　蔥花1湯匙

拌肉料

蔥、薑屑少許　醬油、水各½湯匙　酒1茶匙　太白粉1茶匙　胡椒粉少許

魚香料

辣豆瓣醬1湯匙　醬油、糖各1茶匙　鹽¼茶匙　麻油、太白粉各½茶匙　水2湯匙

作法

1. 絞肉加入拌肉料拌勻，調成肉餡。
2. 藕削去外皮，切成薄片，平擺在菜板上，撒一層太白粉，每2片中夾上絞肉餡，做成藕夾。
3. 麵粉加水調成麵粉糊，藕夾沾裹麵糊後，用熱油炸熟。
4. 用1湯匙油炒香魚香料，撒下蔥花，放下藕夾一拌即可裝盤。

Tri-Color Mushrooms

Ingredients:
12pcs Mushroom, 12pcs Straw mushroom, 225g Needle mushroom, Green cabbage, Green onion.

Sauce:
❶ 6pcs Green onion, sectioned, 1C Soupstock, 1/2t Salt, Sugar, Cornstarch paste, 2T Milk.
❷ 6pcs Green onion, sectioned, 2/3C Soup stock, 1-1/2T Soysauce, 1/2t Sugar, Cornstarch paste.
❸ Green onion, shredded, Green pepper, shredded, Red chilli, shredded, 1T Oyster sauce, 1/2C Soup stock, Cornstarch paste.

Methods:
1. Trim the green cabbage and blanch in boiling water, arrange in a Benz's-car-sign design to divide into three spaces for three mushrooms.
2. Heat 1T oil to stir fry green onion, add mushroom and ❶. Cook for 3 minutes. Pour on the plate.
3. Heat 1T oil to stir fry green onion, add straw mushroom and ❷, cook for 1 minute. Pour on the plate.
4. Use the same way to cook needle mushroom and ❸. Pour on the plate.

Lotus Root's Cake— Szechuan Style

Ingredients:
Lotus roots, 150g Minced pork, 1T Green onion, chopped.

Sauce:
❶ Green onion & Ginger, chopped, each 1t, 1/2T Soysauce, 1/2T Water, 1t Wine, 1t Cornstarch, 1/4t Pepper.
❷ 1T Hot bean paste, 1t Soysauce, 1t Sugar, 1/4t Salt, 1/2t Sesame oil, 1/2t Cornstarch, 2T Water.

Methods:
1. Mix minced pork with ❶, stir to very sticky.
2. Peel lotus roots, cut into thin slices against the grain, sprinkle cornstarch, put the pork between every two lotus root slices like burger shape.
3. Mix flour with water to make batter, use this to coat lotus root burger and deep fry in hot oil to done, drain.
4. Heat 1T oil to cook ❷, add green onion, pour on lotus root. Serve.

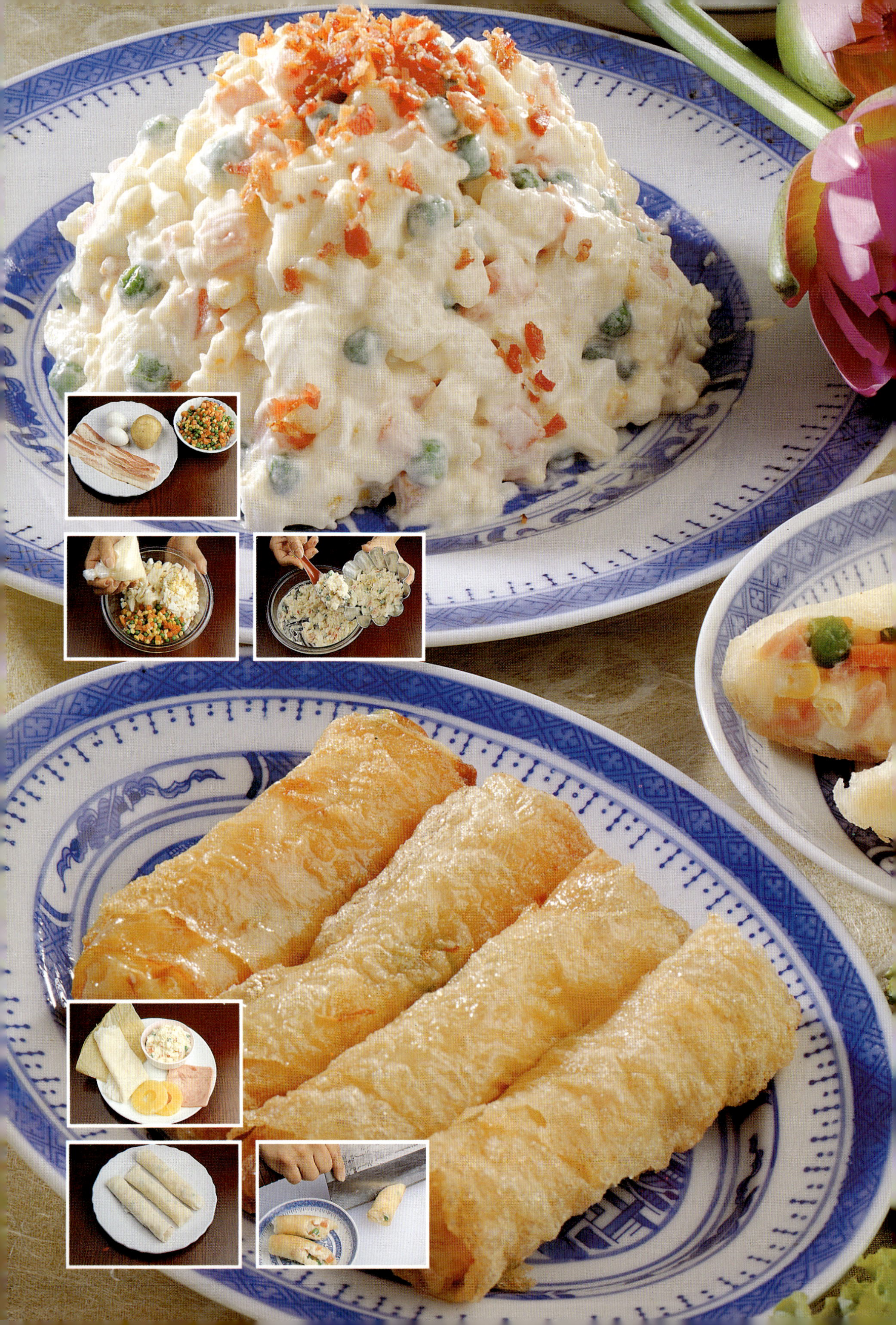

什錦蔬菜沙拉

材料
大馬鈴薯1個　冷凍什錦蔬菜2杯　培根3片　生菜葉數張

調味料
沙拉醬2湯匙　鹽½茶匙　胡椒粉少許

作法
1. 馬鈴薯煮熟去皮，切成1公分四方丁。冷凍蔬菜用滾水燙煮一下，隨即撈出。培根小火煎黃，待冷切小丁。
2. 上項材料放大碗中加調味料拌勻，裝入圓碗中，移入冰箱中略冰過，食前扣在大盤中，撒下培根小丁即可，食時可用生菜或麵包包捲食用。

Assorted Vegetable Salad

Ingredients:
375g Potato, 2C Frozen vegetables (Assorted), 3 slices. Bacon, Lettuce leaves (several pieces).

Dreseing:
2T Mayonnaise, 1/2T Salt, Pepper.

Methods:
1. Boil potato, peel off skin, cut into 1" cubes. Blanch the frozen vegetables in boiling water, drain, Fry the bacon to dry, cut into small cubes.
2. Mix potato, vegetables & dressing into a large mold, freez e for a while, then reverse up-side-down to a plate, sprinkle the bacon. Serve and wrapped with lettuce leaves.

什錦蔬菜沙拉捲

材料
什錦蔬菜沙拉2杯　洋火腿片3片　鳳梨2片　豆腐衣4張或春捲皮5張

作法
1. 上面介紹的什錦蔬菜沙拉中加入洋火腿丁及鳳梨丁拌勻。
2. 豆腐衣切成3小張，包入沙拉，小火熱油炸至外皮酥黃即可瀝出。(用春捲皮包捲可在炸過後再一切為二裝盤)

Vegetable Salad Rolls

Ingredients:
2C Assorted Vegetables Salad, 2pcs Ham slices, 2pcs Pineapple slices, 5pcs Spring roll skin (or Bean curd sheet).

Methods:
1. Mix assorted vegetable salad with ham cubes & pineapple cubes.
2. Cut each bean curd sheet into 3 pieces, wrap in salad mixture, fold into a roll, deep fry in hot oil to crispy. Serve. (Or wrap with spring roll skin).

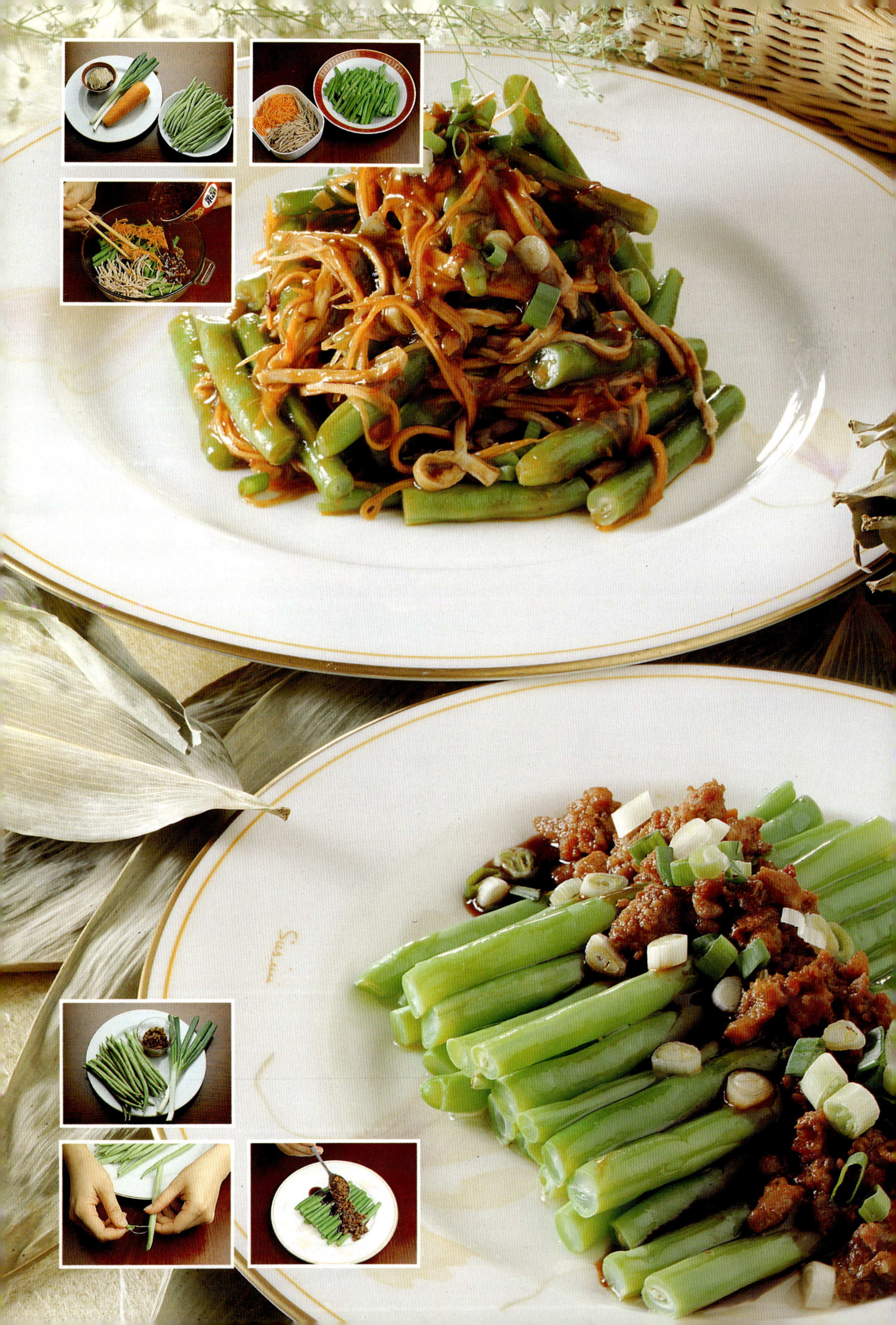

魚香汁拌四季豆

材料
牛肉或豬肉3兩　四季豆半斤　胡蘿蔔絲⅓杯　蔥花1湯匙

魚香料
薑、蒜屑各½茶匙　辣豆瓣醬1湯匙　酒、醬油各½湯匙　水½杯　鹽、糖、味精各少許　太白粉1茶匙　麻油1茶匙

作法
1. 牛肉或豬肉煮熟切絲，胡蘿蔔切絲，用少許鹽抓醃過。四季豆摘除老筋，煮熟瀝出吹涼，全部放在大碗中。
2. 用1湯匙油爆香薑、蒜屑及辣豆瓣醬，加入調勻的魚香料，撒下蔥花，淋入四季豆中拌勻即可。

Green Bean with Szechuan Sauce

Ingredients:
112.5g Pork, 300g Greenbean, 1/3C Carrot, shredded, 1T Green onion, chopped.

Sauce:
❶ 1/2t Garlic, minced, 1/2t Ginger, minced, 1T Hot bean paste, 1/2T Wine, 1/2T Soysauce, 1/2C Water, Salt, Sugar, MSG, 1t Cornstarch, 1t Sesame oil.

Methods:
1. Boil pork and cut into strings, marinate carrot shreds with a little salt. Blanch green bean to done, drain and let cool, put all ingredients in a large bowl.
2. Heat 1T oil to stir fry ginger and garlic, add ❶, bring to a boil, mix with green bean. Serve.

肉燥灼拌四季豆

材料
四季豆半斤或冷凍四季豆2杯　肉燥2湯匙　醬油膏1湯匙　蔥花少許

作法
1. 四季豆摘除老筋，太長的可一切為二，投入滾水中川燙至軟，瀝出放入大碗中，冷凍四季豆僅需一切為二之後在熱水中灼燙10秒鐘。
2. 將熱的肉燥及醬油膏淋入碗中，撒下蔥花拌勻即可裝盤上桌。

＊肉燥作法參考「香菇肉燥蒸鮭魚」的作法。

Green Bean with Minced Pork Sauce

Ingredients:
300g Green bean, 2T Minced pork sauce, 1T Soysauce paste, 1T Green onion, chopped.

Methods:
1. Remove grain ends from green bean, cut each into 2 parts, blanch in boiling water, drain and put into a large bowl.
2. Heat pork sauce and soysauce paste, mix with green onion and green bean. Serve.

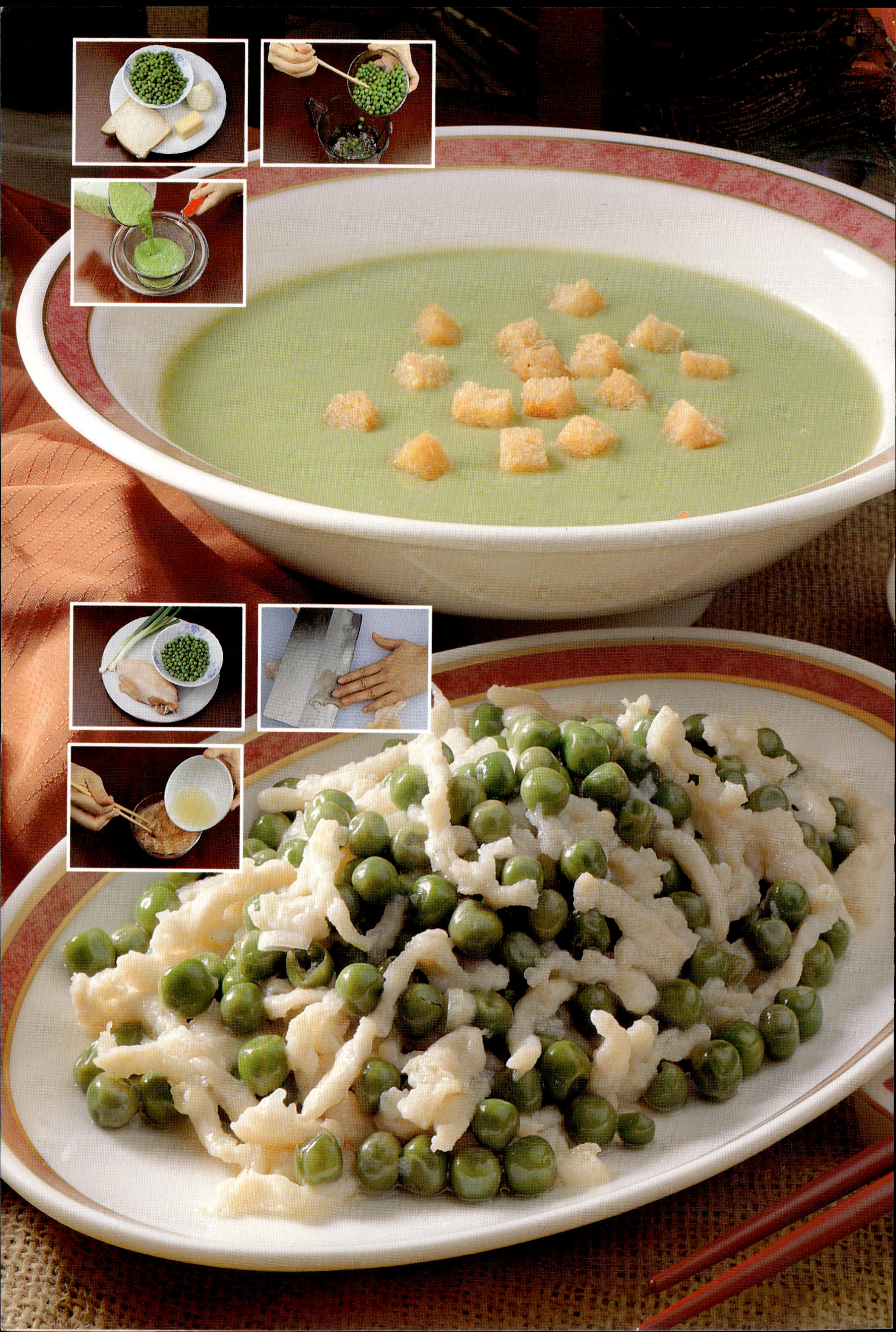

豌豆濃湯

材料
冷凍豌豆2杯　洋蔥屑2湯匙　清湯3½杯　植物性奶油3湯匙　麵粉3湯匙　鹽1茶匙　鮮奶⅓杯　麵包丁2湯匙

作法
1. 將冷凍豌豆解凍後，放入果汁機中，加入清湯(或水)2½杯打碎，過濾1次。
2. 炒鍋中將奶油先溶化，放下洋蔥屑炒香，再加入麵粉炒黃，將高湯1杯慢慢淋下，同時用鏟子將麵糊攪散至均勻，再加入豌豆糊調勻，煮滾後將洋蔥屑撈棄，放鹽調味，加入鮮奶即可裝入個人用湯碟或杯子中，上桌後撒下炸黃之脆麵包丁即可(亦可撒炸酥之培根丁或洋火腿絲)。

Snow Peas Cream Soup

Ingredients:
2C Frozen snow peas, 2T Onion, chopped, 3-1/2C Soup stock, 3T Butter, 3T Flour, 1t Salt, 1/3C Milk, 2T Bread cubes.

Methods:
1. Defroze the snow peas, put into a blender, add 2-1/2C soup stock, blend finely, drain, leave the soup.
2. Heat the butter, stir fry onion, add flour, add 1C soup stock gradually, stir the flour paste evenly, add in snow pea juice, bring to a boil, sieve the onion off, season the soup with salt, add milk. Serve with deep-fried bread cubes (or fried bacon).

炒豌豆雞絲

材料
雞胸半個　冷凍豌豆(青豆)1½杯　蔥屑1湯匙

醃雞料
蛋白1湯匙　鹽¼茶匙　太白粉½茶匙

調味料
酒1茶匙　鹽½茶匙　濕太白粉½湯匙　麻油少許

作法
1. 雞胸肉去皮除筋後，直紋切成細絲，用醃雞料仔細拌勻，醃10分鐘以上。
2. 冷凍豌豆投入滾水中燙一下即刻瀝出。
3. 鍋子燒熱後倒下油1½杯，待七分熱時，放下雞絲用筷子快速將雞絲撥散，待雞絲變白夠熟時便盛出。
4. 另用1湯匙油爆香蔥屑後，將豌豆粒及雞絲一起下鍋，淋下酒及鹽，拌勻後用濕太白粉勾芡，再淋入數滴麻油即可。

Chicken Strings with Snow Peas

Ingredients:
1/2 Chicken breast, 1-1/2C Frozen snow peas, 1T Green onion, chopped.

Sauce:
❶ 1T Egg white. 1/4t Salt, 1/2t Cornstarch.
❷ 1t Wine, 1/2t Salt, 1/2T Cornstarch paste, Sesame oil.

Methods:
1. Remove skin from chicken, cut into fine strings along the grain, marinate with ❶ for 10 minutes.
2. Blanch the snow peas, drain.
3. Heat 1-1/2C oil to 140°C, deep fry chicken shreds, separate with chopsticks. When chicken turns white, drain.
4. Heat 1T oil, stir fry green onion, add chicken & snow peas, add sauce ❷, mix well. Serve.

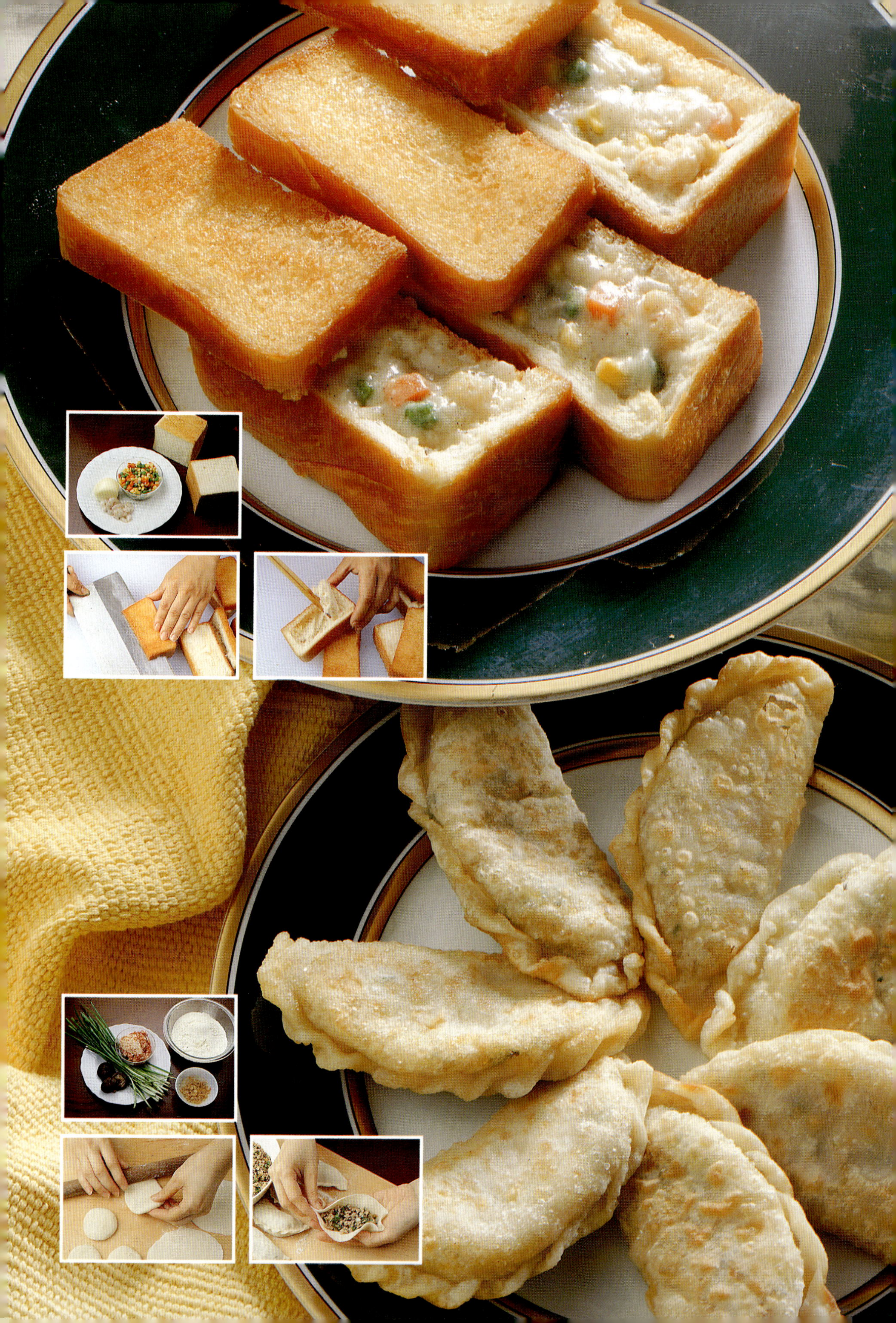

奶油蔬菜盒

材料

小蝦仁3兩　洋葱屑2湯匙　冷凍什錦蔬菜1½杯　土司麵包(未切片)2節　麵粉3湯匙　清湯(或水)2杯

調味料

鹽⅔湯匙　糖、胡椒粉各少許　牛奶2湯匙

作法

1. 小蝦仁洗淨擦乾後，用少許鹽及太白粉抓拌一下，醃10分鐘，用滾水燙一下撈出，冷凍什錦蔬菜亦燙一下。
2. 土司麵包每節對切為二，用油炸黃外表，撈出後切下1公分厚做為蓋子，中間的麵包挖空。
3. 用2湯匙油炒香洋葱屑，待軟後，加入麵粉炒匀，注入清湯及調味料，調拌成糊狀，放下蝦仁及蔬菜拌合，分別盛入4個麵包盒中。

Cream Vegetable in Bread Boxes

Ingredients:
112.5g Shrimp (shelled), 2T Onion, chopped, 1-1/2C Frozen assorted vegetables, 1/2 loaf Bread, 3T Flour, 2C Soup stock.

Seasonings:
2/3t Salt, 1/2t Sugar, Pepper, 2T Milk.

Methods:
1. Clean the shrimp, marinate with salt & corn starch for 10 minutes, blanch and drain. Blanch assorted vegetables in boiling water water and drain.
2. Cut 1/2 loaf of bread into 4 thick sections. Deep fry in hot oil till golden brown, drain and cut 1 cm thick slice as a lid, (Do not cut through). Scoop out the inside bread as a hollow box.
3. Heat 2T oil, stir fry onion, add flour and stir, gradually pour soup in and mix evenly, add seasonings, shrimp, vegetables. Pour into the bread boxes. Serve.

三鮮盒子

材料

絞肉6兩　蝦米2湯匙　香菇4朶　韭菜4兩(或青梗菜)半斤　麵粉2杯

調味料

醬油1湯匙　鹽½茶匙　味精少許　麻油2茶匙

作法

1. 麵粉用半杯滾水燙過(用筷子撥散攪動)，再加入適量冷水，揉成一團，放置20分鐘。
2. 香菇及蝦米均泡軟切小丁，韭菜切屑(青梗菜切碎，加少許鹽醃10分鐘，擠去水分)。
3. 用1湯匙油炒熟絞肉,放下香菇及蝦米炒香，調味後再拌炒一下，盛出待稍涼,拌入韭菜及麻油(青梗菜需下鍋炒一下)。
4. 麵團揉匀後分成乒乓球大小，擀成2½寸直徑圓形，包入3.項韭菜餡料，折好邊線，用火煎黃兩面。

Fried Jumbo Dumplings

Ingredients:
225g Minced pork, 2T Dried shrimp, 4pcs Black mushroom, 150g Leek, 2C Flour.

Seasonings:
1T Soysauce, 1/2t Salt, MSG, 2t Sesame oil.

Methods:
1. Add 1/2C boiling water in flour, stir with chopsticks, add in maderate amount of cold water, knead into a dough, leave for 20 minutes.
2. Soak black mushroom & shrimp, chop finely. Mince leek.
3. Heat 1T oil to fry minced pork, mix with black mushroom, shrimp & seasonings, let cool and mix in leek & sesame oil.
4. Divide dough into small balls, roll out to a 2-1/2" diameter round sheet, wrap in stuffing, pinch and seal to dumplings. Fry both sides to done. Serve.

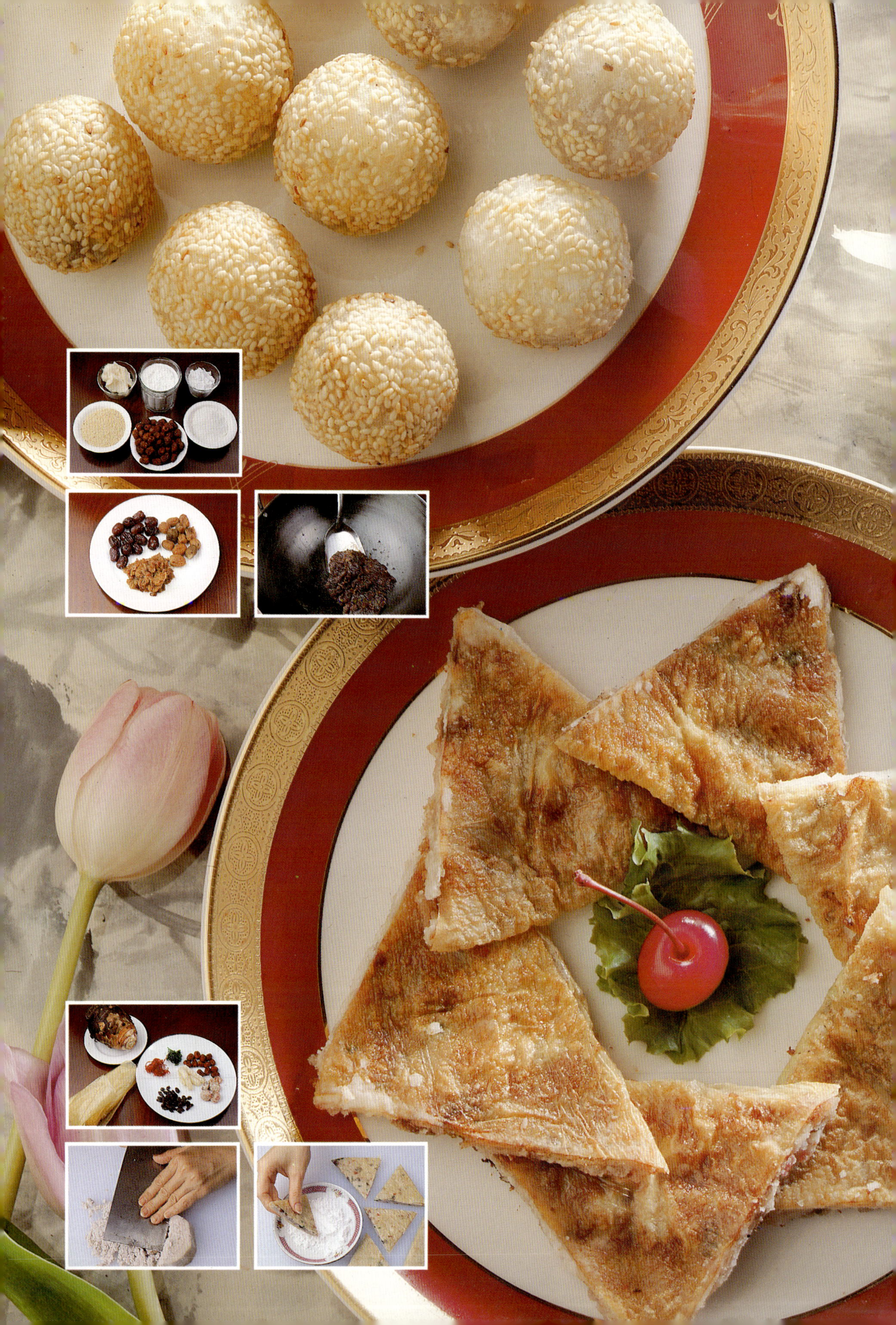

棗泥糯米球

材料
紅棗半斤　油⅓杯　糖½杯　糯米粉2杯　澄粉½杯　豬油2湯匙　糖2湯匙　白芝麻半杯

作法
1. 紅棗洗淨泡脹，加1½杯水蒸30分鐘，待稍涼剝去皮，挖除籽，放入果汁機打成漿，炒鍋中加油及糖，放下棗泥漿，火拌炒至乾香黏稠為止，冷卻分成20小粒待用。
2. 澄粉用滾水半杯沖燙後，倒入糯米粉中，並加豬油及糖，揉成一團，分成20小粒。
3. 每粒糯米皮內包1粒棗泥，擇成球狀。白芝麻倒在托盤中，放下糯米球搖滾，盡量沾滿。
4. 糯米球5～6粒用漏勺托住，放入溫油中慢炸至浮起，再改大火炸至外皮酥硬即可瀝出。

＊可用豆沙代替棗泥餡較方便。

Glutinous Rice Balls with Date Pastes

Ingredients:
300g Red dates, 1/2C Sugar, 2C Glutinous rice powder, 1/2C Flour starch, 2T Lard, 2T Sugar, 1/2C Sesame seeds.

Methods:
1. Rinse and soak the red dates, steam to soft, let cool, peel off skin, discard seeds, beat in a blender to a paste, stir fry in a wok with lard and sugar over low heat to a solidified paste, divide into 20 balls.
2. Mix flour starch with 1/2C boiling water, add glutinous rice powder, lard and sugar, knead into a dough, divide into 20 balls.
3. Wrap inside the dough with a ball of date paste, roll to a ball shape, coat with sesame seeds.
4. Deep fry in warm oil over low heat, when balls rise up, turn to high heat and deep fry for 1 more minute till the surface gets firm. Drain.

♣ You may buy bean paste as stuffing.

八寶芋泥捲

材料
大芋頭1個　豆腐衣2張　八寶料各少許

調味料
糖1湯匙　油1湯匙

作法
1. 大芋頭削皮切成厚片，蒸軟後趁熱壓成泥，拌入糖及油，再加入切成小粒之八寶料，用手搓均勻。
2. 豆腐衣切成長方形，鋪上一層芋泥餡（約1½寸寬½寸厚）捲成扁筒狀。
3. 芋泥捲斜刀切成1½寸寬之菱角形，兩邊切口處沾上太白粉（以免芋泥餡料露出），用少量油煎黃兩面即可。

＊八寶料可選用桂圓肉、橘餅、青紅絲、冬瓜糖或紅棗，切成小粒後可放在碗中蒸10分鐘，使其稍軟更佳。

Sweet Taro Rolls

Ingredients:
1 Taro, 2 Dried bean curd sheet, 1T sugar, 1T Lard.

Eight Treasures:
Candied papaya, wintermelon, raisin, date... etc.

Methods:
1. Peel the taro, cut into thick slices, steam to soft, smash and mix with sugar & lard, mix in minced eight treasures.
2. Cut dried bean curd sheet into rectangle, spread the taro mixture on, wrap and fold into a 1-1/2 cm thick rectangle package.
3. Cut diagonnaly into diamond shapes, coat with cornstarch and fry with a little oil to golden brown.

♣ The Eight Treasures can be Long-gan, candied tangerine, papaya, red date, wintermelon,... etc, mince and steam for 10 minutes to soft.

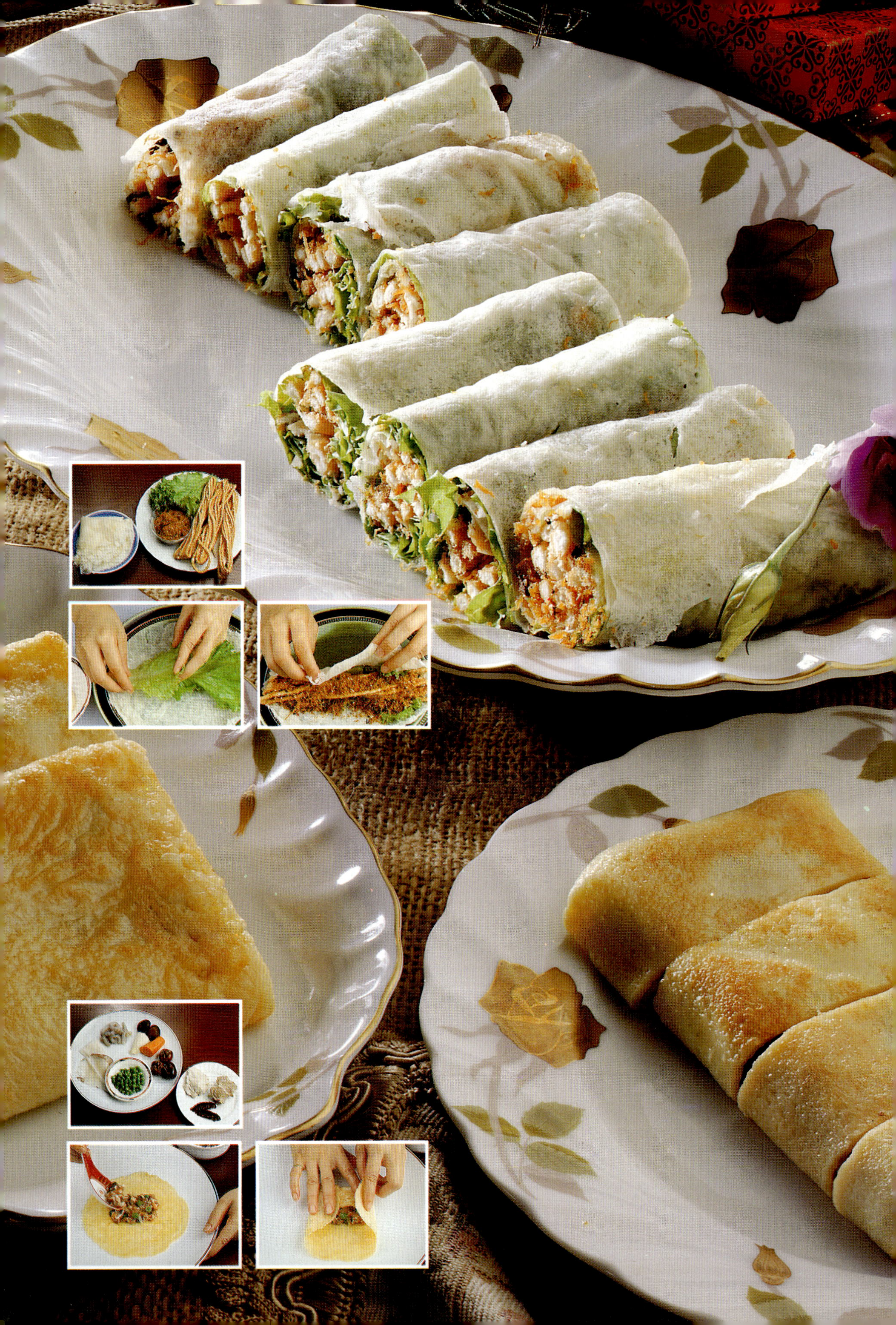

馓子素菜捲

材料
馓子4支　生菜葉4枚　素肉鬆酌量　春捲皮或薄餅4張　沙拉醬酌量

作法
1. 春捲皮塗上沙拉醬，放生菜葉1枚，再塗沙拉醬少許，再放上1支油炸馓子，撒一些素肉鬆或芝麻或花生粉，捲成筒狀。
2. 將頭尾略切除一些，再對切為二即可。

＊可用吃烤鴨用的單餅代替春捲皮。
＊也可以吃葷的，內捲叉燒肉絲、蝦仁、醬肉、肉鬆或加包蘆筍、豆腐乾等。

Crispy Vegetarian Rolls

Ingredients:
4 San-Tsu (Deep Friend Twister Bar), 4pcs Lettuce leaves, 4T Vegetarian meat pulp, 4pcs Spring roll skin, Mayonnaise.

Methods:
1. Rub mayonnaise on the spring roll skin, place a piece of lettuce leave, put 1 San-Tsu on, sprinkle the vegetarian meat pulp, fold and roll into a cylinder.
2. Cut off two ends and cut each roll into halves.

♣ You may use the flour pan sheet (for Pei-jin Duck) to substitute for the spring roll skin.
♣ You may change the vegetarian materials to assorted meat.

歡樂滿堂彩

材料
熟豬肉、香菇、魷魚、海參、雞肉、冬筍、蝦仁、青豆、胡蘿蔔、荸薺、蔥等各少許

調味料
酒1茶匙　醬油½湯匙　麻油1茶匙　胡椒粉少許　濕太白粉酌量

蛋麵糊料
蛋1個　麵粉6湯匙　水½杯　鹽少許

作法
1. 材料可隨意選擇，全部切成小丁，起油鍋用2湯匙油先爆香蔥花，放下所有材料炒拌，加調味料後，用濕太白粉勾芡，此為餡料。
2. 蛋麵糊調成稀糊狀，過濾一次後，用鍋子做成2張8寸大小的薄餅（鍋中塗少許油）。
3. 在薄餅中鋪上餡料，做成6寸長、2½寸寬的長方形，用剩餘的蛋麵糊封口。
4. 用少量油將薄餅煎黃，趁熱切成長條形盛盤。

＊此菜是為清理春節過後的各種生、熟剩餘材料而設計的。

Assorted Meat in Soft Cake

Ingredients:
Pork, Black mushrooms, Squid, Sea cucumber, Chicken, Bamboo shoot, Shrimp, Snow peas, Carrot, Waterchesnuts, Green onion.

Seasonings:
1t Wine, 1/2T Soysauce, 1t Sesame oil, Pepper, Cornstarch paste.

Flour Batter:
1 Egg, 6T Flour. 1/2C Water, Salt

Methods:
1. Cut every ingredients into small cubes. Heat 2T oil to stir fry green onion, mix with every ingredient and seasoning. Thicken with cornstarch. This is the stuffing.
2. Mix batter, sieve, make 2 thin round pan cake, about 8" diameter.
3. Put 4T stuffing on the pan cake, fold and make a 6" x 2-1/2" rectangle package.
4. Fry the rectangle cake with a little oil to golden brown. Cut into sections and serve.

♣ You may use all kinds of food from the New Year left-over dishes as stuffing.

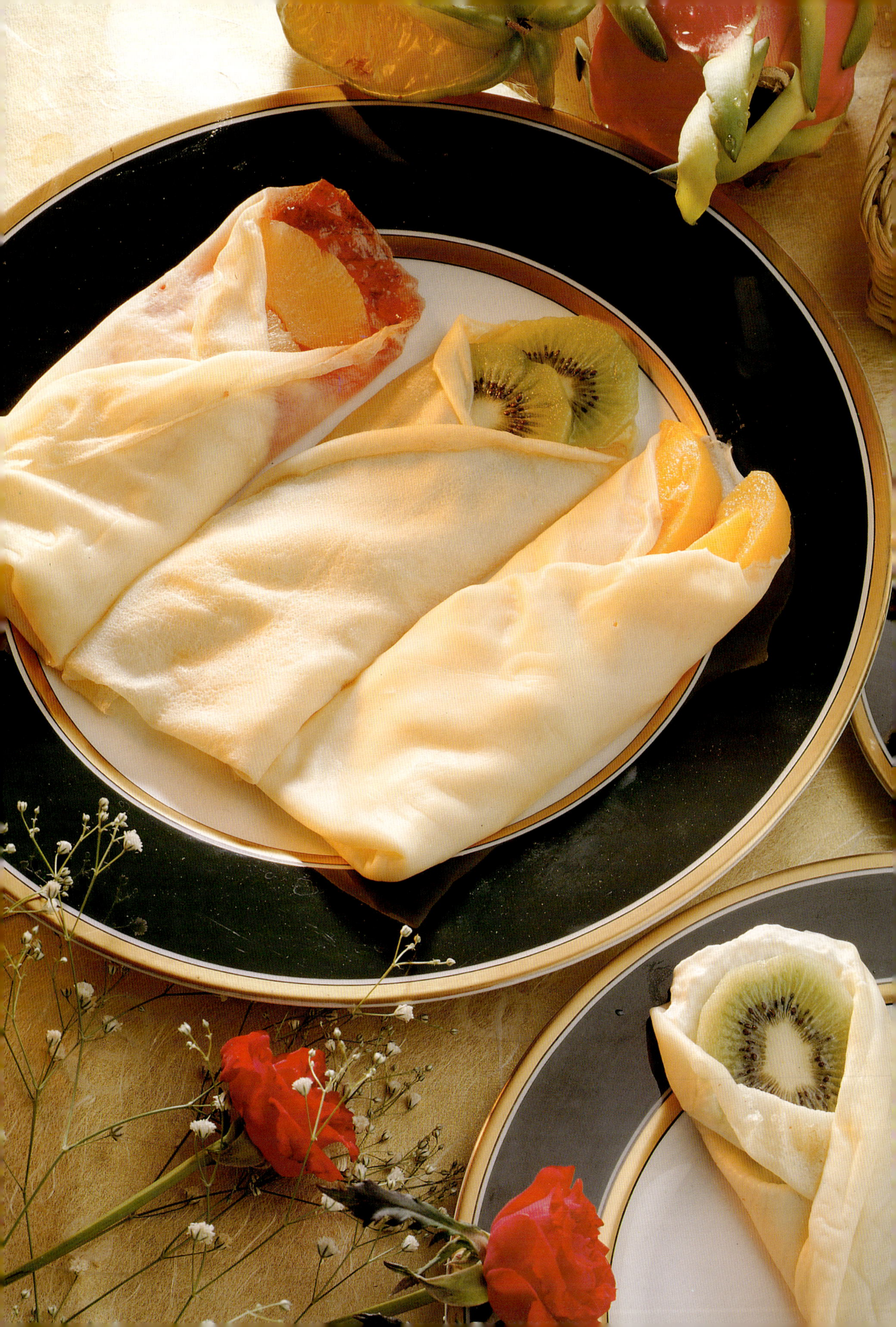

奶油水果淋餅

材料
蛋2個　麵粉1杯　牛奶½杯　水酌量　新鮮水果隨意　新鮮奶油酌量

作法
1. 蛋打散後，加入麵粉、牛奶及水，仔細調成稀麵糊（用篩子過濾一次）。
2. 平底鍋燒熱，刷上少許的油，倒下一大勺麵糊料，迅速轉動鍋子，成為一張薄餅，小火煎熟。
3. 可選用香蕉、草莓、奇異果或罐頭的水蜜桃、橘子瓣等各種喜愛的水果，包入軟餅中，罐頭的鮮奶油整罐搖晃一下，噴出一些，一起包入薄餅中。

French Crêpe

Ingredients:
2 Eggs, 1C Flour, 1/2C milk, Moderate of water, Assorted vegetables, Fresh cream.

Methods:
1. Beat the egg, add in flour, milk, water to stir into a paste, sift once.
2. Brush some oil on a pan, pour 4T paste in, shake the pan to form a round thin sheet. Fry over low heat till firm. Pour out on a board.
3. Choose banana, strawberry, kiwi, peach, tangerine or any other fruit to be wrapped inside, spread some fresh cream on. Serve.

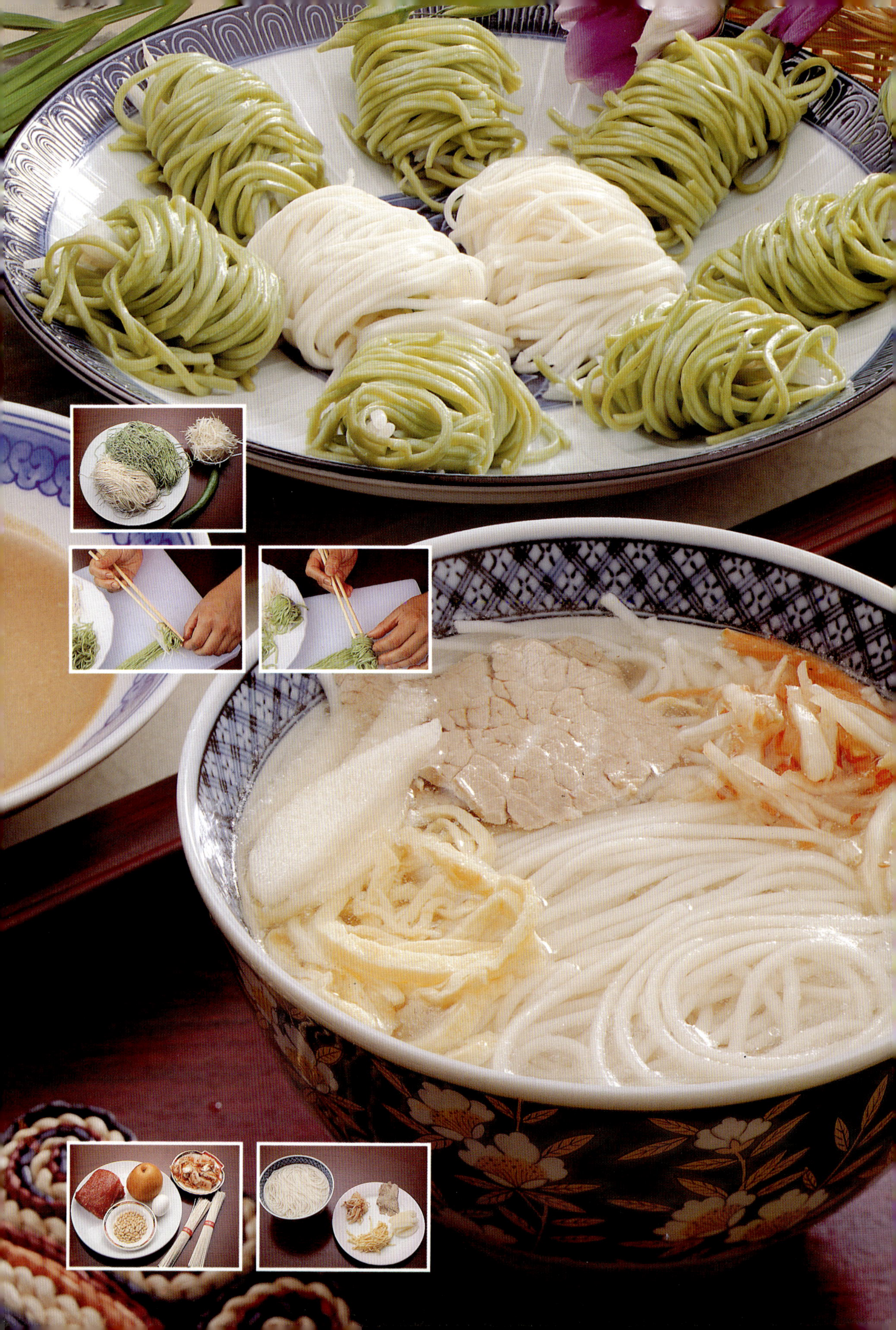

翡翠涼麵捲

材料

翡翠細麵半斤　普通細麵半斤　黃瓜1條　綠豆芽4兩

糖醋汁

糖、醋各2湯匙　冷開水½杯　淡色醬油1湯匙　麻油1茶匙　味精少許

芝麻汁

芝麻醬1湯匙　淡色醬油、冷開水各1½湯匙　糖、麻油各1茶匙　醋½湯匙　花椒粉¼茶匙

作法

1. 將翡翠麵與白細麵分別煮熟，撈出用冷開水沖涼瀝乾，各分成6份。
2. 豆芽摘根燙熟沖冷，黃瓜切絲。
3. 每一份麵條攤長在菜板上，在一端平放1雙竹筷子，中間夾放少許豆芽，將麵條包著筷子捲起，捲好後將筷子抽掉成一個筒狀。白細麵中夾放黃瓜後捲好，做好後分別排放在大盤中。
4. 兩只碗中分別調好兩種汁，隨大盤一起上桌。

Jade Color Cold Noodle Rolls

Ingredients:
300g Green color noodles, 300g White noodles, 1 Cucumber, 150g Bean sprouts.

Sauce:
❶ 2T Sugar, 2T Vinegar, 1/2C Water, 1T Soysauce, 1t Sesame oil, MSG.
❷ 1T Sesame paste, 1-1/2T soysauce, 1-1/2T Water, 1t Sugar, 1t Sesame oil, 1/2T Vinegar, 1/4t Brown pepper corn powder.

Methods:
1. Boil the two color noodles, rinse cool, drain, divide into 6 parts.
2. Blanch bean sprouts, rinse cool, drain, shred the cucumber.
3. Spread each portion of noodle on a board, put chopsticks on one end of green noodles, place 1T bean sprouts, wrap and roll the noodle from one end to the other to make a bun roll. While with the white noodle put in cucumber shreds, fold and roll. Arrange all on a large plate.
4. Serve with two kinds of sauce.

韓國涼麵

材料

牛肉(全瘦腿肉)半斤　韓國泡菜½杯　水梨1個　蛋皮絲½杯　松子2湯匙　細麵12兩　香菜少許

煮肉料

蔥2支　薑1片　酒1湯匙　水4杯　鹽1湯匙　胡椒粉¼茶匙

作法

1. 牛肉放入煮肉料中小火煮1小時，牛肉夾出切薄片，湯過濾待冷，冷後如果湯上有浮油要撇除乾淨。
2. 水滾後，放下細麵煮熟，撈出沖過冷開水，瀝乾放入大碗中(或分裝4個麵碗)。
3. 淋下冷牛肉湯，麵上並放泡菜絲、水梨絲和牛肉數片，再加少許蛋皮絲即可食用。
* 也可加入炸過之松子及香菜屑以增香氣。

Cold Noodles Korean Style

Ingredients:
300g Lean beef, 1/2C Korean pickle, chopped, 1 Pear, 1/2C Egg sheet, shredded, 2T Pine nuts, 450g Noodles, Chinese parsley.

Seasonings:
2 Green onion, 1 Ginger slice, 1T Wine, 4C Water, 1t Salt, 1/4t Pepper.

Methods:
1. Cook beef with seasonings over low heat for 1 hour, drain and cut into thin slices.
2. Boil the noodle to done, drain and rinse cool, divide and put into 4 bowls.
3. Pour the beef soup on noodles, place beef, pickles, pear slices, egg shreds, Chinese parsley, fried pine nuts on top. Serve.

台灣凱斯股份有限公司
K's Collection Taiwan Co., Ltd.

台北市光復南路 555 號 4 樓
TEL : 7581212 FAX : 7296228

國立中央圖書館出版品預行編目資料

創意家常菜：Creative Chinese home dishes
／傅培梅, 程安琪, 林慧懿編著. -- 初版. --
臺北市：韜略出版；[臺北縣] 中和市：三友
總經銷, 1995 [民84]
　　面；　公分.--（十八般廚藝系列；1）
ISBN 957-9211-20-5(平裝)

1.食譜 – 中國

427.11　　　　　　　　　　　　　84004111

◇十八般廚藝系列 01◇　　　　　　　ISBN 957-9211-20-5

創意家常菜
Creative Chinese Home Dishes

編著者／傅培梅・程安琪・林慧懿
翻譯／林慧懿　　　　　　　編輯執行／鄭淑娟・張雅茹
發行人／程顯灝　　　　　　美術編輯／曙鬱
出版者／韜略出版有限公司　　攝影／陳弘暐
地址／台北市仁愛路四段122巷63號9樓　餐具提供／台灣凱斯股份有限公司
印刷／王陽印刷股份有限公司
台北總經銷／三友圖書公司
地址／中和市中山路二段327巷11弄17號5樓
電話／(02) 240-5600・240-5707
傳真／(02) 240-9284
香港總代理／萬里書局
地址／香港北角英皇道499號18 F
電話／25623879
新加坡總代理／諾文文化事業私人有限公司
地址／3 Shenton Way ＃02-08 Shenton House Singapore
　　　　　　　　　　　　　Singapore 0106
電話／3230478
傳真／3230478
登記證／局版台業字第3859號
二版四刷／1999年1月
定價／新台幣290元

版權所有・翻印必究

◆本書如有污損缺頁，請寄回本公司更換◆